A RATIONAL
ANIMAL

A Rational Animal
and other Philosophical Essays
on the Nature of Man

BY

ANTONY FLEW

M.A.(Oxon.), D.Litt.(Keele)

Professor of Philosophy,
University of Reading

CLARENDON PRESS · OXFORD
1978

Oxford University Press, Walton Street, Oxford OX2 6DP

OXFORD LONDON GLASGOW
NEW YORK TORONTO MELBOURNE WELLINGTON
IBADAN NAIROBI DAR ES SALAAM LUSAKA CAPE TOWN
KUALA LUMPUR SINGAPORE JAKARTA HONG KONG TOKYO
DELHI BOMBAY CALCUTTA MADRAS KARACHI

© *Antony Flew 1978*

British Library Cataloguing in Publication Data

Flew, Antony
    A rational animal.
    1. Philosophical anthropology
    I. Title
    128'.3   BD450   77–30284
    ISBN 0–19–824576–9

*Printed in Great Britain by
Cox & Wyman Ltd,
London, Fakenham and Reading*

In memory of

GILBERT RYLE

who never forgot some advice of the good David:

'Be a philosopher; but, amidst all your philosophy, be still a man.'

CONTENTS

PROLOGUE

THE present book, as its sub-title indicates, is a collection of philosophical essays on the nature of man. So it should be no surprise that the questions pursued are often seen as arising in the context of various human sciences. The *first* prefatory point which does perhaps need to be made is that, because the book is a collection, the distribution of attention is not what it would have been in a systematic treatise. Such a treatise would not, for instance, have given so large a part to the philosophy of psychoanalysis. It would also have addressed several topics which are not here introduced at all. The sufficient justification for this apparently unbalanced balance is that I am using space where but only where I believe that I happen to have a contribution to make.

Second, again because this is a collection and not a treatise, I do not begin or even end with any comprehensive statement about our human nature. It is I think sufficient, but also necessary, to say now that what I shall be expounding and defending belongs to the Aristotelian as opposed to the Platonic-Cartesian tradition; and that the emphasis throughout will be on the fundamental yet widely uncongenial fact that we can, and cannot but, make choices. The Aristotelian insists that we essentially are, that we do not merely contingently inhabit, things of flesh and blood; and he has freed himself from Aristotle's own Platonic hangups about the separable or separated intellect, and its putative eternity (Flew, 1964, 'Introduction' and *passim*; and compare Flew, 1976a, Part Three).

Emphasis upon the inexpugnable reality of choice is, of course, not common to all who by the previous criterion count as Aristotelians. For, notwithstanding that it is—as I shall argue—something of which every human science has to take account, it is at the same time something which many practitioners of these sciences are inclined to ignore or even to deny; if only because they assume that it must be inconsistent with the very possibility of what they believe that they must, as human scientists, be trying to do. And everyone—scientist and layman both—who becomes aware of having made a major wrong decision finds in this rueful awareness a strong incentive to persuade himself that really there was no alternative.

Yet emphasis upon the human peculiarity of choice is also Aristotelian, though not Aristotelian as opposed to Platonic. This comes out well, and in a way very relevant to the problems of our Chapter Five, in the second of the two Objections to which St. Thomas offered his Five Ways as the answer. This succinct challenge could fairly be put into the mouth of Strato of Lampsacus, next but one after Aristotle as Head of the Lyceum, and the first to develop his ideas into a total and unqualified scientific naturalism: 'Furthermore, what can be accounted for by fewer principles is not the product of more. But it seems that everything which can be observed in the world can be accounted for by other principles, on the assumption of the non-existence of God. *Thus natural effects are explained by natural causes, while contrived effects are referred to human reason and will.* So there is no need to postulate the existence of God' (Aquinas, I Q2 A3: italics supplied).

Third, although this is a collection, and although most of its material has been somewhere in some form in print before, there was no question of idly posting a pile of old offprints to the publishers. (I hope that some colleagues, who will perhaps follow me in nothing else, may adopt a similar approach to the production of books of papers.) For a start, I have put whatever notes I could not manage to work smoothly into the text at the end, numbered consecutively throughout the whole volume; I have compiled a single unified Bibliography, to include all works to which reference is made; and I have inserted cross-references, and removed unintended overlaps between chapters. I have also imposed a uniform system of sectioning and subsectioning, and of typographical conventions. (In particular I have removed, except from passages quoted, all italics employed for purposes other than emphasis or the marking of titles of books and journals: the full naturalization of such indispensable Latin immigrants as 'a priori' and 'a posteriori' is now all of two centuries overdue, since they were apparently first used in English—by Berkeley— over a quarter of a millennium ago!)

But, as well as trying in these editorial ways to pull the various papers together, I have also more or less drastically revised, rearranged, and rewritten all the previously published material; so much so that sometimes it seemed proper to give fresh titles to the results. The bibliographical history which follows can serve as both programme notes and the basis for due acknowledgements.

The title of Chapter One 'The Darwinian Framework' refers both to the structure of Darwin's theory and to the biological background from which the rational animal evolved. Materials are drawn mainly from 'The Structure of Darwinism' (© Antony Flew, 1959), published in 1959 in a special centenary number of *New Biology* by Penguin Books of Harmondsworth. But the final subsection recovers some of the ground of my reviews of two best-selling books by Desmond Morris for *New Humanist*, published by Pemberton Books of London for the Rationalist Press Association. 'Powers, Checks, and Choice in Malthus' is really a new paper with a new thesis. But it does recycle some materials which have appeared earlier in one or both of two places: a paper on 'The Structure of Malthus' Population Theory' in *Philosophy of Science: the Delaware Seminar*, Vol. I, edited by Bernard Baumrin and published in 1963 in Newark by the University of Delaware Press; and the introduction (© Antony Flew, 1970) to my edition of *Malthus: An Essay on the Principle of Population*, published in 1970 by Penguin Books. Chapter Three 'Hume and Historical Necessity' is a revised version of an article published in 1976 in both Spanish and English, in *Teorema* (Valencia): the first draft was originally commissioned as a contribution to a Hume Colloquium held at Oberlin College, Ohio in 1973. Chapter Four 'Sartre and Unconditional Responsibility' is based upon part of 'Is there a Problem of Freedom?', commissioned by Dr. E. Pivcevic for his collection on *Phenomenology and Philosophical Understanding*, published in 1975 by the Cambridge University Press.

Chapter Five is a special case. It recycles a lot of material from a paper with the same title, 'A Rational Animal', commissioned by Dr. John Smythies for his collection on *Brain and Mind*, published in 1965 by Routledge and Kegan Paul of London. But, in a complete rewriting involving considerable extension, some of this material has been—as I understand is said of secret agents—turned round: my conclusions on the issues of Freewill *and* Determinism or Freewill *or* Determinism are now less uncompromisingly Compatibilist than they used to be.

Most of Chapter Six 'Mind/Brain Identity and the Cartesian Framework' first appeared much as it does here now, and under the same title, in the *Journal of Critical Analysis* (Jersey City) in 1975.

Chapter Seven 'Human Psychology and Skinnerian Behaviourism' is a revision of a review article which originally emerged under the title 'B. F. Skinner: Human Psychology Dehumanized' in *Question Six*, published in 1973 by Pemberton Books. *Question*, by the way, is successor to the old *Rationalist Annual*. Chapter Eight 'Motives and Freud's Unconscious' has been completely rewritten. But it remains substantially what first appeared as 'Motives and the Unconscious' in Volume I of the Minnesota Studies in the Philosophy of Science *The Foundations of Science and the Concepts of Psychology and Psychoanalysis*, edited by Herbert Feigl and Michael Scriven, and published by the University of Minnesota Press (Minneapolis) in 1956. Chapter Nine 'Psychoanalysis and Freewill' draws its material from two sources: first, 'Psychoanalysis and the Philosophical Problems of Free Will' in *Psychoanalysis and Philosophy*, edited by Charles Hanly and Morris Lazerowitz, and published in 1970 by the International Universities Press of New York; and, second, 'Splitting Hairs before Starting Hares' published in 1972 in *The Personalist* (Los Angeles).

The final chapter, 'Lenin and the Cartesian Inheritance' is, I suppose, in another way again a special case. It is really a new paper, though it does recycle material prepared for a British Council visit to Poland in 1966, and first published in 1967, in both Serbo-Croat and English, under the title 'A "Linguistic Philosopher" looks at Lenin's Materialism and Empirio-Criticism' in *Praxis* (Zagreb). But what makes this in its own way a special case is that that journal, after a career including much honourable conflict with the state authorities, seems now to have been suppressed finally; although its Editorial Board, with the support of the Croatian Philosophical Association, refuses formally to disband.*

I thank all the editors of the journals and the publishers of the books listed above for their permissions to re-use those materials which are re-employed below. I also thank Mrs. Deirdre Weizmann, Secretary to the Department of Philosophy in the University of Reading, for her helpfulness and patience in managing to squeeze in among many other commitments nearly all the necessary typing and photocopying. Finally I thank the unknown consultant to the Oxford University Press, all of whose uniformly constructive points I have tried to meet below.

December 1976   BUENOS AIRES

---

* British readers, when they learn that this suppression was effected not by ad-ministrative order and official police action but by an exercise of 'workers' control' will be able, although too often reluctant, to recognize the sinister shape of things beginning and to come, the particular realities of—to borrow a coinage from Orwell's prophetic novel *Nineteen Eighty-Four*—Ingsoc. The explanation which the *Praxis* Editorial Board circulated to subscribers and friends included the sentence: '... the printing house in which the Yugoslav edition of *Praxis* has been printed since its first issue sent us a notice saying that the political activists and the governing body of this Organization of Associated Work have taken the decision that in future the service of printing the journal *Praxis* should be discontinued.' For some parallel home truths compare Beloff, *passim.*

I
THE DARWINIAN FRAMEWORK

'WITH the exception of Newton's *Principia* no single book of empirical science has ever been of more importance to philosophy than this work of Darwin' (Royce, 1892, p. 286). It is a claim both clear and drastic. Yet, if such an assessment of *The Origin of Species* is to be faulted, then the charge surely has to be that it still constitutes an underestimate. For, where Newton was concerned primarily with the inanimate background, Darwin attempted to outline and to explain the origin of every form of life, including that of humankind. *The Origin of Species* also happens to be the most immediately accessible of all the great scientific classics: well-written, wide-ranging, clearly argued, and quite untechnical. As such it is ideally suited for use, whether in whole or in part, as a set-text, both for beginning courses in the philosophy of science, and for courses intended to give some vision and understanding of science to people whose previous education has been confined to 'the Arts side'. Both these exercises are relevant to, and as a large part include, our own main present purpose, a consideration of the bearing of Darwin's theory upon the question of the nature of man.

(1) The Deductive Skeleton

In a typically modest and engaging passage of *Autobiography* Darwin says: '. . . *The Origin of Species* is one long argument from the beginning to the end. . . .' (Darwin, 1887, p. 140.) He had said the same in the final chapter of the book itself: '. . . this whole volume is one long argument . . .' (Darwin, 1859, p. 435). A recent interpreter goes further: 'The old arguments for evolution were only based on circumstantial evidence. . . . But the core of Darwin's argument was of a different kind. It did not make it more probable—it made it a certainty. Given his facts his conclusion *must* follow: like a proposition in geometry. You do not show that any two sides of a triangle are very *probably* greater than the third. You show that they *must* be so. Darwin's argument was a *de*ductive one—whereas an argument based on circumstantial evidence is *in*ductive' (Pantin, p. 137: italics original).

But now, was not Darwin a great empirical naturalist, concerned to discover what as a matter of fact *is* the case; although conceivably it might not have been? What business had he with deductive arguments purporting to demonstrate, as in a theorem of geometry, that this or that *must* be so? We have to investigate just what this deductive core amounts to, exactly how much it does prove, and upon assumptions of what kind it proves it.

Darwin's 'Introduction' indicates both that the book has such a deductive skeleton and what that skeleton is: 'As many more individuals of each species are born than can possibly survive; and as, *consequently*, there is a frequently recurring struggle for existence; *it follows that* any being, if it vary however slightly in any manner profitable to itself, under the complex and sometimes varying conditions of life will have a better chance of surviving and thus be naturally selected. From the strong principle of inheritance, any selected variety will tend to propagate its new and modified form' (Darwin, 1859, p. 68: italics supplied). He also promises that in the chapter 'Struggle for Existence' he will treat of this struggle 'amongst all organic beings throughout the world, *which inevitably follows from* the high geometrical ratio of their increase . . .' (ibid., p. 68: italics supplied).

In that chapter the argument is developed: 'A struggle for existence *inevitably follows* from the high rate at which all organic beings tend to increase . . . as more individuals are produced than can possibly survive, *there must in every case be* a struggle for existence, either one individual with another of the same species, or with the individuals of distinct species, or with the physical conditions of life. It is the doctrine of Malthus applied with manifold force to the whole animal and vegetable kingdoms; for in this case there can be no artificial increase of food, and no prudential restraint from marriage. Although some species may be now increasing, more or less rapidly, all *cannot* do so, for the world would not hold them' (ibid., pp. 116–17: italics supplied).

Just as the struggle for existence is derived as a consequence of the combination of a geometrical ratio of increase with finite resources for living, so, in the chapter 'Natural Selection', this in turn is derived as a consequence of the combination of the struggle for existence with variation. Darwin summarizes his argument here: 'If . . . organic beings vary at all in the several parts of their organization, and I think this cannot be disputed; if there be . . . a severe struggle for life, and this certainly cannot be disputed; then . . . I think it would be a most extraordinary fact if no variation had ever occurred useful to each being's own welfare, in the same manner as so many variations have occurred useful to man. But if variations useful to any organic being do occur, assuredly individuals thus characterised will have the best chance of being preserved in the struggle for life; and from the strong principle of inheritance they will tend to produce offspring similarly characterised' (ibid., pp. 169–70). However, Darwin goes on, 'Whether natural selection has really thus acted in nature . . . must be judged of by the general tenour and balance of evidence given in the following chapters' (ibid., p. 170). Nevertheless '. . . we already see how it entails extinction; and how largely extinction has acted in the world's history, geology plainly declares. Natural selection, also, leads to divergence of character; for more living beings can be supported on the same area the more they diverge in structure, habits, and constitution, of which we see proof by looking at the inhabitants of any small spot . . .' (ibid., p. 170).

Since Darwin's work does indeed have this deductive skeleton, Julian Huxley did well to expound his own understanding of Neo-Darwinian theory in similar terms. It can, he said, '. . . be stated in the form of two general evolutionary equations. The first is that reproduction plus mutation produces natural selection; and the second that natural selection plus time produces the various degrees of biological improvement that we find in nature' (Huxley, 1953, p. 38). The idea is excellent, but Huxley's execution is curiously slapdash. For the first equation, as he gives it $(R+M \rightarrow NS)$, is not valid. Reproduction plus mutation would not necessarily lead to natural selection. It is necessary also to bring in the struggle for existence; and that in turn has to be derived by offering the geometrical ratio of increase to the limited resources available for the support of life. So, if we are going to represent Darwin's own basic argument in Huxley's way, we need something more like: first, $GRI+LR\rightarrow SE$; and, second, $SE+V\rightarrow NS$. (To avoid anachronism V—for heritable variation—has in this case to be substituted for Huxley's M—for mutation.)

Of course to make this basic argument, and the equations used to represent it schematically, ideally rigorous, one would have to construct for all the crucial terms definitions to include explicitly every necessary assumption. There are in fact several, many of which when uncovered and noticed may seem too obvious to have been worth stating. Take, for instance, one to which Darwin himself refers, rather obliquely, in a passage already quoted: 'I think it would be a most extraordinary fact if no variation had ever occurred useful to each being's welfare . . .' (ibid., p. 170). It would indeed. He himself at once deploys a powerful reason for believing that this 'most extraordinary fact' has not in fact obtained, by adding immediately after the phrase just requoted: '. . . in the same manner as so many variations have occurred useful to man.' Yet to bring out such assumptions may have a further value. In the present instance it suggests, what has in fact proved to be the case, that one of the main effects of natural selection is to eliminate unfavourable variations. Natural selection not only helps to generate biological improvement. It is essential in order to prevent biological degeneration.

(2) Darwin's Achievement

This is not, however, the place to essay a rigorous formalization, or to reap any harvest incidental to such a task. For the main aim here is to take the measure of Darwin's theory: first by discovering what his theoretical achievement actually was; and then by following out some of the things which it does and does not imply. The first part of this exercise has become the more worthwhile since some recent writers have, through failing to appreciate that achievement, depreciated Darwin's originality. (See, for instance, Himmelfarb.)

It is salutary to recall the full title of Darwin's most famous book. It is *The Origin of Species by Natural Selection*; and to this is added a sub-title, which in the thirties and the forties acquired a sinister ring: *or the Preservation of Favoured races in the Struggle for Life*. For his true claim to originality does not lie in having been the first to assert the evolution, as opposed to the special creation, of species. That he was not. 'The general hypothesis of the derivation of all present species from a small number, or perhaps a single pair, of original ancestors was propounded by the President of the Berlin Academy of Sciences, Maupertuis, in 1745 and 1751, and by the principal editor of the *Encyclopédie*, Diderot, in 1749 and 1754' (Lovejoy, 1936, p. 268; and compare Lovejoy, 1904, *passim*).

Nor was Darwin the first to introduce into a biological context the ideas either of natural selection or of a struggle for existence. Both can be found in the Roman poet Lucretius in the first century B.C., in an account of how in the beginning our mother earth produced both the kinds of living things which we now know and many other sorts of ill-starred monstrosity. But with these latter: '. . . it was all in vain . . . they could not attain the desired flower of age nor find food nor join by the ways of Venus.' The poet concludes: 'And many species of animals must have perished at that time, unable by procreation to forge out the chain of posterity; for whatever you see feeding on the breath of life, either cunning or courage or at least quickness must have kept . . . from its earliest existence' (Lucretius, V. 845–8 and 855–9). Lucretius too was a disciple, clothing in Latin verse ideas which he had himself learnt from the fourth-century Greek Epicurus, who was here in his turn drawing on such fifth-century sources as Empedocles of Acragas (Kirk and Raven, pp. 336–40).

Darwin was actually original on two quite different counts. First, he put all the various elements together to form the conceptual scheme reviewed just now in Section 1. Second, he deployed an enormous mass of empirical material under the controlling guidance of that scheme. He thus: provided very strong reasons for believing that species are in fact the products of natural evolution rather than special creation; and showed how many whole ranges of previously unintelligible biological facts can and must be explained; and released a mighty stimulus to what has since proved to be endlessly fertile inquiry. Of course, once Darwin has done it for us, everything

appears obvious. The premises of his argument are as untechnical as its conclusions. The several deductive moves are
short and easy. To pick out the crucial notions, to bring them
all together, and to apply the conceptual scheme once it was
constructed, were also, I suppose, simple matters. But that
simplicity was the simplicity of genius.

(3) Deductive Arguments with Contingent Conclusions

Many people have suggested that Darwin's theory consists of
a series of made-to-measure tautologies, and hence that it
cannot be genuinely explanatory. Indeed one philosopher of
biology who has recently reviewed the literature complains
'that the number of critics of this kind is legion' (Ruse, 1973a,
p. 30).

   (i) In part the trouble arises from failure to appreciate that
a demonstration may proceed from premises which are all
logically contingent, through various valid deductive moves, to
conclusions which are themselves also logically contingent.
The temptation, to which good men have sometimes
succumbed, is to assume that the necessity that characterizes
any valid deductive inference must characterize the conclusion
of that inference as well. Yet it is quite wrong to argue—with,
among others, Thomas Hobbes—that: since from the proposition that there will be a sea-battle tomorrow it follows,
necessarily if unexcitingly, that there will be a sea-battle
tomorrow; therefore it also follows, again necessarily but this
time disturbingly, that the predicted occurrence of this sea-
battle will be itself a matter of logical or some other sort of
necessity. (See Flew, 1971, VII §§5–6, for discussion of this
sort of case for a strong determinism.)

   It is easy to read David Hume as involved in a similar
misunderstanding of the possibilities and limitations of
deduction and demonstration. For when in his first *Inquiry* he
develops the instrument now nicknamed Hume's Fork, by
explaining the fundamental difference between propositions
stating or purporting to state 'relations of ideas' and propositions stating or purporting to state 'matters of fact and real
existence', he writes: '*That the sun will not rise tomorrow* is no less
intelligible a proposition and implies no more contradiction
than the affirmation *that it will rise*. We should in vain, therefore,

attempt to demonstrate its falsehood. Were it demonstratively false, it would imply a contradiction and could never be distinctly conceived by the mind' (Hume, 1748, IV (i), p. 40). But in Hume's case we should at least notice that he is about to provide, in the final paragraph of the same Part and Section, a seminal account of the nature of applied mathematics. He appears there to be at least part of the time also seized of the crucial point, that valid deductive arguments may follow the links of logical necessity which sometimes bind contingent premisses to conclusions all themselves equally contingent: 'matters of fact and real existence' (ibid., pp. 45–6).

So it is with the deductive skeleton of Darwinism, the uniting framework of *The Origin of Species*. That living organisms all tend to reproduce themselves at a geometrical ratio of increase; that the resources which they need to sustain life and to reproduce are always in finite supply; and that, while each usually reproduces after its kind, sometimes there are variations which in their turn usually reproduce after their kind: all these propositions are none the less contingent and empirical for being manifestly and incontestably true. That there is a struggle for existence; and that through this struggle for existence natural selection occurs: both these propositions equally are none the less contingent and empirical for the fact that it follows, necessarily and as a matter of logic, that wherever the first three hold the second two must hold also.

(ii) A second common source of trouble here—and else-where—is failure to notice precisely which propositions are or are supposed to be either necessarily true and tautological or, as the case may be, self-contradictory. Thus, for instance, one of the very last people to want to minimize scientific achievement, J. J. C. Smart, writes: 'If we try to produce laws . . . which describe evolutionary processes . . . we can do so only by turning our propositions into mere tautologies. We can say that even in the great nebula in Andromeda the "fittest" will survive, but this is to say nothing, for "fittest" has to be defined in terms of "survival"' (Smart, 1963, p. 59).

Certainly, when we come to consider what Darwinism does and does not imply for morality and for politics, it is essential to recognize that it is a theory of the survival of the fittest only and precisely in so far as actual survival is the criterion of fitness to survive. In effect in this context 'fitness' is defined as 'having whatever it may as a matter of fact take to survive'. It is notorious that such biological fitness may be by other and independent standards most unadmirable. An individual or a species can have many splendid physical or mental endowments without these being or ensuring what is in fact needed for survival. Men who are in every way wretched creatures may, and all too often do, kill superb animals; while genius has frequently been laid low by the activities of unicellular beings having no wits at all. (See Flew, 1967, *passim*.)

But thus to deny that evolutionary biology refers to any external and independent criterion of fitness to survive, is not to say that all such claims about the survival of the fittest—whether on earth or within the Andromeda nebula—must be empty tautologies, carrying no implications about 'matters of fact and real existence'. On the contrary: just because Darwin's notion of the survival of the fittest is part of the integrated conceptual scheme described in Section 1 above, to say that within the Andromeda nebula, or anywhere else, the biologically fittest survive, is to take it for granted that there are in those parts living creatures with the tendency to multiply, reproducing generally after their own kind but with occasional variations apt in their turn to reproduce after their kind, and so on. It is also actually to say that in the constant struggle for existence the survivors survive because they happen to possess what in that particular environment turns out to be an edge of advantage over the going competition. This is, of course, a very general statement. But it is clearly contingent, not tautological. One thing which it precludes is the conceivable, false alternative that both those who die before reproducing and those who survive to reproduce, survive or die at random. (For a fuller, more technical treatment compare Ruse, 1973a, pp. 38ff.)

(iii) It is also instructive to examine a third source of trouble, which centres on confusions about falsifiability. Thus A. R. Manser writes: 'The circular definitions of key terms in the original version and its modern variants are such only because they are being used to construct a conceptual scheme, not to give a testable hypothesis' (Manser, p. 34).

(*a*) Enough has already been said about the curious notion that a conceptual scheme cannot contain any contingent and empirically testable elements. It is, nevertheless, just worth noting a further odd error. He says: 'As in the case of "adaptation", other key terms of the theory, such as "variation" and "environment", suffer from circular definitions.' Then, referring to the famous example of industrial melanism in the Peppered Moth (*Biston betularia*), he continues: '. . . if it had not been for the change from light-coloured to dark-coloured forms, no one would have noticed that the blackening of the trees in some areas constituted a change in environment for the species.'

It may well be true that, but for this change, biologists would not have recognized that blackening as a relevant environmental change. But Manser has no right forthwith to infer: 'What is to be counted as a change in the environment depends on a change in the population; here again no independent definition is possible, and thus no explanation is provided by using the term. If a species which has been relatively constant in numbers starts to decline without there being any obvious external cause such as human depredations, the explanation may be sought in a change in the environment. This change is only postulated because there has been a change in numbers, or in some other aspect of the population' (ibid., p. 26).

Certainly we would—or, at any rate, we should—look for explanations for changes only in so far as we know that there are in fact changes to be explained. But, from the mere fact that we might perhaps only happen to notice something under certain conditions, we are not entitled immediately to deduce that the something to be thus noticed must consist wholly or partly in the circumstances required to draw it to our attention. (If anyone is looking for a textbook illustration of the confounding of epistemology with ontology, then they need seek no further!)

(*b*) Noticing that there seems to be no acceptable alternative to a Darwinian theory, Manser rushes to conclude that any such system must on that account be unfalsifiable in principle. It does not follow. The absence of any acceptable alternative may instead be construed as a reason for thinking: not that the system is unfalsifiable in principle; but that it is in fact not false.

Manser's remarks are useful nevertheless. They provide our occasion to recognize a fundamental distinction. He writes: 'Some biologists will admit that one of the strongest motives leading them to accept the theory is the lack of any genuine alternative. Lamarckism is suggested from time to time, but most scientists in the field would regard it as experimentally disproved, though possibly not on very adequate evidence. Special Creation is not often suggested nowadays, and in any case would seem to be ruled out because no experimental test could be devised for it; hence it does not appear to be a genuine scientific theory. Thus from the time it was propounded, Darwinism has never had to deal with serious scientific opposition' (ibid., p. 18).

It would be hard not to wonder why Lamarckism is disqualified as a genuine and falsifiable alternative, when it has apparently been proved to be in fact false; even if we were to waive altogether the question of the putative inadequacy of this proof. 'These reasons,' one of Manser's critics protests, 'make belief today in Lamarckism . . . on a par with belief in a flat earth' (Ruse, 1973a, p. 109). But here the important thing is to contrast two antitheses. On the one hand we have the opposition between evolution and special creation, between naturalistic and supernaturalistic accounts of the origin of species. On the other hand we have oppositions between rival scientific accounts: between, for instance, 'the modern version' of Darwin's evolutionary theory, best known as 'the "synthetic" theory of evolution' and Lamarckism saltation, or orthogenesis (Ruse, 1973a, p. 9 and pp. 107ff.). These are genuine and falsifiable but, it seems, false alternatives to 'the "synthetic" theory'. There are also alternatives to any evolutionary theory at all, although such alternatives can scarcely rate as scientific. Yet we can scarcely avoid the conclusion that these are, because in fact known to be false, in principle falsifiable.

(4) The Limitations and the Possibilities of the Deductive Scheme

The conclusions of the deductive argument developed in Section 1 above are surely proved. For the argument is valid, and its premisses cannot reasonably be doubted. It is, therefore, all the more important to appreciate how little that argument does by itself actually prove.

(i) It certainly does not establish that 'all the various degrees of biological improvement that we find in nature' can be accounted for in these terms. (Huxley, 1953, p. 38.) Indeed by itself it is not even sufficient to show that any new species in fact evolved in this way. At most it proves only that some biological improvement must be effected thus. Darwin needed, and began most abundantly to provide, other facts and other arguments to support his own far wider and more revolutionary assertions: '. . . that species are not immutable; but that those belonging to what are called the same genera are lineal descendants of some other and generally extinct species, in the same manner as the acknowledged varieties of any one species are the descendants of that species. Furthermore, I am convinced that Natural Selection has been the main but not exclusive means of modification' (Darwin, 1859, p. 69). Although Darwin and his successors have built up a mighty case for this most sweeping conclusion, it is one which cannot be complete until the whole science of evolutionary biology is finished; which it will never be.

(a) It therefore is, and will remain, possible for someone without formal inconsistency to accept a Darwinian account of the origin of some species while insisting that others—and in particular our own—nevertheless were, or are, wholly or in part products of special creation. Consider, for example, how in his 1953 Encyclical *Humani Generis* Pope Pius XII reaffirmed the traditional and in his view essential doctrine. It is that—generously—'the teaching of the Church leaves the doctrine of evolution an open question, as long as it confines its speculations to the development, from other living matter already in existence, of the human body'. Nevertheless, 'That souls are immediately created by God is a view which the Catholic faith imposes on us' (Denzinger, §3027).

But although this sort of stance is, and is likely to remain, formally compatible with all the available biological evidence, still it must be, and will surely become ever more, arbitrary and unreasonable; unless, of course, we can excogitate excellent evidencing reasons to warrant some such theological belief system. Darwin at first had some hesitations himself about going the whole hog. Certainly there are in the final 'Recapitulation and Conclusion' moments when we seem to meet the young man who on the voyage of the *Beagle* had devoured Lyell's newly published *Principles of Geology*: '. . . species are produced and exterminated by slowly acting and still existing causes, and not by miraculous acts of creation and by catastrophes . . .' (Darwin, 1859, p. 457; and compare Darwin, 1887, p. 77). Yet there are still reservations too: '. . . the theory of descent with modification embraces all the members of the same class. I believe that animals have descended from at most only four or five progenitors, and plants from an equal or lesser number' (Darwin, 1859, p. 454). Later, however, all doubts about the universal reality of evolution, though not about the particular mechanisms, disappeared; and in *The Descent of Man* he tackled directly the most important and contentious case.

(*b*) Notice further that Darwin's main deductive argument has nothing to say about the mechanisms of variation. Indeed about these *The Origin of Species* is generally reticent. The good reason for silence is given at the beginning of the summary of the relevant chapter: 'Our ignorance of the laws of variation is profound' (ibid., p. 202). One consequence is that the Darwinism of Darwin, if not the Neo-Darwinism of 'the "synthetic" theory', is quite compatible with some inheritance of acquired characteristics. Those familiar with the extent to which such ideas have since been discredited may well be surprised to find the hospitality which Darwin himself is prepared to afford them.

Another consequence is that Darwinism, if again perhaps not all forms of Neo-Darwinism, could perhaps make room for some still unidentified mechanism making the occurrence of favourable variations, and perhaps at the same time of unfavourable, significantly more frequent than favourable mutations, or even unfavourable, are at this time generally thought to be. This corollary should be a consolation for those who suspect that, despite all the achievements of the evolution-ary biologists, there is still at least one vital element missing.

(ii) By itself the basic deductive scheme proves little. But it can be and is employed both as a vastly powerful stimulus and guide to inquiry and as a similarly potent explanatory framework. Both strengths Darwin himself appreciated fully.

(a) In his final chapter, for instance, he makes the first point with particular reference to those recognized great unknowns of variation: 'A grand and almost untrodden field of inquiry will be opened on the causes and laws of variation . . . on the effects of use and disuse, on the direct action of external conditions, and so forth. The study of domestic productions will rise immensely in value. A new variety raised by man will be a more important and interesting subject of study than one more species added to the infinitude of already recorded species. Our classifications will come to be, as far as they can be so made, genealogies; and will then truly give what may be called the plan of creation. The rules for classifying will no doubt become simpler when we have a definite object in view. We possess no pedigrees or armorial bearings; and we have to discover and trace the many diverging lines of descent in our natural genealogies, by characters of any kind which have long been inherited. Rudimentary organs will speak infallibly with respect to the nature of long-lost structures' (ibid., pp. 456–7).

Three paragraphs later Darwin makes a forecast of special interest to us. The greater our knowledge of evolutionary biology, the greater the need for all human sciences to take account of that knowledge: 'In the distant future I see open fields for far more important researches. Psychology will be based on a new foundation, that of the necessary acquirement of each mental power and capacity by gradation. Light will be thrown on the origin of man . . .' (ibid., p. 458).

Consider, for example, two areas of current controversy in the human sciences where assumptions hard if not impossible to reconcile with a Darwinian account of human origins are still commonly made. First, there is the Chomskyan contention that we all possess 'a native equipment that codes the fundamental structural, semantic and illocutionary features of any possible human language . . . native . . . in the sense that its development is spontaneous and genetically determined . . . not . . . that this apparatus is present in the infant at birth. . . .' On this view there is 'one basic conceptual framework, which is the matrix underlying the various natural languages' (Vendler, p. 230).

So far, perhaps, so good. What gives pause is that it is suggested further, though not stated, that this genetically determined framework could not have evolved through a series of independently useful advances. Thus it is proposed that if someone is to learn his first language L 'he cannot learn L word by word, because he will not know what any word in L means until he has mastered L, and he certainly cannot learn L . . . all at once' (ibid., p. 221). Yet the most which this— in an appropriately dyslogistic sense—scholastic argument proves is: not that he cannot learn, step by step and with no such pre-existing framework, whatever is immediately necessary if he is ultimately to be said to know L; but that a man cannot be said really to know the full meaning of any word in L until he knows (a good part of) L.

Second, we have the insistence, which seems nowadays to be endemic among sociologists and the best publicized educationalists, that, even if they do have to concede that there are significant hereditarily determined differences both of talent and of temperament as between individuals; still it must on no account be admitted that there may be—and indeed are—differences, at least on average, in the distribution of such qualities as between certain social and racial groups. (For some truly astonishing examples of this insistence, and for discussion of theoretical and practical issues arising, see the articles on 'Sociology and Equality' and 'The Jensen Uproar' in Flew, 1976b.) In the 'Postscript' to *The Philosophy of Biology* Michael Ruse echoes Darwin's hope that the human sciences will 'incorporate into their theories results first discovered by the biologist.' At a time when a Neo-Lysenkoist, extreme environmentalism is—sometimes all too literally— running riot, it seems naive or wilful to hope for such influence for a science which, in Ruse's book, puts genetics first. Yet no one who wants to see people and society as they really are, and no discipline aspiring to earn the diploma title 'science', can afford to deny or to ignore relevant and fundamental, but to some professionally or ideologically inconvenient, facts.

(*b*) The same theoretical theme possesses great explanatory power. It is employed to reveal connections between what without it are separate and unintelligible brute facts, and to show that—granted its own scarcely contestable assumptions—what has happened and happens is the sort of thing which could have been expected. Before Darwin the conventional wisdom even among biologists was that species are all fundamental natural kinds, created separately. But then he argued 'that the view which most naturalists entertain, and which formerly I entertained—namely, that each species has been independently created—is erroneous' (Darwin, 1859, p. 69: and compare the 'Historical Sketch' which he prefaced to later editions).

On the contrary, he said, the truth is that all species have their places on one single family tree—or maybe four or five at most—and thus they all are in the most literal sense related. And the same account, which brings all living things together into one enormous extended family, also shows the sorts of ways in which many kinds of previously incongruous and unintelligible fact must have come about, and might have been expected. In his final chapter Darwin reviews case after case. For example: 'As natural selection acts solely by accumulating slight, successive, favourable variations, it can produce no great or sudden modification. . . . Hence the canon of "Natura non facit saltum," which every fresh addition to our knowledge tends to make more strictly correct, is on this theory simply intelligible. We can plainly see why nature is prodigal in variety, though niggard in innovation' (ibid., pp. 444–5: the Latin means 'Nature does not take a leap').

Again: 'How strange it is that a bird, under the form of woodpecker, should have been created to prey on insects on the ground; that upland geese, which never or rarely swim, should have been created with webbed feet; that a thrush should have been created to dive and feed on sub-aquatic insects; and that a petrel should have been created with habits and structure fitting it for the life of a hawk or a grebe! . . . But on the view of each species constantly trying to increase in number, with natural selection always ready to adapt the slowly varying descendants of each to any unoccupied or ill-occupied place in nature, *these facts cease to be strange, or perhaps might even have been anticipated*' (ibid., p. 445: italics supplied).

(5) *A New Conception of Species*

'When the views entertained in this volume . . . are generally admitted . . . there will be a considerable revolution in natural history. Systematists . . . will not be incessantly haunted by the shadowy doubt whether this or that form be in essence a species. This I feel sure, and I speak after experience, will be no slight relief. The endless disputes whether or not some fifty species of British brambles are true species will cease. Systematists will have only to decide (not that this will be easy) whether any form be sufficiently constant and distinct from other forms, to be capable of definition; and if definable, whether the differences be sufficiently important to deserve a specific name . . . we shall be compelled to acknowledge that the only distinction between species and well-marked varieties is, that the latter are known, or believed, to be connected at the present day by intermediate gradations, whereas species were formerly thus connected' (ibid., p. 455).

Darwin is thus challenging in the more particular field of biology those very general prejudices about language and classification which John Locke had begun to uncover and to question two centuries earlier in *An Essay concerning Human Understanding*, Book III, 'Of Words'.[1] These are: that all things belong to certain natural kinds, in virtue of 'their essential natures'; that there are no marginal cases falling outside and between these sharply delimited collections of individuals; that there must always be straight yes or no answers to the question 'Is this individual a so and so or not?'; and that men have only to uncover and, as it were, write the labels for, the classes to which nature has antecedently allocated every individual thing. (See Flew, 1971, XII §4.) In the biological field the pictures appropriate to these false assumptions are: that of the first chapter of Genesis, where all creatures are created after their unambiguously different kinds; and that of the same tradition, splendidly illustrated by William Blake, of Adam naming the beasts. They illustrate the approach to biological classification epitomized in the citation of the Swedish Academy honouring Carl von Linnaeus: 'He discovered the essential nature of insects.'

The importance for us of Darwin's new conception of species

becomes apparent as soon as we turn from British brambles to ourselves. For if Darwin was right, then there never has been any sharp, undisputatious naturally given, dividing line between the human and the not human or the not yet human. Nor is there any guarantee that in every case which we may in the future meet we shall be able—once given all the relevant facts—to return an unhesitatingly correct answer to the question: 'Is this a human being or not?' If Darwin was right—and I propose to take it that the continuing successes of evolutionary biology have shown that he was—then our situation is precisely not that presupposed in the statement of Roman Catholic doctrine quoted in Section 4 (i)(a), above: there are no such sharp and absolute divides between one species and another. And it must be wrong to assume that for every term for every true biological species there has to be a 'real essence'—an ultimate and authentic definition corresponding to the principles of construction and classification actually employed by God or Nature—as opposed to the 'nominal essence'—the definition which only epitomizes conventionally correct usage. Sometimes, therefore, the response to a particular question about membership of our own species—a question heavy with practical implications—cannot be simply a matter of first discovering and assembling all the relevant facts, and then applying verbal knowledge available to everyone who is master of any natural language. It will instead require, not a finding on what somehow just is the case, but a new policy decision to determine where a line ought or ought not to be drawn.

So it is just an arbitrary decision to adopt, or not to adopt, what is in the end merely a matter of convention? No, it is not! All decisions are not arbitrary decisions; any more than all conventions are mere conventions. To decide, for instance, whether a one-month-old or a three-month-old foetus is to count as a human being can be a matter of life or death. Whatever such policy decisions are, they most certainly can be, and ought to be, enlightened, responsible, thoroughly and anxiously considered, and in every other way the reverse of arbitrary.

(6) *An Old Model at Long Last Deployed*

In a useful introduction to the philosophy of physics, too ambitiously entitled *The Philosophy of Science*,[2] Stephen Toulmin introduced the notion of the deployment of a model: 'At the stage at which a new model is introduced the data that we have to go on, the phenomena which it is used to explain, do not justify us in prejudging, either way, which of the questions which must normally make sense when asked of things which, say, travel will eventually be given a meaning in the new theory also . . . One might speak of models in physics as more or less "deployed". So long as we restrict ourselves to geometrical optics, the model of light as a substance travelling is deployed only to a small extent; but as we move into physical optics, . . . the model is continually further deployed' (Toulmin, 1953, p. 37).

Darwin's theory made possible a massive deployment of one ancient model which had for centuries been, as it now seems, incomprehensibly confined. This was the model of the extended family. With this was associated the method of representation usually employed to express both actual familial relationships—'the family tree'—and one system of classification—'the tree of Porphyry'. Darwin, as usual, got and made the point himself: 'The terms used by naturalists of affinity, relationship, community of type, paternity . . . will cease to be metaphorical and will have a plain signification'; while 'Our classifications will come to be, as far as they can be made, genealogies. . . .' (Darwin, 1859, p. 456.)

It is remarkable that this familiar model does not seem to have been either originally introduced in an attempt at scientific explanation or later effective towards the production of the theory in which it is more extensively deployed. The various terms appropriate to this model were, apparently, introduced because naturalists noticed analogies which made the idea of family relationship seem apt as a metaphor. But the suggestion that the metaphor might be considerably more than a metaphor, that the model could be deployed, seems almost always to have been blocked by the strong resistance of the accepted doctrine of the fixity of species. It is wrong to attribute this resistance to nothing but 'religious fears and prejudices' (Hume, 1748, I, p. 20). Certainly belief in the evolution of species would be incompatible with the acceptance of the creation myths of Genesis, interpreted literally (to say nothing of the incompatibility between the two myths themselves). But the evolutionary geology of Lyell is equally irreconcilable with a literal reading of the Pentateuch, and that geology was already becoming generally accepted among scientific men when Darwin began to investigate the origin of species (Gillispie, *passim*).

Quite apart from any considerations of ideology we must acknowledge that it just is a most familiar fact that living things as we see them around us in our everyday lives do, with only comparatively infrequent exceptions, appear to belong to various natural kinds; which also mate and reproduce, again with only comparatively minor exceptions, after their kinds. It was precisely this massive and stubborn fact for which the aetiological myth makers of Genesis were trying to account with their theory of the special creation of fixed species. Even after the evolutionary geologists had opened up the vaster time scale needed for a smooth and uniformitarian process of biological evolution, the way of this concept was still blocked by the difficulty of suggesting any mechanisms which could possibly have brought about such an enormous development.

Another secular bulwark of the doctrine of fixed species surely is the unrevolutionary, pre-Lockean, assumption about classification indicated in Section 5 above. For while the general fact of a superficially apparent stability and separateness of ostensible natural kinds is a main source and stay for those false assumptions; still the very same assumptions—all the more powerful because so rarely recognized and formulated —must in their turn provide support for the fundamental error of believing 'that each species has been independently created . . . that species are . . . immutable' (Darwin, 1859, p. 69).

(7) *The Philosophical Implications of Darwinism*

This last section of the present chapter is not the first to refer to what are usually called the philosophical implications, particularly the implications for our understanding of the nature of man. But we need to conclude with something more concentrated and systematic.

(i) The one which was probably pre-eminent in the minds of Darwin's contemporaries was the threat to what has been, and remains, the most popularly persuasive of the traditional types of argument for the existence of God—the Argument to Design. Thus William Paley, in his *Natural Theology*, urges that, just as from the observation of a watch we may infer the existence of a watchmaker, so, by parity of reasoning, from the existence of mechanisms so marvellous as the human eye we must infer the existence of a Designer. Paley explicitly repudiates as an alternative any suggestion 'that the eye, the animal to which it belongs, every other animal, every plant . . . are only so many out of the possible varieties and combinations of being which the lapse of infinite ages has brought into existence: that the present world is the relic of that variety; millions of other bodily forms and other species having perished, being by the defect of their constitutions incapable of preservation. . . . Now there is no foundation whatever for this conjecture in anything which we observe in the works of nature . . .' (Paley, 1803, Vol. I, p. 32).[3]

The work of Darwin and his successors has surely annihilated the Argument to Design in this form. But there is another form, not similarly exposed to scientific attack, which some find in Way Five of St. Thomas Aquinas. Paley contended that there could and would be no naturalistic account of evolution such as Darwin in fact began to provide. Aquinas, they say, was more cautious. He is said to have maintained that whatever basic sorts of order are found in the Universe, including therefore those ultimate natural laws in terms of which our biologists will eventually explain the evolution of the human eye, cannot be intrinsic to the Universe itself, but must always be imposed upon it by an outside Orderer, 'which all men call God'. The equally decisive reply to this was developed in the century before Darwin by Hume. It led to what he liked to call—following Pierre Bayle—not Stratonian but 'Stratonician atheism'. The reply was a question: 'Whatever warrant could we have that the order which we discover in the Universe— the only Universe we know—is not, as it appears to be, intrinsic, but imposed?' (See Hume, 1748, X, and 1779, *passim*; and compare Flew, 1966, §§3.1–3.30, or 1971 VI §5.)

(ii) Darwinism has been taken, or mis-taken, to justify the

most extraordinarily diverse moral and political policies, often mutually incompatible. As a purely scientific theory it could not by itself entail any normative conclusions (conclusions, that is, about what *ought* to be); because it would not, so long as it remained a purely scientific theory, contain any but descriptive premisses (premisses, that is, about what neutrally *is* the case, or *has been*, or *will be*). It is the more necessary for us to insist upon this categorial distinction: because Darwin did employ some terms which invite normative interpretations, and was occasionally himself led momentarily astray; and because there are today many who would like to dismiss any fact/value distinction as an unfounded and ephemeral eccentricity.

We have already noted—in Section 3(ii) above—that the survival of the fittest guaranteed by the theory is not necessarily the survival of anything which we could by some independent standard adjudge most admirable and best. Again, because artificial selection is always for what somebody holds to be good, and because natural selection in a struggle for existence ensures the survival of those who are in that natural biologists' sense fittest; it has seemed to some that here is a ready-made rationale for unrestricted competition, and extinction take the hindmost. But this is wrong. So, if we British want to find reasons for breaking up the state monopolies, then we shall have to look elsewhere; though that search for reasons need, perhaps, be neither long nor hard.

Yet again, the not particularly Darwinian notion of higher animals, combined with the idea that these are among the later products of evolution, may raise a hope that Nature is somehow in favour of progress. *The Origin of Species* is not wholly untouched by this hope, notwithstanding that Darwin had pinned into his copy of *Vestiges of the Natural History of Creation* the memorandum slip: 'Never use the words *higher* and *lower*.' (Darwin and Seward, Vol. I, p. 114n.) For in his final peroratory paragraph Darwin concludes: '. . . from the war of nature, from famine and death, the most exalted object which we are capable of conceiving, namely the production of the higher animals, directly follows. There is a grandeur in this view of life . . .' (Darwin, 1859, pp. 459–60).

There is indeed. And, although his is no more capable than

any other scientific theory of entailing norms to direct choices, we may well find it both exhilarating and illuminating to see our decisions in an evolutionary perspective (Flew, 1967, V). To understand and to accept that fundamental incapability it will help if we come to appreciate why a theory of the origin of species neither does nor could provide guarantees of human progress; whatever you or I may choose to make our criteria of progress. We find our clue in one of Darwin's references to T. R. Malthus, already quoted in Section 1 above. Darwin is speaking of the struggle for existence, an element in his account of the mechanism producing new species suggested—as we shall be seeing in Chapter Two, below—by his reading of the *Second Essay* on population: 'It is the doctrine of Malthus applied with manifold force to the whole animal and vegetable kingdom; *for in this case there can be no artificial increase of food, and no prudential restraint from marriage*' (Darwin, 1859, p. 117: italics supplied).

The point is that what happens in human history is largely determined by human creativity and human choice; or— what is in the present context the same thing—by human failures to be creative or to choose. Furthermore, and to an ever-increasing extent, the fortunes and even the survival of all other species also depend on what men do or do not do. I shall in later chapters have much more to say about the nature, extent, and importance of this crucial phenomenon of choice. Here it is sufficient to remark that every scientific prediction has in some way to be protected against the threat of falsification by human agency.

In many cases this protection is secured by the fact that it is now, and maybe always will be, contingently impossible for any person or group of persons to prevent the event predicted: the astronomers, for instance, forecasting future eclipses of the sun have no need to add any non-intervention clauses. But in other cases the prediction, though appealing to the most respectable physical, chemical, or biological laws, has to be safeguarded with some tacit or explicit UNLESS clause. The aim of the entire exercise may indeed lie precisely in the formulation and eventual satisfaction of that clause: 'We called in a crack firm of civil engineers, and they report that the structure will collapse in the next Force 8 gale unless the following steps are taken.'

The upshot is: even if there were—what I shall later argue that there neither are nor could be—natural laws of human action; still a biological theory containing no reference to choice could not yield guarantees that choices will be made in this sense rather than that. It could not, therefore, underwrite our hopes that the development of events determined by such choices either will or will not proceed in a direction which any of us could by some independent standard rate as progressive; or, for that matter, reactionary.

Further attention to the notion of choice can illuminate another aspect of the reason why premisses neutrally referring only to what *is* cannot by themselves entail conclusions about what *ought* to be. It is not a bit of good to discover that many of the words and expressions which we ordinarily employ are at the same time both descriptive and prescriptive; nor to report that in Hegel or Marx or in anyone else there is no distinction of this kind, and hence that your favourite guru has triumphantly 'transcended such dichotomies'. For no one has ever asserted that the distinctions between ought and is, prescriptive and descriptive, value and fact, always are made:[4] there would be little point in making a fuss about them if they were. Nor do you do any honour to an author by saying only that he does not observe some distinction. For, unless you can go on to say that he demonstrated that it is either not worth making or cannot be made, your fine word 'transcended' becomes a pretentious euphemism for 'muddled and confounded'. Yet the prospect of providing the required demonstration is small. For the notion of ought here clearly refers to contexts of choice. But from a series of strictly neutral statements about what was and is and will be we can scarcely hope to leap directly to a committed conclusion recommending this particular course rather than that, or that.

(iii) The third kind of possible implication bears directly upon the main concern of the present book. We have already noticed—in Section 5 above—that there cannot have been any gross discontinuities in the development of humankind from non-human ancestors; although this is not to say that gaps cannot have been, and have not been, opened up since by subsequent extinctions. Then in Section 6 we noticed that Darwinism implies that all living things are members of one single, enormous, extended family. But the fact of this relationship does not carry the further implication that we ought all to behave to one another as ideal siblings would, or to treat other forms of life as some believe St. Francis of Assisi did.[5] Cain and Abel were both brothers, in the neutral biologists' sense. But it was a moral rather than a logical offence which Cain committed in murdering Abel. The true corollary for us to draw from the fact that we are members of this extended family of all living organisms is that we are inescapably animals, albeit very special and very peculiar animals.

Perhaps the best way of beginning to appreciate what this involves is by reviewing some of the insights and oversights of two best-selling books, *The Naked Ape* and *The Human Zoo*. Both contain much curious zoological information, interestingly retailed.[6] Who, for instance, could resist an account of the unsuccessful attempt to get the London and the Moscow giant pandas to mate, which begins: 'I myself was once the embarrassed recipient of sexual advances by a female giant panda'? This sad story of futile travel and sexual fixation—a story wittily entitled by the advertising agents of British European Airways *To Moscow for Love*—concludes: 'He had matured as a panda's panda, but she was now a people's panda' (Morris, 1970, p. 161).

This is splendid stuff, and fun, if perhaps not quite good clean fun. But both books are also books with a message. This message is not worked out and made precise, and it is usually suggested rather than stated. The fullest and most open statements come at the start and the finish: 'The comparison we must make is not between the city-dweller and the wild-animal, but between the city-dweller and the captive animal. The modern human animal is no longer living in conditions natural for his species. Trapped, not by a zoo collector, but by his own brainy brilliance, he has set himself up in a huge restless menagerie . . .' (ibid., p. 8). The author's stated conclusion is that all leaders and directors 'must become good biologists', realizing that man is 'a human animal, a primitive tribal hunter, masquerading as a civilized, super-tribal citizen and desperately struggling to match his ancient inherited qualities with his extraordinary new situation' (ibid., p. 248).

Now there certainly is something both important and true here. Some of this something I have already said in my own way. Then again it presumably is both correct and to the point to remind us that the enormous and ever-accelerating environmental changes of the last ten thousand years or so have not been accompanied by any significant mutational additions to the human gene pool, as opposed to distributional changes within it. Most important is the insistence that, however special and peculiar we become, we still remain animals: 'Even a space ape must urinate' (Morris, 1967, p. 21). One consequence of seeing people in this way, as Morris makes very plain, is to remove a main obstacle to recognizing the urgency of population problems. For how could the affirmation of a universal natural right to reproduce, regardless of the likely availability of resources, survive the wholehearted acknowledgement of our essential corporeality?

Unfortunately, however, it is not these good things which are most distinctive, and which Morris is most eager to emphasize. Look again at the two passages quoted. In the first Morris is claiming that what—still—is truly natural for man is the life led by our hunting ancestors; while in the second he speaks of man as—now—'a primitive tribal hunter, masquerading as a civilized, super-tribal citizen'.

This will not do. Of course there is a continuity of development from the primitive to the advanced. Of course too, as Morris often and interestingly indicates, there are many similarities between primitive and civilized practices. And, furthermore, of course there is a hereditary animal nature from which man, so long as he remains man, never escapes: 'Even a space ape must urinate.' But what is just not true is that for us now most of what comes naturally, or second naturally, is what would have come naturally to our hunter ancestors; that we are not really citizens of our own countries and children of our own times, but only masquerading as such; that when the chips are down we are not what we are, but what our ancestors were. For to say that this has developed or evolved from that is precisely not to say that, truly or ultimately, this just is that. The one claim is indeed not merely different from, but strictly incompatible with, the other. Evolution implies changes: if, therefore, this evolved from that; then that is not now, and cannot be, the same as this. In a word: oaks are not, and cannot be, really acorns; and civilized men—whether for better or for worse—are not, and cannot be, really primitive apes.

What Morris does is to offer as a, or even the, biologists' point of view a systematic depreciation of environment as opposed to heredity, of what is learnt as opposed to what is instinctual. In this perverse presentation the gaps between men and the brutes, and between civilized men and primitive hunters, must narrow enormously. Yet it is a bizarre sight to see Morris flourishing this supposed insight as a professional trophy. For it requires him to minimize precisely what one would expect any biologist to pick out as the most remarkable peculiarities of our species—the extraordinarily long period between birth and maturity, the incomparable capacity for learning. This learning capacity, together with its main instrument and expression language, provides our unique species with an excellent substitute for the inheritance of acquired characteristics.[7]

An adequate account of man, even an adequate biological account of man, must do justice both to the differences and to the similarities, to the uniqueness as well as to the likenesses. The occupational weakness of Morris, indeed the occupation, is to sacrifice the former to the latter. I end the chapter with two more examples.

(a) First, Morris lists ten conditions of inter-group violence, and then remarks: 'The one condition which I have deliberately omitted from this list is the development of differing ideologies. As a zoologist, viewing man as an animal, I find it hard to take such differences seriously. . . .' (Morris, 1970, pp. 47–8.) This is altogether typical. Yet it is both bad science and inconsistent with the more realistic attitudes which he himself adopts elsewhere. It is bad science because it insists, against the facts, that there are no important and relevant differences between our species and all others. It is inconsistent because elsewhere Morris himself is ready to recognize and to deplore ideology as a real and formidable human phenomenon. The truth itself compels him, for instance, to allow that ideology constitutes a major obstacle to his own enlightened attitude towards population: 'Yet the opponents of contraception persist in their views' (ibid., p. 82).

(*b*) Second, Morris talks of examinations simply as initiation ceremonies: 'These are conducted in the heavy atmosphere of high ritual with the pupils cut off from all outside assistance. Just as in the tribal ritual, no one can help them . . . When the final exams. are over, at university level, the students who have "passed the test" become qualified as special members of the adult section of the super-tribe. They don elaborate display robes and take part in a further ritual called the degree ceremony, in the presence of the academic elders wearing their even more impressive and dramatic robes' (ibid., pp. 238–9).

Certainly a degree ceremony can be aptly and fairly compared with a tribal initiation. So far so good. But it is not zoological or any other sort of realism thus to insist on ignoring the essential and primary function of the antecedent examinations; which is to test learning, and to establish qualifications. It is nevertheless entirely fitting that Morris, dedicated as he is to depreciating the learnt as opposed to the inherited, should want to distract attention from the content and purpose of public examinations.

No doubt this part of *The Human Zoo* proves congenial to all those many, 'teachers' and 'pupils' both, now labouring so strenuously to remove from our educational system every approximation to an objective test of what, if anything, has actually been taught, or learnt (Flew, 1976b, VI).

2

POWERS, CHECKS, AND CHOICE
IN MALTHUS

SECTION I of Chapter One quoted from *The Origin of Species* a comment on the idea of 'A struggle for existence . . . It is the doctrine of Malthus applied with manifold force to the whole animal and vegetable kingdoms; for in this case there can be no artificial increase of food, and no prudential restraint from marriage' (Darwin, 1859, p. 117). In those two final clauses, after the semicolon, Darwin puts his finger on a crucial difference between his own theory and that of Malthus—or, indeed, any other theory which makes any move to embrace the intransigent peculiarity of human beings. The present chapter takes the work of Malthus on population as an example, and considers it mainly in so far as it accommodates or fails to accommodate that peculiarity. This choice of example is for us abundantly justified: partly because Malthus is so often misrepresented, and every opportunity to straighten the record is welcome; partly because his studies refer to overwhelmingly urgent practical issues—issues which arise only and precisely because, whatever our specific differences, we cannot but remain generically animal; and partly because his theoretical framework is both logically and historically close to that of Darwin, which makes it possible to bring out through illuminating comparison what it was that respect for the idiosyncrasy of his human subject matter required Malthus to concede.

(1) Two Historical Paradoxes

Both Darwin and his independent co-discoverer Alfred Russel Wallace stated quite categorically each in his own case that the stimulus of reading Malthus was in fact decisive. Thus, in a letter to Wallace, Darwin confirms the other's conjecture 'that I came to the conclusion that selection was the principle of change from study of domesticated productions; and then reading Malthus I saw at once how to apply this principle' (Marchant, Vol. I, p. 136; and compare Flew, 1970, pp. 49–51).

Apart from providing a worthwhile warning to specialists inclined to neglect their general reading, this well-documented story of the contribution made by a theory of human population to the construction of an account of the evolution of species by natural selection may be seen as one of many paradoxes of the history of ideas. It may be so seen in as much as the actual development was in two different ways from the more complex and the more difficult to the less. These two paradoxes relate to the first and second subsections of the final Section 7 of Chapter One.

(i) In the former we noticed how the work of Darwin ruined the more popular version of the old and respected Argument to Design. For he showed how so much of what may look like the product of design, though certainly not of human design, could come about, and presumably does, without any design at all. Yet already in the previous century Hume and the other Scottish founding fathers of social science had been applying similar evolutionary ideas to social institutions. They thus enforced the surely still more difficult and disturbing conclusion that many of the most remarkable of our own supposed 'special creations' are not, perhaps could not have been, the intended results of intended action.

Less enlightened predecessors told tales of foresight and contract. Hume argued that this was 'mere philosophical fiction, which never had, and never cou'd have any reality'. The fundamental conventions through which 'we maintain society' neither have nor could have originated out of a pre-social state of nature by way of a social contract—if only because promising itself presupposes the essentially social institution of language: 'Two men, who pull the oars of a boat, do it by an agreement or convention, tho' they have never given promises to each other. Nor is the rule concerning the stability of possession the less deriv'd from human conventions, that it arises gradually, and acquires force by a slow progression . . . In like manner are languages gradually establish'd by human conventions without any promise. In like manner do

gold and silver become the common measures of exchange . . .'
(Hume, 1739–40, III(ii) 2, pp. 493, 489 and 490; and compare
Flew, 1976c, II. But then contrast Hume 1739–40, III(ii) 10,
pp. 554ff.).

Institutions, in the same broadest sense, can and very often
do serve important or even indispensable social purposes,
notwithstanding that they were not originally designed so to
do, and notwithstanding that the persons involved may
themselves harbour only other, perhaps less lofty and public-
spirited intentions. In such cases a 'system . . . comprehending
the interest of each individual, is of course advantageous to the
public; tho' it be not intended for that purpose . . .' (ibid.,
III(ii) 6, p. 529). The same profound sociological insight was
later to lead Hume's younger friend Adam Smith to write of
the economically efficient allocation of scarce resources by a
market, and of the individual's participation therein: 'He
generally . . . neither intends to promote the public interest,
nor knows how much he is promoting it . . . he intends only his
own gain, and he is in this, as in many other cases, led by an
invisible hand to promote an end which was no part of his
intention' (A. Smith, IV(ii), Vol. I, p. 400).[8] Nine years earlier
another leader of the Scottish Enlightenment, Adam Ferguson,
had made the point in general: we 'stumble upon establish-
ments, which are indeed the result of human action, but not
the execution of any human design' (Quoted by Hayek,
1967, p. 96n: I give this reference thus indirectly as my thanks
to Hayek for introducing me to Ferguson).

(ii) That first of the two paradoxes has little connection
with Malthus, although his enormously influential work
certainly did concentrate attention upon the fact that private
and intended sexual activities are apt to produce public and
unintended social consequences. But the second, as we begin
to see in the second subsection of Section 7 in Chapter One,
cannot even be understood without appreciating the crucial
difference between the theoretical frameworks of Darwin and
of Malthus. The point is, in short, that Malthus had to take
account of choice, whereas Darwin did not. Certainly Darwin
'came to the conclusion that selection was the principle of
change from the study of domesticated productions'. But *The
Origin of Species* is about natural selection, rather than the

activities of human breeders; and natural selection, unlike what we have learned thanks to Darwin to call artificial selection, involves no choice. So, given that the populations with which he is concerned possess a power to multiply, which can be inhibited only by some external force, and given that the resources available to support these populations are always finite, Darwin infers that 'A struggle for existence inevitably follows . . . It is the doctrine of Malthus applied with manifold force to the whole animal and vegetable kingdoms; for in this case there can be . . . no prudential restraint . . .'.

(2) The Malthusian Framework

The main sources for 'the doctrine of Malthus' on population are four. First, there is *An Essay on the Principle of Population as it Effects the Future Improvement of Society, with Remarks on the Speculations of Mr. Godwin, M. Condorcet, and other Writers.* This was published in 1798 and, as the full title suggests, was an occasional polemic directed at various then fashionable utopians. Second, there is *An Essay on the Principle of Population; or, a View of its Past and Present Effects on Human Happiness; with an Inquiry into our Prospects respecting the Future Removal or Mitigation of the Evils which it occasions.* This was published in 1803, as if it were a second edition of the first item. But in his Preface the author himself said: 'In its present shape it may be considered as a new work . . .' (Malthus, 1803, Vol. I, pp. v–vi). Indeed it may, and should. I shall follow, and recommend, the practice of referring to what library catalogues call the first edition as the *First Essay*, reserving the title *Second Essay* for this second and all later editions. Where the former is a long polemical pamphlet, the latter is a massive two-volume treatise.

Third, there are the appendices to the third and fifth editions of 1806 and 1817, also published separately in the same years, and both reprinted in the sixth and last edition to be revised by the author. Fourth, and finally, there is *A Summary View of the Principle of Population.* This consists in the greater part of the article on 'Population' for the 1824 Supplement to the *Encyclopaedia Britannica.* This *Summary* appeared in 1830, four years before the death of Malthus in 1834, and is thus his own last published statement of his theory.

(i) The foundation of the whole theoretical structure, the very principle of population itself, is in every successive treatment substantially the same. But it is presented most powerfully in the *Summary*: 'In taking a view of animated nature, we cannot fail to be struck with a prodigious power of increase in plants and animals' (Malthus, 1830, p. 119). 'Elevated as man is above all other animals by his intellectual faculties, it is not to be supposed that the physical laws to which he is subjected should be essentially different from those which are observed to prevail in other parts of animated nature' (ibid., pp. 121–2). 'All animals, according to the known laws by which they are produced, must have a capacity of increasing in a geometrical progression' (ibid., p. 123).

(ii) The next stage, again the same in every successive treatment, is: first to assert 'that population, *when unchecked*, increases in geometrical progression . . .' (ibid., p. 138: italics supplied); and then to argue that the means of subsistence, under circumstances the most favourable to human industry, could not possibly be made to increase faster than in an arithmetical ratio' (Malthus, 1803, Vol. I, p. 10). It is from a comparison between these misleadingly precise, yet by the same token powerfully persuasive, supposed ratios that Malthus then proceeds to derive his first conclusion. This becomes more cautious with the passage of the years. Thus he maintains in the *First Essay*: 'By that law of our nature which makes food necessary for the life of man, the effects of these two unequal powers must be kept equal. This implies a strong and constantly operating check on population from the difficulty of subsistence' (Malthus, 1898, p. 14). In the *Summary* he claims to have proved only that 'it follows necessarily that the average rate of the *actual* increase of population over the greatest part of the globe . . . must be totally of a different character from the rate at which it would increase, if *unchecked*' (Malthus, 1830, p. 143: italics original). There is however no need to repeat here the detailed criticism of the comparison of the ratios which I have offered elsewhere, nor to redevelop the constructive contention that he could perfectly well have proved all he really needed in more prudent if less exciting ways (Flew, 1970, pp. 17–21 and 31–43).

(iii) Having to his own satisfaction established that powerful checks must be always or almost always operating to offset the mighty multiplicative power of population 'The great question, which remains to be considered, is the manner in which this constant and necessary check on population practically operates' (Malthus, 1830, p. 143). But, of course, like almost every social scientist, Malthus always had, in addition to this speculative and academic interest in how things are, a practical concern with how they ought to be. This duality of interest led him to mix two entirely different systems of classification.

The neutral one divides all recognized possibilities into positive and preventive: 'foresight of the difficulties attending the rearing of a family acts as a preventive check; and the actual distress of some of the lower classes, by which they are disabled from giving the proper food, and attention to their children, acts as a positive check' (Malthus, 1798, pp. 62–3). Here in the *First Essay* the handling of this distinction is a little awkward. Later the two categories are construed as mutually exclusive and together exhaustive: the preventive comes close to including everything which prevents a birth; while the positive embraces all the various kinds of cause of death.

In addition to this neutral system Malthus also employs another, which is from the first offered as comprising exhaustive though surely not in every context exclusive categories. This cuts right across the neutral system. It is itself not neutral but belligerent. Thus he concludes in the *First Essay*: 'In short it is difficult to conceive any check to population which does not come under the description of some species of misery or vice' (ibid., p. 108). But in his Preface to the *Second Essay* Malthus announces the admission of a third category 'another check to population which does not come under the head of either vice or misery; ... I have endeavoured to soften some of the harshest conclusions of the *First Essay*' (Malthus, 1803, Vol. I, pp. vii–viii: italics and a capital supplied). This member of the trinity is Moral Restraint, very narrowly defined as one of 'the preventive checks, the restraint *from* marriage which is not followed by irregular gratifications'.[9]

With this one vitally important modification, the old claim to exhaustiveness is repeated: 'the checks which repress the superior power of population ... are all resolvable into moral

restraint, vice and misery' (ibid., pp. 15 and 24: italics
supplied).

(iv) To complete his theoretical structure Malthus makes the
point that the values of the various possible checks do not vary
entirely independently: 'The sum of all the positive and
preventive checks, taken together, forms undoubtedly the
immediate cause which represses population . . . we can
certainly draw no safe conclusion from the contemplation of
two or three of these checks taken by themselves because it so
frequently happens that the excess of one check is balanced by
the defect of some other' (ibid., p. 256). Although his general
statements about the relations between the various checks
considered as variables are usually, like this one, curiously
weak, his particular arguments again and again depend on
the subsistence of far stronger connections. Thus in the *First
Essay* he remarks that the failure of Richard Price, after
supposing that all the checks other than famine were removed,
to draw 'the obvious and necessary inference that an unchecked
population would increase beyond comparison, faster than the
earth, by the best directed exertions of man, could produce
food for its support' was 'as astonishing, as if he had resisted
the conclusion of one of the plainest propositions of Euclid'
(Malthus, 1798, pp. 340–1). Again, in the *Second Essay*,
Malthus quotes with approval the remark of a Jesuit mission-
ary: 'if famine did not, from time to time, thin the immense
number of inhabitants which China contains, it would be
impossible for her to live in peace' (Malthus, 1803, Vol. I,
p. 226). Most significant of all, the whole force of the argument
for Moral Restraint lies in the contention that this check might
be substituted for those others which Malthus classed as
species of Vice or Misery.

(3) Powers, Checks, and Choice

The theoretical scheme outlined in Section 2 above, is in
important ways both like and unlike some famous frameworks
in the natural and biological sciences.

(i) It is like classical mechanics, for instance, in that the
master question for Malthus too is in form negative: 'The
natural tendency to increase is everywhere so great that it will
generally be easy to account for the height at which the

population is found in any country. The more difficult, as well as the more interesting, part of the inquiry is, to trace the immediate causes which stop its further progress ... What becomes of this mighty power . . . what are the kinds of restraint, and the forms of premature death, which keep the population down to the level of the means of subsistence?' (ibid., Vol. I, p. 218.) Earlier in the *Second Essay* Malthus had quoted the question which Captain Cook asked of New Holland in his *First Voyage*, 'By what means are the inhabitants of this country reduced to such a number as it can subsist?'; remarking that 'applied generally' it may 'lead to the elucidation of some of the most obscure, yet important, points in the history of human society. I cannot so clearly and concisely describe the precise aim of the first part of the present work as by saying that it is an endeavour to answer this question so applied' (ibid., Vol. I, p. 67).

(*a*) Newton might have spoken in parallel terms. For, as stated in Book I of the *Principia*, the First Law of Motion runs: 'Every body continues in its state of rest or of uniform motion in a right line *unless it is compelled to change that state by forces pressed upon it.*' (Italics supplied.) Since in actual fact most, if not all, bodies are in motion relative to some other bodies, and since this motion never continues for long in a right line, the questions arise: Why do bodies *not* continue in a state of rest or of uniform motion in a right line, what forces operate to prevent this, and how?

Malthus himself was, I believe, always both well aware of and well pleased with this similarity. He had learnt his way around Newtonian physics in the course of a rich and strenuous undergraduate career, which climaxed in becoming ninth Wrangler in 1788. (Flew, 1970, pp. 8–9.) In the *First Essay* he expresses admiration for 'the grand and consistent theory' and 'the immortal mind' of Newton, and argues strongly that 'the causes of population and depopulation have probably been as constant as any of the laws of nature with which we are acquainted' (Malthus, 1798, pp. 159, 363, and 126–7).

It is worth labouring this comparison. For many critics, including some who must surely have themselves read Malthus, fail altogether to grasp the relation between the power and the checks. For instance, in his own elaborate polemic on *The*

Malthusian Controversy Kenneth Smith remarks that Francis Place's 'advocacy of birth control was the beginning of a movement which can completely nullify the geometrical or any other ratio' (K. Smith, p. 325). Later he says: 'Malthus opposed birth control, yet it has become so widespread that where it is practised the notion of a geometrical ratio can have no validity at all' (ibid., p. 329). Yet, obviously, the spread of birth control has not the slightest tendency to invalidate Malthus's basic principle of population. Can Kenneth Smith, one wonders, really have remained innocent of what contraception is intended to prevent?

Nor is this a momentary lapse, quickly recovered. For a page or two later Smith shoots again—and again into his own goal: 'Man cannot live without food . . . What then becomes of the geometrical series? It is reduced to the rate of food production in each period? . . . The invalidity of Malthus' ratios could never have escaped detection if he had stated the real series of increase and hence deduced all that it implied . . . Although his illustrations and proofs have a first appearance of careful inductive work, the basis of all his ideas is the postulate of the geometrical ratio which he does not find in practice' (ibid., p. 331). One might as well argue that the invalidity of the First Law of Motion would never have escaped detection if only Galileo and Newton had stuck to stating the real observed motions of bodies!

Indeed, before dropping this aspect of the comparison, we should perhaps remark that the reality of the power of multiplication, though not of course any precise formulation of the strength of that power, is just about as much a matter of observed fact as the subsistence of any power could be. Malthus can and does appeal directly to observational evidence, as Galileo and Newton here could not. After deploying the considerations repeated in Section 2(i) above, Malthus reviews evidence of what has in fact happened with practically isolated human populations in peculiarly favourable, although not of course ideal, conditions: 'It may be safely asserted . . . that population, when unchecked, increases in a geometrical progression of such a nature as to double itself every twenty-five years' (ibid., p. 138). It is now known that even that formidable rate is in some unfortunate regions being, although that is scarcely the right word, bettered. But Malthus also insisted, as was and remains true, that 'in no state that we have yet known has the power of population been left to exert itself with perfect freedom' (Malthus, 1803, Vol. I, p. 4).

(b) Sometimes he pressed the comparison with physics too hard. Thus in the *1817 Appendix* he defends his talk of a natural tendency, which in fact is always to a greater or lesser extent checked by counteracting forces, by appealing to the practice 'of the natural philosopher . . . observing the different velocities and ranges of projectiles passing through resisting media of different densities'. He complains that he cannot 'see why the moral and political philosopher should proceed upon principles so totally opposite' (ibid., Vol. II, p. 485). So far, so good. Unfortunately he is then inclined to misinterpret his contention that the power of populations to multiply is inordinately greater than their capacity to produce food; to construe it as if it were the same thing as saying, or at any rate involved, that population always does, and inevitably must, press hard upon the means of subsistence.

The crucial difference was brought out well by Archbishop Whately in 1832, in the ninth of his *Lectures on Political Economy*. Whately distinguished two senses of the word 'tendency': in one a tendency to produce something is a cause which, operating unimpeded, would produce it; in the other to speak of a tendency to produce something is to imply that that result is in fact likely to occur. Malthus, misled perhaps by his favourite physical paradigm, seems to have slipped without distinction: from the first interpretation, which comes easily to the theoretical natural scientist, to the second, which belongs rather to the discussion of practical and human affairs.

(ii) Malthus certainly understood the relation between the Principle of Population and its possible checks. He also saw and relished the analogy between this and the relation in classical mechanics between the First Law of Motion and possible impressed forces. But, equally certainly, he had no similarly clear appreciation of the fundamental difference between our animal power to multiply and the disposition epitomized in that law. For, although Malthus, especially in the *Second Essay*, did introduce into his theoretical framework ideas which are needed if proper account is to be taken of the peculiarity of human populations, he seems never to have seen, much less stated, that this was what he was doing, and why he had to do it.

Consider again the statements quoted in Section 2(i) above: 'In taking a view of animated nature, we cannot fail to be struck with a prodigious power of increase in plants and animals'; 'Elevated as man is above all other animals by his intellectual faculties, it is not to be supposed that the physical laws to which he is subjected should be essentially different from those which are observed to prevail in other parts of animated nature'; and 'all animals, according to the known laws by which they are produced, must have a capacity of increasing in a geometrical progression'.

We have to make and to insist upon a fundamental distinction between two senses of the word 'power'. In one sense, the only sense in which the word can be applied to inanimate objects and to most of animate nature, a power simply is a disposition to behave in such and such a way, given that such and such preconditions are satisfied. Thus we might say that the bomb ('the nuclear device') dropped at Nagasaki possessed an explosive power equivalent to that of so many tons of TNT, or that full-weight nylon climbing rope has a breaking strain of (a power to hold up to) 4,500 pounds. Let us, for future ready reference, label this 'power (physical)'. In another sense, the sense in which the word is typically applied to people, and perhaps to people only, a power is an ability at will either to do or to abstain from doing whatever it may be. Thus we might say that in his heyday J. V. Stalin had the power of life and death over every subject of the Soviet Empire, or that a fertile pair of people of opposite sexes have the power to start a baby. Call this 'power (personal)'.

Much more must be said both about this second sense of the word 'power', a sense which essentially involves the possibility of choice, and about the inexpugnable realities to which in that sense the word necessarily refers. But for the moment let it suffice to quote briefly from Locke's great chapter 'Of Power'. The sentences chosen both explain what is meant by having or not having the power to do or to refrain from doing something at will, and indicate the utterly familiar differences in terms of which this distinction is and has to be defined.

Locke speaks with his customary common sense and caution: 'everyone, I think, finds . . . a power to begin or forbear, continue or put an end to several actions in himself . . . We have instances enough, and often more than enough in our own bodies. A Man's Heart beats, and the Blood circulates, which 'tis not in his Power . . . to stop; and therefore in respect of these Motions, where rest depends not on his choice . . . he is not a *free Agent*. Convulsive Motions agitate his legs, so that though he wills it never so much, he cannot . . . stop their motion (as in that odd disease called *chorea Sancti Viti*,) but he is perpetually dancing: He is . . . under as much Necessity of moving, as a Stone that falls or a Tennis-ball struck with a Racket' (Locke, II(xxi) 7 and 11, p. 237: the Latin means 'St. Vitus's dance').

The passages of Malthus requoted in the second paragraph of the present subsection do not recognize our fundamental distinction between two senses of the term 'power'. On the contrary: he insists that 'Elevated as man is above all other animals by his intellectual faculties, it is not to be supposed that the physical laws to which he is subjected should be essentially different . . .'. This must, surely, be presumed to preclude the suggestion that the 'prodigious power of increase' is in man a power in an importantly different sense. But of course at other times Malthus, like everyone else, recognizes the difference which there in fact is. He recognizes it implicitly even in the *First Essay*, every time that he condemns some check by allocating it to the category Vice. It comes out a deal more clearly in the *Second Essay*, because of the new emphasis on 'moral restraint . . . Of the positive checks, those which appear to arise unavoidably from the laws of nature, may be called exclusively misery; and those which we obviously bring upon ourselves, such as wars, excesses, and many others which it would be in our power to avoid, are of a mixed nature. They are brought upon us by vice, and their consequences are misery' (Malthus, 1803, Vol. I, p. 8). All this is nevertheless at best very far from what we need. We need at the beginning an explicit and categorical statement that the great power from which all the theory construction starts is a power which entails choice.

(4) The Practical Moral

The failure to meet this requirement is perhaps the more remarkable since this particular conceptual framework was originally designed as a guide to political and social action or inaction. Although its fundamental principle also generated the speculative question which Malthus by his own later work showed to be of great heuristic value, his theory always retained this essentially practical character. The evaluative-prescriptive method of classifying checks remained alongside the value-neutral descriptive one. Malthus also throughout retained the argument of the comparison of the ratios to support simultaneously, and without sufficient distinction, both the speculatively stimulating conclusion that some checks *are* operating everywhere, and the practically crucial contention that there always *must be* checks. Although he made one practically important addition, the category of moral restraint, and various minor alterations, in the *Second Essay* and after, it always remained essentially the conceptual framework of the *First Essay* with which Malthus approached all population questions.

It should therefore not surprise us that these ideas are more suitable for the rough and ready understanding of broad trends, and for guiding the wide lines of general policy, than for assisting in detailed demographic analysis. It was, for instance, left to David Booth, one of Malthus's early critics, to bring out the crucial importance for such analysis of age and sex distribution, and particularly of the proportions of women of child-bearing age.[10]

However, for a rough yet practically vital understanding of the population explosions now occurring in so many of the backward countries ('the developing countries'), Malthus's simple model of an enormous power of increase opposed by various counteracting forces is necessary and perhaps sufficient. For it can bring out that in these countries the application of modern medical knowledge weakens the positive check, while in most of them nothing or virtually nothing is being done to produce a proportionate strengthening of the preventive. And if, as is surely possible, the fallacious argument of the comparison of the ratios is replaced by a soundly based and valid argument for the slightly weaker conclusion that the power of increase is so enormous that it must always be checked in the fairly short run, then Malthusian ideas can be used to support some enormously important general practical conclusions.

Thus if Malthus's facts and arguments, so amended, are correct, and if it is accepted that there can be no right to the physically impossible, then it is surely preposterous to assert or assume that every (married) couple has a right to produce as many children as it wishes, regardless of what others may be doing or wanting to do; and that all these children will have a right to support in childhood and a right as adults to earn a living, to marry, and to have a similarly unrestricted right to produce children with similar rights in their turn. It is pre-posterous, that is, unless you also make the gigantic and even more preposterous assumption that the sum of all these separate possible desires will always work out providentially to a practically manageable birth-rate. Malthus himself always drew, and insisted upon, the conclusion that these suggestions are indeed irresponsible. The importance of this conclusion can be appreciated by considering how widely and how bitterly it has been resisted—and still is.

Again, it must surely be unsound in principle to offer as a scheme for raising average standards of living a plan for increasing production, unless: on the one hand, you have good independent reason to believe that any parallel increase in population will be less than proportionate; or, on the other hand, your scheme itself makes provision for securing this as an objective.[11] This is a conclusion which guided Malthus in all the political and social arguments of the second part of the *Second Essay*, although he is very much open to criticism both for his general pessimism and for the narrow-ness of his ideas about the licit means of securing the necessary check.

The importance of this conclusion too can best be appreci-ated by considering how until Malthus it had been almost entirely overlooked, and how it is still with discreet cowardice ignored by so many official reports and plans dealing with the problems of raising living standards in the backward countries. William Nassau Senior, in his perhaps over-generous summing up of the agreement reached in his controversy with Malthus, puts the point judiciously: 'no plan for social improvement can be complete, unless it embraces the means both of increasing production, and of preventing population making a proportionate advance' (Senior, p. 90).

3
HUME AND HISTORICAL NECESSITY

In Chapter Two we looked at one famous attempt to introduce
into the territories of the study of man a conceptual scheme
modelled on the paradigm of classical mechanics. In particular
we attended to the way in which Malthus accommodated, or
failed to accommodate, the reality of choice. The present
chapter will be equally concerned with that same fundamental.
But the discussion takes the form of a consideration of one of
Hume's contributions to the analytical philosophy of history—
the longest established and the most comprehensive of what he
called the moral subjects.

(*1*) *Contingent Necessity and Contingent Pseudo-Necessity*

In Section VIII(i) of the first *Inquiry* Hume develops his
reconciling project with regard to the question'Of Liberty and
Necessity'. In the corresponding section of the *Treatise* there
is no such suggestion of appeasement. But now, Hume says,
'it will not require many words to prove, that all men have ever
agreed in the doctrine of liberty as well as in that of necessity,
and that the whole dispute, in this respect also, has hitherto
been merely verbal' (Hume, 1748, p. 104).

It is, surely, to this part of the first *Inquiry* that we must trace
the ancestry of one characteristically philistine contention of
the old original Logical Positivists. For they used to urge that,
since philosophical problems are, as they have to be, conceptual, therefore all such problems must by the same token
rate as—merely—verbal. They are, as the favoured phrase
had it, not real problems to be solved but pseudo-problems
to be dissolved. There is more to be said about this, and
different. (See, for instance, Flew, 1953, pp. 5–6.) But that
more is not going to be said here and now.

(i) By the end of his third introductory paragraph Hume is
ready for business: 'We shall begin with examining the doctrine
of necessity.' He continues, in a fresh paragraph: 'It is univer-

sally allowed, that matter, in all its operations, is actuated by a
necessary force, and that every natural effect is so precisely
determined by the energy of its cause, that no other effect, in
such particular circumstances, could possibly have resulted
from it. The degree and direction of every motion is, by the
laws of nature, prescribed with such exactness, that a living
creature may as soon arise from the shock of two bodies, as
motion, in any other degree or direction than what is actually
produced by it. Would we, therefore, form a just and precise
idea of *necessity*, we must consider whence that idea arises, when
we apply it to the operation of bodies.' (ibid., pp. 91–2: italics
original.)

(*a*) There are two things to notice at once about this first
statement. One is that, characteristically, Hume is insisting
that to elucidate the meaning of a term we have to consider:
not, what follows necessarily from, or what is necessarily
incompatible with, assertions containing that term; but, rather,
'whence that idea arises'. This is dangerous. For, however
illuminating it may prove to discover the answer to that
second question, the present meaning of a term is not determined by the origins of anything, but by its present correct
usage. It is, therefore, entirely possible for the meaning of
some contention to be significantly wider than the sum of all
the statements which in fact are, or ever could be, offered in
its support (Flew, 1961, pp. 132–5). It is also, surely, at least
conceivable that someone might possess an unlearnt capacity
to employ certain words in what is in fact the correct way;
although to say this is neither to say nor to deny that anyone
could know, and know that he knew, (part of) a public
language without ever having employed (the corresponding
part of) his verbal capacities.

(*b*) The other point to seize is that Hume is here talking
about laws of nature in the fullest and hardest sense. In this
sense whatever is 'prescribed' by a law of nature is contingently
necessary; while anything which is logically incompatible
with a law of nature is contingently impossible. It is not just
that, from a law of nature proposition stating that all A's
must be followed by B's, and given that an A is now occurring,
it follows necessarily that a B will occur. That conclusion would
follow with the same logical necessity, given again that an A

is now occurring, from the weaker statement that all A's are in fact followed by B's. Rather it is that, from the law of nature proposition, plus the second premiss as before, it also follows necessarily, that the B which will occur will occur inevitably— that it must be in fact impossible to prevent its occurrence.

Here lies the crucial difference between a law of nature proposition—one of the two species within the genus nomological—and a 'merely empirical' generalization. The former is, in Kantian terms, apodeictic; though both the necessity and the impossibility asserted are, of course, contingent. In the previous paragraph, for instance, the various logical necessities refer to the relations between propositions. They belong to the linguistic world of, in Humean terms, 'the relations of ideas'. But some of these propositions make claims about contingent necessities, which are supposed to obtain in the non-linguistic world of 'matters of fact and real existence'. The nature of such contingent necessities and contingent impossibilities needs to be discussed extensively. But at this stage it is both necessary and sufficient to take two points only: first, that they are not the logical necessities and logical impossibilities involved in the relations of ideas; and, second, that they are what Hume starts by talking about.

Once we have seen that this is where Hume starts, it becomes interesting to notice more recent writers who, sharing Hume's concern to make out that the human sciences are in fundamentally the same case as the non-human, begin with the same stress upon inflexible natural laws. H. T. Buckle, for instance, in a much-quoted passage from the first chapter of his *History of Civilization in England*, commended the belief 'that every event is linked to its antecedent by an inevitable connection, that [every] such antecedent is connected with a preceding fact; and that thus the whole world forms a necessary chain, in which indeed every man may play his part, but can by no means determine what that part shall be' (Buckle, Vol. I, p. 9). Later, after citing some remarkable year-to-year regularities in vital statistics, he continues: 'In a given state of society, a certain number of persons must put an end to their own life. This is the general law; and the special question of who shall commit the crime depends of course upon special laws ...' Nevertheless, 'the power of the larger law is so irresistible, that neither the love of life not the fear of another world can avail anything towards even checking its operation' (ibid., Vol. I, p. 28).

(ii) It is on these lines that Hume too starts: 'The actions of matter,' as he put it in the *Treatise*, 'are to be regarded as instances of necessary actions; and whatever is in this respect on the same footing with matter, must be acknowledged to be necessary' (Hume, 1739–40, II(iii) 1, p. 400). But in the first *Inquiry*, in the paragraph following our previous citations, when we should be hearing 'whence that idea arises, when we apply it to the operation of bodies', we read nothing of unsuccessful attempts to prevent consequences, which we thus come to believe must have been inevitable. Instead we find Hume speaking only of regularities: of 'the constant *conjunction* of similar objects, and the consequent *inference* from one to the other' (ibid., p. 12: italics original).

Obviously any analysis on these lines of what Buckle meant by 'necessity', or what Hume himself has just meant, must be too weak. For it would be quite reasonable to affirm the proposed analysis, while at the same time undertaking to try to break the conjunction which in all previous observation had appeared to be constant. 'You have,' someone might sensibly suggest, 'fallen into the habit of expecting things to go in the future as they have been going in the past. But in the present case there is perhaps no physical necessity about this at all.'

Notice here that every element in Hume's account of causality can be accommodated within a slightly revised version of the famous Occasionalist example of the two clocks. Yet, as we all know, that example was originally developed in the century before Hume by Arnold Geulincx in order to illustrate the notion of a non-causal constant conjunction.

Suppose two mechanically ideal clocks, clock one a split second fast on clock two. Let A's be the events of the telling of four o'clock by clock one, and let B's be the events of the telling of four o'clock by clock two. To provide for the spatial as well as the temporal contiguity of the members of the corresponding pairs of the two series of events, let the two clocks be touching. Now, there will be a constant conjunction between A's and B's, sustained for as long as anyone chooses to specify.

So, surely, the Humean observer will form the strongest habits of association between impressions of A's and ideas of B's; and so on.

But, of course, this still is not an example of a causal connection. It is not, because no one believes that the constant conjunction between A's and B's would survive an even moderately strenuous attempt to break it. 'There is, therefore,' our same sensible someone might say, 'no real connection.' We have no warrant here for asserting any subjunctive conditional; no warrant, that is, for saying that if an A were not to have occurred no B would have occurred. Indeed we know very well that if A's were to be prevented—perhaps by the destruction of clock one—this would by no means guarantee the non-occurrence of B's; while, correspondingly, we have no reason for maintaining that the occurrence of A's renders the non-occurrence of B's contingently impossible. The crux is that statements of 'brute fact' constant conjunction can be analysed in terms of the notion of material implication: not as a matter of fact A and not B; 'This is true or the Pope's a Jew', as the stock Belfast example has it. Notoriously, no such material implication proposition entails any subjunctive conditional. But the notions both of a cause and of a law of nature are nomological: causal propositions are the other species of nomologicals. And nomological propositions have as such to entail subjunctive conditionals. It is, therefore, precisely the idea of contingently necessary connection which is and must be left out by any Humean analysis of these notions in terms of constant conjunction.

The crucial gap is not one which could be filled by some story about our associations of ideas. For it is a gap in an account of what nomological propositions say about the universe around us. This Humean account is epitomized in two definitions in Part II of Section VII. The second makes a cause 'an object followed by another, and whose appearance always carries the thought to that other'. We should certainly not be surprised to find Hume confessing that 'these definitions be drawn from circumstances foreign to the cause'. He was, although on his own principles without warrant, warmer when to the first he added—as if this could be either equivalent to or a consequence of a mere statement of constant conjunction:

'Or, *in other words*, where, if the first object had not been, the second never had existed' (Hume, 1748, p. 87: italics supplied).[12]

(iii) Hume starts, as we have seen, with talk of physical necessity in the strongest sense. He next proceeds not to fulfil his promise to 'consider whence that idea arises, when we apply it to the operation of bodies'. Instead he provides us with an account of a necessity which would be at most psychological and not physical. Yet in fact it is not any kind of necessity at all, since the psychological associations to which Hume refers certainly do not stop us forming any idea we choose, with or without any other we choose. So it should be no surprise that what he actually discusses, and tries to reconcile with our liberty of action, is, neither the necessity of natural laws, nor the inevitable consequence of effects upon their causes; but instead that large measure of regularity and uniformity in conduct which most certainly is both pre-supposed and revealed both in the progress of the human sciences and in the day-to-day business of living.

(*a*) For us, therefore, the most remarkable thing about these interesting pages on the presuppositions of critical history, and everyday life, is what they are usually so scrupulous not to say.[13] Certainly we are told one or two things about necessity and impossibility, things which surely have to be construed in the sort of full-blooded sense indicated in our Section 1(i) above. Particularly is this so when Hume provides a 'trailer' for the forthcoming attractions of Section X 'Of Miracles'. For here he is arguing—whether rightly or wrongly—that some testimony about people has to be dismissed because what is reported just is known to be contingently impossible. The critical historian will have no truck with Quintus Curtius, who 'describes the supernatural courage of Alexander by which he was hurried on singly to attack multitudes'. And, 'Should a traveller . . . bring us an account of men . . . entirely divested of avarice, ambition or revenge, who knew no pleasure but friendship, generosity and public spirit, we should immediately . . . prove him a liar with the same certainty as if he had stuffed his narration with stories of centaurs and dragons, miracles, and prodigies' (ibid., p. 94).

Nevertheless it remains the rule that where in this Section

VIII Hume is speaking of people his appeal is, not to any supposed necessities or impossibilities, but rather to the subsistence of regularities in human behaviour, regularities which enable us to make progress in accounting for past and in predicting future human conduct: 'Were there no uniformity in human actions, and were every experiment . . . irregular and anomalous, it were impossible to collect any general observations concerning mankind, and no experience, however accurately digested by reflection, would ever serve to any purpose' (ibid., p. 93).

This characteristic appeal is several times backed by a claim which is neither closely analysed nor ever sufficiently illustrated: 'The same motives always produce the same actions: The same events follow from the same causes' (ibid., pp. 92–3). Construed as the contention that the same desires are in fact always followed by the same performances, the first part of this statement is contingently false. Desires always can be inhibited, and often are. When inhibited they result in no performance at all. Construed alternatively as the modest thesis that all desires tend to express themselves in appropriate action, it becomes a logically necessary truth.

There is, however, one instructive exception of another kind: '. . . when we consider how aptly *natural* and *moral* evidence link together and form only one chain of argument, we shall make no scruple to allow that they are of the same nature and derived from the same principles. A prisoner who has neither money nor interest discovers the impossibility of his escape as well when he considers the obstinacy of the jailer as the walls and bars with which he is surrounded, and in all attempts for his freedom chooses rather to work upon the stone and iron of the one than upon the inflexible nature of the other' (ibid., pp. 99–100: italics original).

This is as true as it is well said. But it is also in the present context misleading. For Hume, like so many others since, is overlooking the essential relativity of all contingent necessity. What is impossible for one man at one time may be entirely possible for another man at the same time, or for the same man at another time. What is always and for ever impossible for any man singly, or even for all men together, may be possible for God. The gaoler who is to his prisoner altogether inflexible may be clay in the hands of his masterful wife or of his adored daughters. Perhaps then our prisoner happens to be a victim of the world's most populous prison system? Perhaps his gaoler is one of those legendary iron Bolsheviks, wholly impervious to any and every ordinary human claim? Still, if that gaoler is to be an agent at all, it has to be the case that even a Bolshevik, in the most fundamental sense, can if he chooses do other than he in fact does.

In Section 1(ii) we saw that Hume started from the strong notion of physical necessity, a notion contained in the idea of a descriptive law of nature. But, as we have been seeing in the present Section 1(iii), when he is supposed to be showing how what is supposed to be the same idea of necessity applies equally to human behaviour, we meet for the most part only such apparently much weaker concepts as uniformity or regularity, and explanation or prediction in terms of motives. It is exceptionally, and at the very end of this attempted demonstration, that we meet again a case where Hume is prepared to speak of 'a train of causes, cemented together by what we are pleased to call a *physical* necessity' (ibid., p. 100: italics original). By thus generally averting his attention from any genuine necessity Hume succeeds in making his 'reconciling project' seem much easier than it is.

(b) Before, however, we proceed to that, and consequently to the aforementioned most fundamental sense of 'could have done otherwise', it is worth noticing again, as at the end of Section 1(ii), a resemblance between Hume and one of our own contemporaries committed to a similar contention of the basic identity of the natural and the human sciences. In a justly celebrated and much reprinted article on 'The Function of General Laws in History', after first proclaiming his devotion to 'rational scientific anticipation which rests on the assumption of general laws', C. G. Hempel goes on to offer as his example of 'a historical explanation' an account of what we have all since learnt to call the bureaucratic Parkinson's Disease: 'People who have jobs do not like to lose them; those who are habituated to certain skills do not welcome change; those who have become habituated to a certain kind of power do not like to relinquish their control . . . Thus, government offices and bureaus, once created, . . . institute drives, not only to fortify themselves against assault, but to enlarge the scope of their operations' (Hempel, 1942, pp. 39 and 40; and compare C. N. Parkinson).

Critics have long since pointed out that all these statements of what Hempel himself now most significantly starts to call 'general regularities' are, even if construed only as universal generalizations, false. Alan Donagan, for instance, deals swiftly and faithfully with the first three: 'My charwoman would not mind losing her job in the least; after becoming habituated to loading a fruit-grading machine during a summer vacation, I welcomed returning to study; and power can disgust as well as corrupt' (Donagan, 1964, p. 14). It is also, I suppose, possible to find the odd case, the very odd case, of an office which has accepted or even campaigned for its own diminution or dissolution.

I have no wish to minimize this first deficiency, already so often pointed out by Hempel's critics. Whether or not importance is important, truth is (Austin, 1961, p. 219). But, even allowing that some such generalizations could be so hedged and qualified as to become true, there remains a second and somewhat less thoroughly rehearsed objection. It is that they would still not even begin to look like laws. For they would at best, or at worst, state only that in such and such situations people in fact do act in such and such ways. Yet from a statement of this form we are not entitled to infer, what it is essential that a law of nature must entail, that it is impossible for those concerned to behave in any other way.

Nor can this second objection be evaded by maintaining that the laws which govern human behaviour are probabilistic. Suppose this means that we can at this time say only that it is probable that this suggested law does in fact obtain. Then we must still demand to be shown some examples which are, both, as candidates for belief, at least plausible, and, as subjects of analysis, properly nomological in form. Alternatively it must surely mean that the probability enters into the formulation itself. In that case putative laws presumably state that such and such a proportion of the people concerned will in such and such conditions in fact act thus and thus. Suppose we waive the question of where here is the element of contingent necessity, which alone could justify calling such regularity statements laws. It is still enough to point out that statistical 'laws' must as much be incapable of determining—as opposed to merely probabilifying—even what any particular individual will in fact do. Much less can they show that it must be impossible for him to behave in any other way.

(2) *The Nature of Agency*

Hume's handling of the other side of the alleged antinomy is extremely brief: '. . . it will not require many words to prove that all mankind have ever agreed in the doctrine of liberty as well as in that of necessity' (Hume, 1748, p. 104). This terseness is no doubt to be attributed in part to Hume's new concern for the more self-indulgent type of reader: 'the state of the argument here proposed . . . will not much disturb his ease by any intricate or obscure reasoning' (ibid., p. 91). But it is also, surely, at least in some part the consequence of Hume's lively awareness of what Locke had had to say 'Of Power'. For it is as certain as without direct testimonial evidence this sort of thing can be that Hume had that chapter most in mind, perhaps open before him, when he wrote both Part I of the immediately preceding Section VII 'Of the Idea of Necessary Connection' and these few paragraphs of the present Section VIII 'Of Liberty and Necessity'.

(i) It is there, as we began to see in the previous chapter, that Locke develops his account of the nature of the will and of the essential liberty of the agent as such: 'This at least I think evident, that we find in ourselves a *Power* to begin or forbear, continue or end several actions of our minds, and motions of our Bodies . . . This *Power* . . . thus to order the consideration of any *Idea*, or the forbearing to consider it; or to prefer the motion of any part of the body to its rest, and *vice versa* in any particular instance, is that which we call the *Will*' (Locke, II(xxi) 5, p. 236: italics and punctuation original).

Locke explains and illustrates these conceptions in the passage quoted earlier. It will bear representation, this time in modern dress: 'We have instances enough, and often more than enough, in our own bodies. A man's heart beats, and the blood circulates, which is not in his power by any thought or volition to stop; and therefore in respect of these motions, where rest depends not on his choice, nor would follow the determination of his mind, if it should prefer it, he is not a free agent. Convulsive motions agitate his legs, so that though he wills it ever so much, he cannot by any power of his mind stop their motion, (as in that curious disease *chorea Sancti Viti*), but he is perpetually dancing; he is not at liberty in this action, but under as much necessity of moving, as a stone that falls, or a tennis ball struck with a racket.'

Remembering all this, Hume asks: 'what is meant by "liberty" when applied to voluntary actions? We cannot surely mean that actions have so little connection with motives, inclinations and circumstances that one does not follow with a certain degree of uniformity from the other, and that one affords no inference by which we can conclude the existence of the other.' No, the word in this context 'can only mean "a power of acting or not acting according to the determinations of the will"; that is, if we choose to remain at rest, we may; if we choose to move, we also may' (Hume, 1748, p. 104: punctuation modernized). And if that is indeed what, and all which, is meant by 'the freedom of the will', then—Hume concludes—such liberty is obviously compatible with the subsistence of those regularities which alone make possible the explanation of conduct, and even some measure of prediction.

(ii) In fidelity to what he sees as his own peculiar insight into the nature of causal necessity, Hume has to insist 'that men begin at the wrong end of this question concerning liberty and necessity when they enter upon it by examining . . . the operations of the will' (ibid., p. 102). It is nevertheless from Locke's treatment of these that Hume extracts a seminal suggestion. This seminal suggestion is, in effect, that the crucial concept of action can be defined ostensively by reference to a familiar and undeniable difference. This is the difference: between the case of those parts of our bodies which we can move at will; and the case of those other parts which we cannot so move. It is, it is suggested, in terms of this difference that we have to understand what we earlier called the most fundamental sense of 'can if he chooses do other than he in fact does'. For it is essential to the idea of action that it has to be true of any agent, that, in this sense, he can if he chooses do other than he in fact does.

It is most important to recognize that and how this basic

sense differs from others which are more usual and less fundamental. Both the person who, in the everyday and untechnical
sense, acts of his own free will, and the person who acts under
compulsion, act. So when we say of the latter that as things
were he had no choice, or that in the circumstances he could
not have done other then he did, these charitable phrases
need to be construed with caution. If he really did act, albeit
under compulsion, then it cannot be true: either that he had
literally no choice; or that, in the most fundamental sense, he
could not have done otherwise. The point, rather, is: not that
he had no alternative at all, but that he had no tolerable
alternative; and not that, in that sense, he could not have done
otherwise, but that, although of course he could, it was not
reasonable to expect this. The case of the recalcitrant business-
man, who receives from the Godfather in the film of that name
'an offer which he cannot refuse', is vitally different from that
of the errant mafioso, who is without warning gunned down
from behind. The former is an agent, however reluctant, but
the latter, in that very moment of sudden death, ceases to be.
(See Chapter Four, below.)

Hume has, to his own satisfaction, reduced the necessity
both of cause and of natural laws to constant conjunction and
the possibility of inference. So, as long as any regularities to
which our predictions and explanations of conduct refer can
be similarly analysed in terms of nothing stronger than
material implication, it seems that Hume's 'reconciling
project' can go through at the trot. Your private predictions
of my electoral behaviour—well-grounded though they be
upon your long knowledge of my unfashionable political
convictions—do not to any degree constrain my choices. Nor
does the fact that we can readily explain the mendacity of that
other lot in this particular affair, in terms of their usual clear-
headed but unscrupulous appreciation of their own party
interests, have any tendency to show that, in the most fundamental sense, they could not have behaved in any other way.

The truth is, indeed, quite the reverse. To offer any explanation of behaviour as conduct is to presuppose the contrary.
Certainly we may be able, in the light of the evidence available
to us, to conclude that those people could not have done
otherwise: where this means that it would not have been

reasonable to have expected—in the purely descriptive sense of 'expect'—that they would in fact do otherwise. Again, we may be able, in the light of that same evidence, to conclude that they could not have done otherwise: where this means that it would not have been either right or proper to have expected—in the prescriptive sense of expect—that they should do otherwise.[14] Yet before we can even raise these questions whether, in such inferential or prescriptive interpretations, those people could not have done otherwise, we have to take it as given that, in the most fundamental sense, the sense which is essential to the whole idea of conduct, they could have. And, of course, it is not inconsistent with this modal claim to maintain that in fact they did not.

(3) Agency and Contingent Necessity

The role of the reconciler is not, however, so easy when once we begin to try to come to terms with the contingent necessity expressed by nomological propositions. Consider first a bizarre passage from later in that same first chapter of Buckle's *History*. Buckle has been reviewing the regularities noticed by Quetelet in the criminal statistics: 'Nor is it merely the crimes of men which are marked by this uniformity of sequence. Even the number of marriages annually contracted, is determined, not by the temper and wishes of individuals, but by large general facts over which individuals can exercise no authority' (Buckle, Vol. I, p. 32).

Although even Buckle cannot at this point quite bring himself to misdescribe 'this uniformity of sequence' and other similar 'large general facts' as laws of nature, he does nevertheless insist on drawing the false conclusions which would follow from that misdescription. From the observation of an actual regularity in conduct, nothing can be deduced about any incapacity. But from a law of nature embracing certain forms of conduct it would follow that none of the agents concerned could have behaved otherwise; and that, surely, in what we have labelled 'the most fundamental sense'. Since the contrary of this last is essential to the concept of conduct, the upshot seems to be that there cannot be laws of nature which embrace the behaviour of agents as such. So, though it will usually in one way or another refer to some laws of nature, or to some causal connections, by which the agents concerned were limited, or of which they took advantage, the explanation of conduct as conduct cannot be in terms of the self-contradiction of natural laws of human agency.

It is this conclusion which constitutes the decisive objection to the programme of assimilating explanation in the social sciences to explanation in the natural sciences. So long as the former continue to provide explanations of conduct—explanations, that is, in terms of the desires and purposes of agents—they will, by the same token, not be providing explanations in terms of natural laws. There is, therefore, no call to be surprised that Hempel and his supporters have been altogether unable to point to any authentic laws of nature discovered by our social scientists. We have already seen, in Section 1(iii) above: both that Hempel's own candidates were not even true; and that they contained no hint of the required contingent necessity.

In *The Poverty of Historicism* Sir Karl Popper offers some suggestions which may seem at least on the second count more promising: '. . . every natural law can be expressed by asserting that *such and such a thing cannot happen* . . . This way of formulating natural laws is one which makes their technological significance obvious, and it may therefore be called the *"technological form"* of a natural law.' Popper then offers his list of 'such sociological laws and hypotheses'. One is: 'You cannot have full employment without inflation' (Popper, 1957, p. 61: italics original). This is outstanding among the suggestions so far noticed, since in Britain at any rate at least its non-nomological analogue is very likely true: 'You will not in fact have full employment without inflation.' You may, come to think of it, even have inflation and formidable officially recognized unemployment (over and above, that is, that constituted by massive overmanning and abysmal productivity).

Popper's suggestion will, nevertheless, not do at all. He has failed altogether to take account of what, in the same earlier Section 1(iii), I labelled 'the essential relativity of all contingent necessity.' Suppose that we do allow that no government which is subject to electoral pressures, and at the mercy of powerful labour monopolies,[15] can possibly bring about a state of full employment without inflation. It still remains true that the

impossibility intrinsic to a genuine law of nature is not just an
impossibility for some particular person or group only. It is
supposed to obtain universally, for all men without exception,
and at all times.

For this to apply in the present example, however, it would
have to be the case, as we all know it is not, that the citizens
themselves are each and all simply unable to restrain the
inflationary pressures constituted by their own claims; that
they are all victims of what is literally a sort of inflationary St.
Vitus's dance.

Suppose for a moment that, with a world-weary generosity,
we are willing to concede that all the various groups and
individuals making the inflationary running, in both the
ordinary everyday senses of these words, could not do other than
they do. Even suppose, that is to say, that we are willing to allow:
not only that it would be utterly reasonable to predict that
they will act as they will; but also that it would be unreasonable
to reproach them for so acting. Still, the fact remains, to concede all this is not merely consistent with saying, it actually
presupposes, that, in the most fundamental sense, they always
could restrain themselves. When Luther thundered at the Diet
of Worms 'Here I stand. I can no other. So help me God', he
was not denying, he was presupposing, that, in the most
fundamental sense, he could!

Since there cannot be laws of nature which embrace the
behaviour of agents as agents, and since there is no possible
question but that the subjects of history and of the other social
sciences are agents, there remains one severe challenge to the
reconciler. It is to try to show that the familiar and undeniable
facts of agency can leave room for natural law to extend its
sway over these same agents considered simply as organisms.
(See Chapter Five below.)

(4) Historical Necessity and Historical Inevitability

Hume's treatment here 'Of Liberty and Necessity' is very
much the work of a man who was both a philosopher in the
narrower modern sense and a very wide-ranging social
scientist. Certainly he does begin with physics: 'Matter, in
all its operations, is actuated by a necessary force, and . . .
every natural effect is so precisely determined by the energy of

its cause that no other effect, in such particular circumstances, could possibly have resulted from it' (Hume, 1748, p. 91). Certainly too he does want to maintain what later came to be called a unity of science thesis: 'When we consider how aptly *natural* and *moral* evidence link together and form only one chain of argument, we shall make no scruple to allow that they are of the same nature and derived from the same principles' (ibid., p. 99).[16] But in trying to show that 'all men have ever agreed in the doctrine . . . of necessity' Hume's dominant concern is that of a moral rather than a physical scientist. He wants to make out that it is both a presupposition and a finding of both our practical lives and of every attempt at social science, and in particular history, that there is a fundamental regularity and uniformity in human nature and human conduct.

Thus he writes: 'As it is from past experience that we draw all inferences concerning the future, and as we conclude that objects will always be conjoined together which we find to have always been conjoined, it may seem superfluous to prove that this experienced uniformity in human actions is a source whence we draw *inferences* concerning them' (ibid., p. 98: italics original); 'This experimental inference and reasoning concerning the actions of others enters so much into human life that no man, while awake, is ever a moment without employing it' (ibid., p. 99). 'Would you know the sentiments, inclinations, and course of life of the Greeks and Romans? Study well the temper and actions of the French and English: you cannot be much mistaken in transferring to the former *most* of the observations which you have made with regard to the latter. Mankind are so much the same, in all times and places, that history informs us of nothing new or strange in this particular . . . Nor are the earth, water and other elements examined by Aristotle and Hippocrates more like to those which at present lie under our observation than the men described by Polybius and Tacitus to those who now govern the world' (ibid., p. 93: italics original). 'It seems almost impossible, therefore, to engage either in science or action of any kind without acknowledging the doctrine of necessity . . .' (ibid., p. 99).

Yet, at the end of the day, after Hume has talked a little

about necessity and a lot about history, almost nothing has
been said about historical necessity and historical inevitability.
He begins, as we saw in Section 1(i) above, with a reference to
an authentic contingent necessity. But this is a physical not a
sociological or historical necessity; and, of course, Hume's own
patent account fails altogether to take the measure of any
notion of contingent necessity. When quickly he proceeds to
history and human affairs generally what we are offered as
necessity is not the real thing, but only the well-known Humean
substitute. There are, I think, just two exceptions to this
negative assessment. First, he does make a covert and oblique
appeal to something stronger than he can accommodate
officially, when he urges us to dismiss tales of psychological
impossibilities as being on all fours with 'stories of centaurs
and dragons, miracles and prodigies'. (See Section 1(iii)
above; and compare Flew, 1961, VIII.) Second, and more
directly relevant, in order to show 'how aptly *natural* and
moral evidence link together' he says: 'A prisoner who has
neither money nor interest discovers the impossibility of his
escape as well when he considers the obstinacy of the jailer as
the walls and bars with which he is surrounded. . . .' (See,
again, Section 1(iii) above.)

These two exceptions still do not bring us very close to
twentieth-century talk of historical necessity and historical
inevitability. Presumably Hume, living in the world before
Hegel, had himself heard little such talk. The apparent
distance between these two worlds is one good reason to conclude the present chapter with a final section applying ideas
and distinctions developed in the three earlier sections to
E. H. Carr's interesting and widely read meditations on his
trade—his George Macaulay Trevelyan Lectures on *What is
History?*. For not only is Carr one of our most distinguished
creative historians. His own main work has also been a study
of a great empire under the rule of a highly ideological élite
which professes to be, in Popper's sense, historicist. A second
reason is to do my mite to break down an unfortunate, you
might even say divisive, intellectual barrier. In a recent article
on 'The Autonomy of Historical Understanding' Louis Mink
noticed, and rightly regretted, 'the absence of discourse'
between analytical philosophers of history and historians

considering the nature and implications of historiography. There is, he said, an 'extraordinary difference in writing by representatives of the philosophical revival and of the historical revival, between footnotes and bibliographies. The later invariably cover both revivals with at least quantitative fairness; the former infallibly reveal the hermetic limits of each' (Mink, pp. 24–5).

(i) It looks as if Carr, like so many of us so often, wants to have things both ways: 'The human being is on any view the most complex natural entity known to us, and the study of his behaviour may well involve difficulties different in kind from those confronting the physical scientist. All I wish to establish is that their aims and methods are not so fundamentally dissimilar' (Carr, p. 64). When, however, Carr is considering questions about historical inevitability what is in the ascendant is the lack of fundamental dissimilarity, rather than the possible difference in kind. For instance: arguing against Popper's claim in *The Open Society* that 'everything is possible in human affairs', Carr insists, very much in the spirit of Hume, upon universal causal determinism as a presupposition, not only of all serious work in both the natural and the human sciences, but also of all sensible practical life. 'Determinism' Carr here defines, explicitly following Samuel Alexander, 'as the belief that everything that happens has a cause or causes, and could not have happened differently unless something in the cause or causes had also been different' (ibid., p. 87).

Carr like Hume thus takes it that '*natural* and *moral* evidence link together and form only one chain of argument'. Yet, whatever may be the correct answer to the question of the ultimate compatibility of such determinism with the realities of human action, this is immediately wrong. For the personal sense of the word 'cause' in which we speak of the causes of actions is not the same as that in which we talk of the physical (and non-human) causes of physical events. No doubt it is true to say, construing the word in the latter interpretation, that these physical events 'could not have happened differently unless something in the cause or causes had also been different'. But it is most emphatically not true that if I give you cause for celebration, then you cannot but find yourself celebrating.

For, in the sense of the word 'cause' in which we speak of the causes of actions the man who suggests the cause of another's action does not deny, but rather presupposes, that the other person could, in the fundamental sense, have done something which he did not do.[17]

Certainly we must also recognize that when, on a particular occasion, a person has in this sense been given cause to celebrate, and is in fact celebrating, then it may also be true that there are contingently sufficient physiological preconditions for the actual present behaviour of the organism; although these sufficient conditions may well have to be construed in material implication terms as mere constant conjunctions, and not as fully causes in the other, physical sense. However, for the moment, be that as it may. For there is no doubt but that the historian in his professional capacity has no dealings with any such hypothetical sufficient physiological conditions. It is enough for him if he can explain in terms of the operative desires and purposes of the agents concerned what actually happened. He is, therefore, constantly seeking, and finding, causes. But this he does in a sense of 'cause' in which it is false to say that what happened, in our fundamental sense, 'could not have happened differently unless something in the cause or causes had also been different'.

(ii) Carr is certainly not, in the new sense improvidently imposed by Popper upon that already overworked word, a historicist. Carr does not believe, that is to say, that there are laws of historical development. He nevertheless reaches by other routes many of the conclusions definitive of the Popperian historicist.[18] For instance: Carr derides every suggestion that the great men of history should be subject to moral assessment: 'Sir Isaiah Berlin', poor fellow, 'is terribly worried by the prospect that historians may fail to denounce Genghis Khan and Hitler as bad men.' (Carr, p. 40.) To this Carr counters: 'But what profit does anyone find today in denouncing the sins of Charlemagne or of Napoleon?' (ibid., p. 72.) This last is, by the way, for Carr's purposes an extraordinarily inept choice of example: almost as unfortunate as to have chosen from his own special field either Lenin or Stalin. For the profit of denouncing Charlemagne's sins or Napoleon's lies, of course, in the continuing contemporary relevance of the choices made

by these men. Although Carr himself commends Pieter
Geyl's 'fascinating monograph . . . *Napoleon For and Against*',
Carr sees this only as a study of 'how the successive judgements
of French nineteenth-century historians on Napoleon reflected
the changing and conflicting patterns of French political life'
(ibid., pp. 39–40). Certainly it is this. But it also shows how the
presentation of these assessments was in turn part of those
political conflicts; a possibility which in other contexts Carr is
himself eager to stress (e.g. pp. 60ff.).

Again, Carr's historian, like history for the historicist, is
always on the winning side: 'Good historians,' he suspects,
'whether they think about it or not, have the future in their
bones'; and 'the history of cricket' is 'presumably studded with
the names of those who made centuries rather than those
who made ducks and were left out of the side' (ibid., pp. 102
and 120).

Although he does not believe in laws of historical development, Carr does have something to say about laws in general.
He notices that 'the word "law" came down trailing clouds of
glory from Galileo and Newton' (ibid., p. 52). He also mentions
Gresham, Adam Smith, Burke, Malthus, Lassalle, and Marx
as pioneers who defended various putative laws in the field of
the social sciences. This, Carr thinks, has quite gone out:
'though scientists, and even social scientists, still sometimes
speak of laws, so to speak, for old time's sake, they no longer
believe in their existence in the sense in which scientists in the
eighteenth and nineteenth century universally believed in
them. It is recognized that scientists make discoveries and
acquire fresh knowledge, not by establishing precise and
comprehensive laws, but by enunciating hypotheses which
open the way to fresh enquiry' (ibid., p. 53).

Like so many others Carr thus misses the point which is
here crucial. For what is at issue is not whether propositions
are held tentatively, albeit with a strong heuristic concern,
and on the basis of evidence by which they are probabilified
rather than proved. It is the different question of what nomological propositions essentially imply. The true reason why
Malthus's Principle of Population is not a law of nature but a
power (personal) is that it has always been the case that sexual
intercourse is, in the basic if not the other senses distinguished

in Section 2(ii), above, something which we can, if we choose or if we have to, do without.

(iii) When he starts his explicit treatment of historical inevitability Carr is at his most eirenic: 'Historians, like other people, sometimes fall into rhetorical language and speak of an occurrence as "inevitable" when they mean merely that the conjunction of factors leading one to expect it was overwhelmingly strong' (ibid., p. 90). If this were all, then it would be entirely innocuous. For this suppositious inevitability involves no real contingent impossibility. It applies wherever, in our terms, it would not have been reasonable to have expected— in the purely descriptive sense of 'expect'—that they would in fact do otherwise.

But no one who has seen the significance of Carr's commitment to the notion that the work of the historian both presupposes and supports an Alexandrine universal causal determinism will expect such merely inferential necessities to be all. He will not be disappointed. For Carr, while all the while pooh-poohing 'this charge of inevitability . . . and . . . the vehemence with which it has been pursued in recent years', proceeds at once to much harder stuff: 'Nothing in history is inevitable except in the formal sense that, for it to have happened otherwise, the antecedent causes would have had to be different' (ibid., p. 90).

This, now, is no merely formal claim. For if it is to be taken, as it is, as presupposing Carr's kind of universal causal determinism, then the contention is most substantial. Carr, like so many others, has totally failed to appreciate that it is a quite different sense of 'cause' which is central in history; as well as in all the other studies which attempt to explain the conduct of persons as agents. In this *different* sense, which is the one which is relevant here, a cause is whatever is an agent's reason for acting as he does; while the historian's ability to specify what conditions the agent did in fact take as his reasons does not preclude, but presupposes, that, even given those same conditions, that agent, in our fundamental sense, could have done otherwise. It is by failing to appreciate this crucial distinction between two senses of 'cause' that Carr in less than one page succeeds in getting from a harmless beginning to a conclusion more ruinous than the historicism of Marx himself:

'When a society has discovered the natural law that determines its own movement, even then it can neither overleap the natural phases of its evolution, nor shuffle them out of the world by a stroke of the pen. But this much it can do: it can shorten and lessen the birth-pangs' ('Preface' to *Capital*; and quoted in Popper, 1957, p. 51).

For Carr the universal inevitability, unqualified by any partly saving sentence about birth-pangs, is not a consequence of a law of development but a presupposition of critical history: 'Last term here in Cambridge I saw a talk to some society advertised under the title "Was the Russian Revolution inevitable?" I am sure it was intended as a perfectly serious talk. But if you had seen a talk advertised on "Were the Wars of the Roses inevitable?" you would at once have suspected some joke. The historian writes of the Norman Conquest or the American War of Independence as if what happened was bound to happen, and as if it was his business simply to explain what happened and why; and no one accuses him of being a determinist . . . When, however, I write about the Russian revolution of 1917 in precisely this way—the only proper way to the historian—I find myself under attack from my critic for having by implication depicted what happened as something that was bound to happen.' (ibid., pp. 90–1: he cannot, I take it, be intending the 'as if' and the 'and as if' to carry the usual negative implications. For why ever should Carr insist that he and other historians must professionally pretend that something is true which he and they believe is not true?)[19]

Carr ought to congratulate himself, rather than complain, that he is attacked precisely and only for holding what he has just so very clearly explained that he does hold; and what he mistakenly but most emphatically believes that every historian is by his cloth required to hold. But of course Carr also believes things which are true, and incompatible with these false and demoralizing doctrines. It is, no doubt, his awareness of such inconsistent 'deviations into sense' which gives him this unfounded feeling of being unfairly done by.

Carr's position, and in particular Carr's failure to recognize the fundamental inconsistency of that position, may be illuminatingly compared with that of Isaac Deutscher. In the Introduction to his *Stalin: A Political Biography* Deutscher writes: 'The historian . . . cannot help being a determinist, or behaving as one if he is not: he has not done his job fully unless he has shown causes and effects so closely and naturally interwoven in the texture of events that no gap is left, unless, that is, he has demonstrated the inevitability of the historic process with which he is concerned . . . Thus, the approach from the historian's angle, accounts for the much debated undertone of inevitability that runs through this book. As a partisan I had repudiated many of the deeds of my chief character which as a biographer I demonstrate to have been inevitable' (Deutscher, p. xv).

Let us round off the present subsection with two specimen assertions inconsistent with the sort of determinism which Carr elsewhere holds, mistakenly, to be both presupposed and discovered by the work of historians and other social scientists. First he pays just tribute to the 'epoch-making work' of Malthus: 'Today nobody believes in such objective laws; but the control of population has become a matter of rational and conscious social policy.' (There is no friend of mankind but wishes that this was indeed everywhere true!) Second, without apparent qualms, Carr tells us that 'it is a condition of social life that normal adult human beings are responsible . . .'. He also tells us, with a confidence which surely could not survive even the most cursory acquaintance with the literature of criminology: 'It would not, I feel sure, occur to any of those engaged in investigating the causes of crime to suppose that this committed them to a denial of the moral responsibility of the criminal' (ibid., pp. 137 and 89; and compare Flew, 1973, especially III).

(iv) However, as we have seen, Carr is also fully committed to the disastrous view that for historical explanation to be possible what happens in history must happen inevitably. For this is an immediate and undenied consequence of what he takes to be the historian's inescapable professional commitment to an Alexandrine universal causal determinism: 'the belief that everything that happens has a cause or causes, and could not have happened differently unless something in the cause or causes had also been different'. The consequence is indeed immediate and inescapable, since the 'everything' precludes any intervention from outside the system, while the whole formulation makes it quite plain that the 'cause or causes' here are of what we have distinguished as the physical kind; which does necessarily necessitate (Section 1(ii) above; and compare Flew, 1961, VI).

The instruments for disposing of this disastrous view have been provided already. First, we have to realize that when historians discover what it is proper for them to call the causes of conduct they refer either to the situations which these people saw as their reasons to act thus and thus, or else to the desires, purposes, intentions or other reasons which they had for so acting; and such reasons are not necessitating physical causes. Second, we must remember that in the everyday senses of 'could not have done otherwise', both prescriptive and descriptive, to show that someone could not have done otherwise is precisely not to show that they were subject to any altogether inescapable fundamental necessity (Section 3 above; and compare Chapter Four below). Third, we need to recognize the often realized possibilities of confusion indicated in Section 1(i)(b) above. From the statement, for instance, that there will be a sea-battle tomorrow it follows necessarily, if boringly, that there will be a sea-battle tomorrow. But it is quite another thing, and quite unwarranted, to infer from the same premiss the excitingly different conclusion that this sea-fight will occur absolutely inevitably and altogether inescapably; that all the participants are going, if warning quotes may now be introduced to neutralize the usual implications of agency, to 'play out' their parts either as conscious puppets or as prisoners in their own bodies (Flew, 1971, VII §5; and, for the final phrases, compare Baier).

Granted that the essential tools have been provided already, two final points nevertheless remain. First, Carr writes: 'The trouble about contemporary history is that people remember the time when all the options were still open, and find it difficult to adopt the attitude of the historian for whom they have been closed by the fait accompli.' This is bad: 'Let us get rid of this red herring once and for all' (Carr, p. 92). Certainly it is impossible now to undo, or to do, what has been done, or not done. But what Carr was supposed to be maintaining, yet has momentarily ceased to maintain, is that everything was either inevitable or else impossible then. And, as was made plain in

Section 1(iii), above, in the discussion of the essential relativity of contingent impossibility, we cannot validly argue that because something is impossible for everyone now it must also have been impossible for anyone then.

Second, Carr does take note of the enormous importance of 'accidents' in history, quoting Gibbon's remark that 'an acrimonious humour falling on a single fibre of one man may prevent or suspend the misery of nations'. But then he says that 'this question has nothing to do with the issue of determinism' (ibid., p. 92). This is perfectly true, in that these 'accidents' are specified as such by reference not to all possible conditions but only to such rather splendid creatures as 'profound social causes', or 'deep-seated breakdown in the system of international relations'. They are not, that is, defined as either physically or personally uncaused. The point of calling them accidental is: to indicate that they cannot be explained as the outcome of such 'profound social causes'; rather than to suggest that they cannot be explained at all.

But Carr is not really content to settle for this. For at other times he wants, and is inclined to believe that the historian must always require, his explanations of great events to be in terms only of deep, wide, and mighty causes: 'It is easier,' he suggests, 'to attribute the Bolshevik revolution to the stupidity of Nicholas II or to German gold than to study its profound social causes, and to see in the two world wars of this century the result of the individual wickedness of Wilhelm II and Hitler rather than of some deep-seated breakdown in the system of international relations' (ibid., pp. 40–1).

But if what are from this point of view 'accidents' are possible, then there may be, as in fact there are, major developments for which no explanation of the favoured kind can properly be given. And, furthermore, that such a major development depended at some stage upon such an 'accidental' fact as the availability of one particular man, must make that development at least at that stage not inevitable, in a sense additional to that in which no human action is ever inevitable. For any such 'accident' could surely have been stopped: not just by some mighty collective social force; but by something comparatively trivial, like the illness, or the assassination, of one individual.

Without Lenin, for instance, would the Bolsheviks ever have been persuaded to attempt their coup in a country in which—in Marxist terms—the possibilities of capitalism had quite clearly not been exhausted? And, had the attempt been made without Lenin, would the Bolsheviks have achieved and maintained power? (Hook; and compare, for instance, Plekhanov, Szamuely, and Conquest, 1972.) Or again, could not the whole Bolshevik position have been undermined in— say—July not by 'profound social forces' but simply by a piece of good intelligence work proving the extent of their dependence upon German money? (Carmichael.)

Grant that it is not after all a presupposition of critical scientific history that there have to have been profound social causes guaranteeing the success of any successful movement. Grant too that it is enough to explain how they succeeded without showing, what in the most fundamental sense is always false, that they could not have failed. Then we can begin to ask, in each particular and individual case, when, and how far, and by whom, and upon what contextual assumptions, what actually happened was or was not inevitable. Such questions are, of course, questions for historians rather than philosophers. But they must be settled by the historians through open-minded examinations of evidence; neither prejudiced by unlovely personal preferences for the apologetics of victorious power (Hayek, 1944, pp. 138ff. and *passim*); nor begged by a general philosophical misreading of the presuppositions of historiography.

4
SARTRE AND UNCONDITIONAL RESPONSIBILITY

I WANT now to apply, and in so doing further to develop, ideas about choice and agency which were first introduced in Section 2 of Chapter Three. The subject of this application is the discussion of 'Being and Doing: Freedom' in *Being and Nothingness* by Jean-Paul Sartre. There is a kernel of most important truth here, though that truth is falsified by exaggeration, and obscured by rather than, as Sartre thinks, derived from, its Heideggerian integuments. There is a need for sometimes conjectural interpretation as well as criticism because of the considerable and, as it seems to me, gratuitous, and therefore scandalous, obscurity and mystification of so much of this author's philosophical writing and, presumably, thinking. Writing not of *Being and Nothingness* but of the even more formidable *Critique of Dialectical Reason* Mary Warnock complains 'of the almost impossible difficulty of reading the latest book, in which all the worst features of French and German philosophical writing seem to have come together to produce a book which must tax the perseverance of the most enthusiastic, and in which, of his earlier philosophical style, only the deliberate obscurity is left. I believe that it is positively *wrong* to write in such a way' (M. Warnock, p. 12: italics original).

There was an older time when they ordered these things better in France. For it was not thus in the seventeenth century, with Descartes or with Bayle. And in the eighteenth century among the *Maxims* of the Marquis de Vauvenargues we find waiting for the copy-book of Sartre: 'Obscurity is the kingdom of error'; 'Clearness is the ornament of deep thought'; and—straight to the heart—'For the philosopher clarity is a matter of good faith'.

(1) Telling it as Sartre Sees it

The most exciting thing in our subject chapter, and indeed for my money the most exciting thing in all Sartre, is the dramatic conclusion: 'that man, being condemned to be free, carries the weight of the whole world on his shoulders; he is responsible for the world and for himself as a way of being'. Sartre glosses this as involving responsibility 'in its ordinary sense of "consciousness (of) being the incontestable author of an event or of an object"' (Sartre, 1943, p. 533/639).

My main aim in the present Section 1 is to show that no such conclusion can be derived from those distinctive notions from which, I think, Sartre thinks that he has derived it. In the following Section 2 I shall try to show how what is both important and true might have been, and should be, justified.

(i) The first part of Sartre's chapter is called 'Freedom: the First Condition of Action'. It begins: 'It is strange that philosophers have been able to argue endlessly about determinism and freewill, to cite examples in favour of one or other thesis, without ever attempting first to make explicit the structures contained in the very idea of action ... We should observe that an action is on principle intentional. The careless smoker who has through negligence caused the explosion of a powder magazine has not acted' (ibid., p. 433/508).

This is not a promising start. For the opening statement takes for granted three things which, given a tolerably competent philosophical training, Sartre should have known to be untrue: first, that the terms 'determinism' and 'freewill' each have, at least in the present context, a single clear and unambiguous sense; second, that in these senses the two are manifestly incompatible; and, third, that what has traditionally been rated a paradigm philosophical problem is not after all in essence philosophical—not, that is, a special kind of problem about concepts—but is instead a question of which of two alternative factual theses happens to be correct.[20] This misunderstanding and this misrepresentation of the issues is the more unfortunate, and none the less mistaken, for being well nigh universal among philosophical laymen. The truth is that philosophical problems must be, in Humean terms, primarily if not exclusively concerned with 'the relations of ideas' rather than with 'matters of fact and real existence'.

The endless arguments of which Sartre speaks are generated by the seeming, and perhaps actual, incompatibility of the various assumptions and implications of applying two different ranges of concepts, both of which we think we have excellent justifying reasons for employing, and neither of which could we lightly or even possibly abandon. On the one hand are all the notions involved in the ascription or repudiation of responsibility: 'He acted of his own freewill'; 'She had no choice'; 'We could have treated them decently.' On the other hand are the characteristic ideas embraced in such claims as that everything which happens has a cause, or that everything which happens could—in principle, of course—be subsumed under universal laws of nature. The great question is whether and, if so, how and how far the presuppositions of those two universes of discourse are logically compatible. In another, less secular age the key word was not 'determinism' but 'predestination'; and then the master question was how, if at all, any authentic human responsibility is to be reconciled with the basic theist claim that we are all the creatures of an omnipotent and omniscient God.[21]

In the contemporary context the master question arises because, while what we take to be our everyday knowledge of human beings seems to show that it is often truly said that we and others could have done differently, still both the natural and the social sciences might appear to presuppose and to reveal that in reality nothing ever could have been or could be other than it was, or is, or will be. One kind of answer to this comprehensive philosophical question is to contend that the two sets of notions are largely, or even completely, compatible. Such contentions are now usefully labelled Compatibility Theses. The opposite response is to urge that on the contrary, they are incompatible. Contentions of this kind are now called, correspondingly, Incompatibility Theses.

It was distressing, at the start of the previous chapter, to see Hume dismiss his own presentation of a Compatibility Thesis as a 'merely verbal' exercise; as if any such grappling with a conceptual problem upon which so much hangs could be on a level with some such genuinely trivial contest as that between, on the one side, spokesmen for those athletic Americanisms 'elevator' and 'automobile' and, on the other side, protagonists of their effete Olde World alternatives 'lift' and 'car'. It is distressing now to see Sartre begin by simply begging the question in favour of an Incompatibility Thesis; and then proceed with his exposition as if he was altogether unaware that Compatibility Theses have also been maintained, widely, powerfully, and respectably.

Nor are the spirits raised by the second two statements in the passage quoted. The first of these expresses what is for Sartre a fundamental. It was, therefore, sloppy to offer nothing to meet the obvious if perhaps easily surmountable objection that people are often truly said to have acted unintentionally. The third statement is, surely, just plain false. For although the careless smoker had no intention of causing the explosion he presumably was acting, and acting negligently, when he dropped his unextinguished cigarette end and failed to tread it out.

(ii) Having thus to his own satisfaction established that the key concept is action, and that this is always and essentially intentional, Sartre proceeds at once to deduce that 'action necessarily implies as its condition the recognition of a *desideratum*, that is, of an objective lack or again of a *négatité* . . . This means that from the moment of the first conception of the act, consciousness has been able to withdraw itself from the full world of which it is consciousness and to leave the level of being in order frankly to approach that of non-being'. Warming to this heady Heideggerian work Sartre continues: 'Consciousness in so far as it is considered exclusively in its being, is perpetually referred from being to being and cannot find in being any motive for revealing non-being' (ibid., pp. 433–4/508–9). After a short discussion of two interesting historical examples Sartre concludes: '(1) No factual state whatever it may be . . . is capable by itself of motivating any fact whatsoever. For an act is a projection of the for-itself towards what is not, and what is can in no way determine by itself what is not. (2) No factual state can determine consciousness to apprehend it as a *négatité* or lack' (ibid., pp. 435–6/510–11).

The first of these last three sentences is, I am sure, to be construed and defended as a made-to-measure necessary truth:

like Hume's 'Reason is . . . the slave of the passions'. The point is that it must be impossible to deduce from even the fullest wholly neutral and detached description of a man's environment what that man will want to do in that environment, as he perceives and structures it as his situation. Thus interpreted as a tautology, what is said is illuminating. This is what Sartre is after when he argues, for instance, that 'it is in and through the project of imposing his rule on all of Gaul that the state of the Western Church appears objectively to Clovis as a cause of [a motive for—A.F.] his conversion' (ibid., p. 448/ 524: 'apparait objectivement à Clovis comme un motif de se convertir').

But the second utterance, which is offered as a reason for the first, will not do at all. The high metaphysical assertion that 'what is can in no way determine what is not' is falsified whenever today's causes produce tomorrow's effects. Much more important to us here is that this second statement expresses a crucial and quite unwarranted shift: from questions of what can, or cannot, be deduced from propositions about the environment only; to questions whether prior states of the agent could in any way determine either the consciousness or the behaviour of that agent. An argument which is sufficient to support the first claim, that no description of a man's environment is by itself adequate to entail any conclusion about what he will decide to do, does not even begin to warrant any contention that there neither are, nor can be, corresponding physiological conditions within the man himself. (For consideration of other reasons for so contending, see Chapter Five below.)

The third statement can be satisfactorily defended when it is read as a variation on the first. But we have now to distinguish —as Sartre never, it seems, does distinguish—between, on the one hand, such properly a priori claims about deducibility and non-deducibility, and, on the other hand, substantive contingent contentions that there could not be physiological sufficient conditions of—say—his seeing the head of that spectacular pass as just the place to put his projected bistro.

If you do not appreciate this distinction you may well misconstrue these non-deducibilities as warranting Incompatibilist conclusions; and hence, if you also believe that motivation and decision are realities, as showing that many claims which have been and will be made by psychologists and physiologists must be false. Since Sartre satisfies both protases we ought not to be surprised by his drawing precisely this conclusion. If we were to admit, he says, 'that human reality can be determined to action by a prior state of the world . . . Then these acts disappear as acts in order to give place to a series of movements. Thus the notion of conduct is itself destroyed with Janet and with the Behaviourists. The existence of the act implies its autonomy' (ibid., pp. 476–7/556).

(iii) A few sentences after the three discussed in the previous sub-section Sartre further concludes: that 'as soon as one attributes to consciousness this negative power with respect to the world and itself, and as soon as the nihilation forms an integral part of the positing of an end, we must recognize that the indispensable and fundamental condition of all action is the freedom of the acting being'; and 'Thus at the outset we can see what is lacking in those tedious discussions between determinists and the proponents of freewill' (ibid., p. 436/511).

What the poor bores ought to do is 'to ask how a cause (or motive) can be constituted as such'. For 'the motive makes itself understood as what it is by means of the ensemble of beings which "are not", by ideal existences, and by the future. Just as the future turns back upon the present and the past in order to elucidate them, so it is the ensemble of my projects which turns back in order to confer upon the motive its structure as a motive. It is only because I escape the in-itself by nihilating myself towards my possibilities that this in-itself can take on value as cause or motive. Causes and motives have meaning only inside a projected ensemble which is precisely an ensemble of non-existents' (ibid., p. 437/512–13: the crux in the French is 'un motif (ou un mobile)').

The key motions, which are what set Sartre off into successive orgies of pretentious verbosity and elaborate mystification, are the harmless necessary truths that a motive for action has to be a desire to bring something about, while what is to be brought about cannot actually be the case unless and until it has in fact been brought about. Sartre seems to think that he may derive the important conclusion 'that the indispensable and fundamental condition of all action is the freedom of the acting being' from these favourite notions. This is strongly suggested by the dark saying that 'we must recognize' that conclusion 'as soon as we attribute to consciousness this negative power with respect to the world and itself, and as soon as the nihilation forms an integral part of the positing of an end'. It appears to be confirmed by Sartre's statement of the outcome of the preceding discussion: 'either man is wholly determined (which is inadmissible, especially because a determined consciousness—i.e. a consciousness externally motivated—becomes itself pure exteriority and ceases to be consciousness) or else man is wholly free' (ibid., p. 442/518). And, since Sartre proposes to make a great song and dance around the idea that desire is a sort of directedness at what is not presently the case, there is no doubt but that he ought to be looking for some real work for that idea to do.

Whatever the difficulties of determining what Sartre did actually want to say, it is quite clear that no kind of consciousness could by its mere occurrence logically necessitate the crucial and fundamental possibility of action, and hence of acting alternatively in either one way or another. Unless the key word 'consciousness' is to be arbitrarily so redefined as to make this sentence the expression of a worse than futile necessary truth, it is false to say that 'a consciousness externally motivated . . . ceases to be consciousness'. For it just is not contradictory to suggest that some unfortunate might be totally —but totally—paralysed while nevertheless possessing, if not exactly enjoying, every kind of consciousness. This nightmare supposition is, it may be recalled, one of the recurrent themes of the stories of Edgar Allan Poe.

Sartre is much given to alluding to Descartes, at least so long as this can be done without requiring any precise reference to the actual words of the master. He might here have learnt from Descartes's example the dangers of assuming that mere consciousness is logically connected with things with which it is not so connected. For it was, it may be recalled, Descartes who, having committed himself to employ the word 'thought' to cover all and only modes of consciousness, was then, as might have been expected, apt to backslide into a pair of complementary assumptions: that such 'thought' is necessarily ratiocinative; and that ratiocination is necessarily conscious.

Thus his proposed 'two very certain tests' for deciding whether some man-shaped bodily machine is occupied by an incorporeal thinking substance are both tests of intellectual capacity rather than criteria for consciousness. Thus too it is at least in part the same confusions which require him to move from the premiss that the brutes possess no ratiocinative powers to the scandalous conclusion that they must also be, by the same token, wholly insensible (Descartes, 1637, IV–V, Vol. I, pp. 101–12 and 115–16; 1644, I(ix), Vol. I, p. 222; and compare Cottingham).[22]

(2) *Telling it as it is*

The reason, I suggest, why Sartre believed that some such necessary connections obtain, although not of course precisely those connections assumed by Descartes, is that Sartre does from time to time introduce into his ecstatic contemplations of nihilating consciousness the more pedestrian notion of acting to realize one project as opposed to alternative possible projects. But, of course, by thus conjoining the idea of acting with that of consciousness he has done nothing to demonstrate that any element of the former can be derived from the latter alone. If we are to provide some justification for even a qualified version of the desired dramatic conclusion, then we need to sober down from the verbal intoxication of nihilating and not-being. We have on the morning after to remember what Sartre himself said at the very beginning: it is essential 'first to make explicit the structures contained in the very idea of action'.

(i) So consider again the archetypal Protestant hero: 'Here I stand. I can no other. So help me God.' These splendid words are not, as I have remarked before, to be construed at the foot of the letter—as the French would say if only they spoke English. Luther was not claiming to have fallen victim to a sudden general paralysis. For to say, in either or both of the everyday senses of 'could have done otherwise', that I could not have done otherwise, is not merely inconsistent with, but presupposes, the truth of the assumption that, in the fundamental sense, I could. What, as we all know, he meant— and said—was: not that his legs were paralysed, and that the words were pouring from his mouth uncontrollably; but that none of the alternative courses of action open to him were acceptable.

Again, consider the people who do something not of their own freewill but under compulsion. It may be the Bank Manager who opens the safe and hands out its contents in face of the threatening machine guns of Mr. 'Legs' Diamond and his business associates. Or it may be my younger daughter who says something rude to her teacher because a horrid boy threatened to spoil her pretty new frock if she did not. The excuse that they acted under compulsion does not imply that there was no alternative possible course of action which they might have chosen. There was in each case a very obvious alternative available. It is precisely that alternative to which their respective excuses refer. The point is: not that the agent had no alternative; but that, although there was an alternative, it was one which the agent could not properly be blamed or punished for not choosing.

(a) Both the person who does something of his own freewill, and the person who does the same thing under compulsion, act. There therefore must have been some alternative which they might have chosen. It is for this reason, and for this reason only, reasonable that we should—as we do—require more formidable alternatives to excuse more serious offences. Had our Bank Manager been able to plead only that 'Legs' Diamond had threatened to spoil the Manager's natty executive suit, his excuse would, even in our softer and more permissive period, have been unacceptable. Nor on the other hand would the fact that the alternative was his own death necessarily be sufficient. For it is not obvious that we ought to receive as a full excuse, as opposed to weighty extenuation, your plea that you assisted the S.S. at Oradour or Lidice, or the much-renamed Cheka in *The Gulag Archipelago*, only because they would have killed you had you, like too few others, refused.

The cases where a person acts, or refrains from acting, under compulsion are totally different from cases where the person does not act at all. Suppose that I am overpowered by a team of skilful strong-arm men, who throw me willy nilly out of the window. Suppose too that I fall through the roof of your greenhouse, and that your treasured orchids are ruined by that fall. Then, however excusable in the excitement of the moment, it would be incorrect for you to demand to know why I did such damage to those precious orchids, or for me to explain that I acted only under compulsion. For there is no conduct of mine to be explained or excused. I did not do or refrain from doing anything. I did not act under compulsion. I did not act at all. The responsible agents were the defenestrators. I was simply a missile victim.

(*b*) Having thus reminded ourselves of the ordinary meaning of the expression 'of his (or her) own freewill' we can and must distinguish this from a more technical but less precise sense in which people claim to believe in or to repudiate freewill, or Free Will, or perhaps *libertarian* freewill. For, whatever the issue there in dispute may be, it is surely obvious that it is not simply whether or not people ever do, in the ordinary sense, act of their own freewill rather than under compulsion. It is much more likely: either that one contestant is affirming and the other denying something rather special about a select few make-or-break decisions; or that each is offering a rival account of what is essentially involved in any authentic action at all, not in free action only. The temptation, as we shall be seeing in Chapter Five, is to mis-take it that the familiar facts of everyday action prove either more or less than they do prove Dr. Johnson was, I suggest, at least half-wrong when with swingeing Johnsonian finality he pronounced his own last word: 'We know our will is free, and there's an end on't' (Boswell for 10/X/1769).

(ii) What has been said in the previous Section 2(i), and the anticipations in the previous Chapter Three, is a mere sketch for prolegomena to the analysis of the concept of action. Yet even that is enough to indicate the sound and simple justification for a qualified and weakened version of Sartre's own dramatic conclusion. For it is both true and enormously worth saying that wherever people were agents they chose to do what they did do, and they always could have done other than they did. If they do nothing where as agents they could do something, that too is part of their conduct: 'Not to choose is, in fact, to choose not to choose' (Sartre, 1943, p. 481/561: the 'en effet' translated 'in fact' might perhaps here for once have been better rendered as 'in effect').

It would, therefore, even be correct to say that every agent is as such abandoned; if only that meant only that he cannot help making some choice—perhaps the final choice of suicide: 'I am abandoned in the world . . . I bear the whole responsibility without being able, whatever I do, to tear myself away from this responsibility . . . and suicide is one mode among others of being-in-the-world' (ibid., pp. 555–6/641).

I will not resist the temptation to point out, by the way, that, all of a quarter of a millennium before Sartre, a very sober and undemonstrative Englishman anticipated the substance of this existentialist insight; although this anticipator had no truck with the dramatics of nothingness, facticity, or abandonment. In that same chapter 'Of Power' John Locke wrote: 'For it is unavoidably necessary to prefer the doing, or forebearance, of an Action in a Man's power . . . a Man must necessarily *will* the one, or the other, of them; upon which preference, or volition, the action, or its forebearance, certainly follows, and is truly voluntary: But the act of volition, or preferring one of the two, being that which he cannot avoid, a Man, in respect of that act of *willing*, is under a necessity, and so cannot be free . . .' (Locke, II(xxi) 23, pp. 246–7: italics original).

All this is true because in the intended senses of the words it is necessarily true. It is enormously worth saying because there are truths which we are for ever concealing from ourselves under too easily misunderstood excuses: 'I could not have done otherwise', 'I had no choice', and so on. For just as it would be inept to claim that, in the superficial sense, you could not have done otherwise unless, in the fundamental sense, you could; so when we say, in some correspondingly superficial and usual sense, that we had no choice, we are taking it for granted that, in the fundamental sense, we had.

To insist in this way upon the inescapable responsibility of the agent as such has point and value. Compare the more particular case of responding to the excuse of a general and chronic lack of time by insisting, equally tautologically, that everyone's day contains no less and no more than the same twenty-four hours. If I have time for this but not for that it can only be: not because I have less time in the days of my life than other people do; but because I choose to spend my time not upon that but upon this.

(iii) I have been trying to show that part of the conclusions of Sartre must be true of all agents as such. But part is not all; and there is also the question of how often, if ever, we in fact are agents. Since it is essential to this notion that any agent qua agent must in the fundamental sense have been able to do otherwise, anyone who like Sartre wishes to make much of our agency owes it both to his public and to Truth herself to try somehow to come to terms with suggestions that science can make no room for such possibilities.

Sartre is, as I indicated earlier, ruinously inhibited by his combined ignorance of and contempt for his boring predecessors. It may indeed be true that 'the notion of conduct is itself destroyed with Janet and with the Behaviourists'. (See, for instance, Chapter Seven below.) It certainly is true that, in some sense, 'The existence of the act implies its autonomy' (Sartre, 1943, pp. 476–7/556). But we are entitled to at least a reference to some other work in which the errors of this alleged denial of the reality of conduct are dealt with more fully and at closer quarters. In particular we have a right to hear more, especially in so long an essay, about what Sartre takes it that this essential autonomy of action involves; and how we are supposed to know that we are indeed, in his understanding, agents.

Apart from the short way with Janet and the Behaviourists we appear to have only one text: 'Does this mean that one must view freedom as a series of capricious jerks comparable to the Epicurean *clinamen*? Am I free to wish anything whatsoever at any moment whatsoever? . . . Inasmuch as it has seemed that the recognition of freedom had as its consequence these dangerous conceptions which are completely contradictory to experience, worthy thinkers have turned away from a belief in freedom' (ibid., p. 452/529). The subsequent pages, giving as much of an answer as we are going to get from Sartre, are characteristically opaque. My own best guess, as unconfident as it is unflattering, is that his reply is in effect to maintain that these *clinamina* do have to be happening but not all the time; notwithstanding that his account of our freedom is surely supposed to apply not just to a few spectacular make-or-break conversion decisions but to the everyday and all the time life of any agent whatsoever. (I am sorry: that was a lapse—to borrow a phrase from Elizabeth I at Tilbury—into 'mere English'. The new word is not, of course, 'life' but 'being-in-the-world'.)

(iv) Besides maintaining, without stated warrant and in some sense most insufficiently explained, that we are agents, Sartre often makes what seem to be quite reckless claims about the massive scope of that agency: 'man being condemned to be free carries the weight of the whole world on his shoulders; he is responsible for the world and for himself as a way of being. We are taking the word "responsibility" in its ordinary sense as . . . being the incontestable author of an event or of an object. In this sense the responsibility of the for-itself is overwhelming, since he is the one by whom it happens that there is a world. Since he is also the one who makes himself be, then whatever may be the situation in which he finds himself, the for-itself must wholly assume this situation with its peculiar coefficient of adversity, even though it be insupportable' (ibid., pp. 553–4/639).

It is magnificent. But it is not the truth. Nor is it, if I understand it, even consistent either in itself or with many of the considerations urged in its support. It is not consistent, since if there is a 'situation in which he finds himself', then it surely cannot be the case that 'he is the one by whom it happens that there is a world'. Nor is it in fact without crucial qualification true that 'he is the one by whom it happens that there is a world'. For, even if the word 'world' is charitably read as referring to the world as seen in terms of his projects, still those projects themselves, as Sartre himself frequently remarks, involve and indeed embrace intransigent objective facts.

Nor will it do to say 'that the situation, the common product of the contingency of the in-itself and of freedom, is an ambiguous phenomenon in which it is impossible for the for-itself to distinguish the contribution of freedom from that of the brute existent'. Sartre the for-himself appears to be making precisely this supposedly impossible distinction a few sentences later, when he admits that 'whether the rock "to be scaled" will or will not lend itself to scaling . . . is part of the brute being of the rock'. He makes it again though in a less direct way when later on the same page he utters the reckless falsehood: 'The rock will not be an obstacle if I wish at any cost to arrive at the top of the mountain' (ibid., p. 488/568–9). Yet the most press-on-regardless assault may simply, and perhaps fatally, be defeated by the brute being of the rock; while, if the assault succeeds, its success will have been precisely in overcoming what, though they were by the very attempt chosen, were at the same time recognized as actual, ontologically autonomous, obstacles.

5
A RATIONAL ANIMAL

THE feature of the human condition with which we have been mainly concerned in the last three chapters has been choice; and, again in the main, the concentration has been on what is most fundamental and most elementary. But Chapter Three did also bring out that this possibility of doing or not doing at will is presupposed by every explanation of human conduct as such. For explanation of this kind, which is characteristic both of history and of the other human sciences, explains why—for what reasons—the agent did or abstained from doing whatever it may have been. It is always, and rightly, taken for granted that every explanation of doing leaves open the possibility that the agent, precisely because he was truly an agent, in the most fundamental sense, could have done otherwise; and hence that any corresponding prediction can at most guarantee, not that he will necessarily and unavoidably, but simply that he will in fact, act or not act thus and thus. Often agents themselves provide true and sufficient explanations of their own conduct; they have and give their own actual reasons for what they do or do not do. And, as well as reasons of that sort, they also have and offer reasons for believing that something is or is not the case. Let the former be called reasons as motives, and the latter reasons as evidence.

In the present chapter I shall begin to explore the relations or lack of relations between these rational aspects of our nature, and our nature as organisms; a topic which was in Chapter Three and Chapter Four deliberately deferred. It is for us of central importance. The philosophical mainstay of the Platonic-Cartesian tradition has always been, and remains, the conviction that these rational characteristics—and perhaps some others too, such as consciousness—cannot really belong to creatures of flesh and blood. Our nature, or at least our nature under the Sun, must be dual: a kind of Webb partnership, the corporeal Sidney mated for life to the incorporeal

Beatrice. If we are to defend any Aristotelian view of man, then we have to rebut this challenge. And it is, surely, only such a view which can be squared with the demands of a comprehensively scientific and naturalistic world-outlook.

(1) A Statement of the Two Theses

I shall proceed by examining two theses. To explain what they are I must first develop a distinction just touched upon and hinted at in earlier chapters.

(i) In its full form it is a distinction between two sorts of question, two kinds of answers, two categories of explanation. It is so fundamental, and each of the two alternatives embraces so many subdivisions, that it becomes perhaps apt to speak of categories rather than, more modestly, of classes, sorts, or kinds. On the one side are the questions, answers, concepts, and explanations which refer to mechanisms and other things incapable of purpose, intention or rationality; as well perhaps as to the non-rational aspects of objects to which those other ideas may in other aspects apply. On the other side we have those questions, answers, concepts, and explanations which refer to reasons, purposes, wishes, intentions, and so on.

Having said this we need at once to remove two possibilities of misunderstanding. First, the word 'mechanism' has just been employed in that very broad sense in which all electrical processes, as well as more old-fashioned arrangements of wheels, pumps, and pendula, count as mechanical; and not in the narrower sense in which electrical is contrasted with mechanical engineering. Second, the rational is here opposed to what is incapable of rationality. It is in this sense and only in this sense that the species homo sapiens has been defined as that of the rational animal. To that definition it is irrelevant to object, as Bertrand Russell so often made play of objecting, that too many men—and women—are in truth very irrational. For to be rational, in this sense of capable of rationality, is not merely not inconsistent with, but is a precondition of, being irrational; irrational, that is, as opposed to, in the commendatory or diploma sense, rational. (In the same way only a moral being, a being capable of morality or immorality, can be truly said to be actually immoral.)

Returning to the original and main distinction, the home of

the first of these two categories is the sphere of the natural sciences and of those technologies which teach us to manipulate non-human nature and the non-human aspects of human beings. The concepts of the second of these two categories belong to the human sciences— and especially to history, the Queen of the Human Sciences—as well as to academically lay discourse about human conduct. The members of two of the pairs of senses distinguished in earlier chapters fall on opposite sides of this great divide. Both powers (physical) and causes (physical) belong in the first category, while powers (personal) and causes (of agency) fall into the second.

(ii) Both the theses to be discussed accept as fundamental the categorial division just now indicated. But one maintains that the two categories are so different as to be logically incompatible; while the other urges that they are so far separated that members of the first have no logical relations with members of the second—other than the relation, if we can call it such, of logical compatibility (Smythies, p. 131).

(a) Take as a bold, clear statement of the former Peter Winch's manifesto in *The Idea of a Social Science*: 'I want to show that the notion of a human society involves a scheme of concepts which is logically incompatible with the kinds of explanation offered in the natural sciences' (Winch, 1958, p. 72). Or, again, consider Alasdair MacIntyre's claim that 'human behaviour can only be understood in terms of such distinctive concepts as purpose, intention, consciousness, rationality, morality, and language. And these concepts rule out the possibility of causal explanation, in the sense in which mechanical explanations are causal explanations' (MacIntyre, 1960, p. 91).

(b) The second thesis is stated by A. I. Melden in *Free Action*, equally boldly: 'absolutely nothing about any matter of human conduct follows logically from any account of the physiological conditions of bodily movement' (Melden, p. 201; but compare and contrast p. 215).

(c) We need mnemonic labels to identify these two theses. So, since we ordinary mortals find it virtually impossible— even were we inclined to try—to remember what arbitrarily affixed letters or numerals were arbitrarily affixed to, let us name the first the Conflict and the second the Co-existence

Thesis. (By the way: many writers and speakers will insist on identifying distinguished senses only as the first and the second, or as Sense A and Sense B. So it is perhaps worth these two or three parenthetic sentences to insist that for anyone wishing to be heard and understood the model has to be the popular discrimination between 'funny' (ha ha) and 'funny' (peculiar). To fail to provide mnemonic descriptions is inconsiderate— some might even apply what is to them the terrible word 'divisive'. Such bad, thoughtless practice becomes still more tiresome when it is found—where I have myself sometimes met it—among people preening themselves upon their identification with the popular masses.)

(2) A Partial Special Case of the Conflict Thesis

This thesis is in part presupposed by the further and more specific claim that any comprehensive scientific naturalism must be self-refuting. The contention here is that, if there could be a fully comprehensive account in terms of physiology, and perhaps ultimately of physics and chemistry, of all the ongoings in and around human organisms; then we, as being such organisms, could never know that this account was true. The argument is that, if the sufficient reason why I believe such and such a proposition is that I am in such and such a physiological condition, then there can be no room left for me to have—or even for there to be—good evidencing reasons to warrant that belief.

(i) Although rarely noticed in the philosophers' trade journals this contention appears to have been, and to be, both widely and respectably maintained. Thus, in his *Beyond Realism and Idealism*, W. M. Urban asserts: that 'in deriving mind and knowledge from nature as science conceives it, he [the "naturalist"] must assume that his own account of nature is true. But, on his premises, the truth of this account, like that of any other bit of knowledge, is merely the function of the adjustment of the organism to its environment, and thus has no more significance than any other adjustment. Its sole value is in its survival value. This entire conception of knowledge refutes itself . . .' (Urban, p. 236). Again, in a similar context in his very widely circulated study *Miracles*, C. S. Lewis urges: 'A theory which explained everything else in the whole universe but which made it impossible to believe that our thinking was valid, would be utterly out of court. For that theory would have reached by thinking, and if thinking is not valid that theory would, of course be itself demolished. It would have destroyed its own credentials' (Lewis, pp. 18–19).[23]

That this contention does take for granted the partial truth of the Conflict Thesis comes out most clearly from a third formulation, by a scientist who later disowned the whole argument, J. B. S. Haldane: 'If my mental processes are determined wholly by the motions of atoms in my brain, I have no reason to suppose that my beliefs are true . . . and hence I have no reason for supposing my brain to be composed of atoms' (Haldane, p. 209). He was obviously presupposing that there cannot be room simultaneously for accounts: both of the physiological mechanics of the origins of a belief; and of the evidence which was sufficient to warrant the believer to hold it to be true. Of course Haldane's minimum presupposition here is considerably narrower than the full Conflict Thesis: for that covers the entire category of rational and purposive concepts, not very precisely delimited; whereas Haldane is immediately concerned only with those required for the logical assessment of human discourse, concepts which we shall soon be finding reason to allocate to another category or subcategory.

(ii) Suppose that someone, let us say a man called Jones, emits from his mouth noises within the range of variety which would be rendered in the notation of the English language as: 'The massacre in the Katyn forest was the work of the Russians'; or 'In Euclidean geometry the square on the hypotenuse is equal to the sum of the squares on the other two sides'.

(a) The most usual response, and the one which would almost always be at least logically appropriate, would be to construe these ongoings as significant utterances; and to respond with questions or other remarks about the truth of the corresponding propositions, or about the reasons—which may not be the same as Jones's reasons—for holding them to be true. This is one sort of response: and the relevant notions are those of the truth of propositions, the validity of arguments, evidence for conclusions, logical grounds and logical implications, and so on. For ready reference we may label the kind of assessment which is involved in this sort of response Subject Assessment.

(b) A second sort of response is to treat the Jones performance as an action: which, usually, it will have been. Here the appropriate remarks refer to Jones's purposes, motives and intentions; and questions may also be raised about whether what he did was moral or immoral or morally neutral, legal or illegal, good or bad manners, and so on. Thus we may, for instance, ask: 'Why did he make a remark which he must have known would touch all the Communist delegates, and their fellow-travellers, on the raw?'; or 'Do you have to keep rubbing in the fact that you did geometry at O level, or to be so pedantic about its being Euclidean?' A mnemonic label for the kind of assessment which is involved in this sort of response might be Action Assessment.

One rather special case of Action Assessment, which in the present context perhaps deserves separate mention, is that seen in the work of the psychoanalyst. For the psychoanalyst is professionally committed to treating every utterance, and indeed every piece of non-verbal movement too, as an expression of his patients' (probably unconscious) intentions, motives and purposes. (See Chapter Eight below.) Consider, for example, the methodological manifesto of Dr. Charles Berg, a leading English Freudian, in his *Deep Analysis*: 'To achieve success the analyst must above all be an anlyst. That is to say he must know positively that all human emotional reactions, all human judgements, and even reason itself, are but the tools of the unconscious, that such seemingly acute convictions which an intelligent person like this possesses are but the inevitable effect of causes which he buried in the unconscious levels of his psyche' (Berg, 1946, p. 190).

It is also, surely, significant that even compulsive symptoms, at least when it is thought that they are susceptible of some analytic interpretation, should be called obsessive acts or obsessive actions. (See again, Chapter Eight below.) However, having added that comment, it is necessary further to insist that, if what has been said in the last three chapters about an essential of action is correct, then neither 'reflex actions' nor— in so far as they too are irresistibly compulsive—'obsessive actions' are, properly, actions.

(c) A third possible response is to think of Jones as an organism, and of his utterances as so much acoustic disturbance: which indeed he is, and they are. Then the appropriate questions will be about the mechanisms responsible for the production of these particular disturbances on this particular occasion; though it would be unrealistic to expect to get any but the sketchiest and most inadequate answers for a very long time to come. This third response can be labelled the Physiological Approach. Whereas both Subject and Action Assessments require notions from the second of the two categories distinguished earlier, the Physiological Approach demands only those of the first. What the Conflict Thesis in its most comprehensive form maintains is that where Subject or Action Assessment is possible, there the questions of the Physiological Approach cannot arise; and, of course, the other way about also. The present particular partial special case of this most comprehensive Conflict Thesis insists only that, where there is room for the Physiological Approach, there there cannot also be room for Subject Assessment; and, as before but in general, the other way about too.

(iii) The right reply is to deploy the corresponding partial special case of the Co-existence Thesis. For the example just developed in Section 2(ii) above, brings out clearly that questions about the evidencing reasons for believing such and such a proposition, and questions about the physiological sufficient conditions of having a disposition to create acoustic disturbances of the sort conventionally construed as the utterance of that proposition, are too different to be rivals for the occupation of the same area of logical space: the reasons *for* in the one case and the reasons *why* in the other are not reasons in the same sense.

The same example has also, surely, made it clear that no one has any business to try to pass off even the most comprehensive set of answers to any one of the three quite different sorts of questions there distinguished as if this single set could by itself constitute an exhaustive account of the nature of man. The physiologist, for instance, will in his professional capacity perceive 'all the ongoings in and around human organisms' in physiological terms; and his story may be the truth and the whole truth about those particular aspects of the men and women who are among the objects of his study. Yet this comprehensive but necessarily limited professional account cannot as such shut out other and complementary questions which other people—to say nothing of the physiologist himself in his lay capacities—may want to raise. These include questions about the motivating reasons for what they did; questions about the evidencing reasons for what they said; and questions of many many other kinds, with which we are not here concerned. All the physiological, or the physical, or the financial, or the aesthetic, or the political aspects of whatever it may be are all the physiological, or the physical, or the financial, or the aesthetic or the political aspects: they are none of them separately, nor even all of them together, all the aspects.

(a) Rashly exclusive claims are often made on behalf of various disciplines; and, where the possibility of Subject Assessment is among the exclusions, such claims are indeed—in the way suggested by Urban, Lewis, and Haldane—self-refuting. Consider again, for instance, the formidable manifesto quoted just now in Section 2(ii), above. Dr. Berg maintains that a psychoanalyst 'must know positively that all human emotional reactions, all human judgment, and even reason itself, are but the tools of the unconscious, that such seemingly acute convictions which an intelligent person like this possesses are but the inevitable effect of causes which lie buried in the unconscious levels of his psyche'. The most, perhaps excessively, charitable interpretation of this passage is to construe it as intended only as a statement of the limitations of interest required of an analyst in his working hours: every utterance as well as every non-verbal movement is to be treated solely as a symptomatic act; and the only questions to be asked, whether silently or aloud, are those belonging to the realm of Action Assessment—as extended by the introduction of the notions of unconscious motivation, planning and so on. If so, fair enough; no doubt.

But the temptation, to which others if not Berg himself certainly have succumbed, is to take it that the discoveries, methods, and presuppositions of psychoanalysis warrant or demand the deflationary metaphysical claim that there is no room anywhere for Subject Assessment; that there is no proper place—even among those fortunate enough to enjoy rude mental health—for the notions of logic, evidence and validity; that no one ever has, and knows he has, good and sufficient reasons for believing any proposition to be true. To do this is to provide one more example of the illegitimate conversion of the necessary limitations of a professional interest into an aggressively contractionist metaphysic. Against this move it is a decisive objection to urge that any system of ideas which really did carry this implication would thereby undermine its own claims to consideration. Psychoanalysis cannot possibly have shown that all argument is just so much unwarranted rationalization, because the supposed demonstration would be self-discrediting in just the way in which it has been supposed that any naturalism must be which insists that man is a part of nature.

Similar, and similarly misguided, claims might be made on the basis and on behalf of physiology; or even of physics and chemistry. Someone might say—they often have said—that people are merely very, very, complex organisms the workings of which are, in principle, comprehensible in physiological and ultimately, in physical and chemical terms. Of course, if such claims are to be construed as stating only that people are complex organisms; that we neither contain nor are incorporeal substances; and that all our physiological aspects are appropriate subject-matter for the investigations and the theory construction of physiologists; then these claims are to the Aristotelian, though not to the Platonic-Cartesian, unexceptionable. But if—as the insertion of the word 'merely' may suggest—they are intended to imply that physiology, or even physics and chemistry, can compass not just the physiological, or even the physical and the chemical, but all aspects of man; then, presumably, they must also carry the false and self-refuting implication that the universe contains no place for the notions of good or bad, sufficient or insufficient, evidencing reasons.

Today sociological varieties of this error are the most popular. We are, for instance, regularly assured by those claiming to be Marxists that it has been revealed to them that our beliefs are nothing but elements in a system of false consciousness; a system which is, they say, merely an expression of the wishes and interests of our class, and of the limitations of the period in which we live. Too often our would-be instructors offer no account of how it is supposed that they and their teachers contrive to overcome these universal handicaps, and upon what grounds they think themselves entitled to believe that their revelation itself constitutes—nothing but?—the known objective truth.

(b) Words like 'merely', and such expressions as 'nothing but', have to be watched. They often get slipped in unnoticed, though they may be crucially important. Certainly if they have any but a purely emphatic function then it cannot be right to proceed immediately, without further reason given, from the premiss that this is that to the conclusions that this is merely that, that this is that and nothing else, and so on. Yet try an experiment. Say to a group of students, or of any others whom you can find to listen, 'Man is an animal'; and notice how many of your hearers will, in all good faith, be willing to misreport you as having said that man is merely an animal.

Confronted with any claim that people are *merely* very complex organisms, and so on, the first thing is to get clear what this particular *'merely'* is intended to exclude. If, for instance, the point of the assertion was to reject the idea that people are incorporeal substances, which as such might significantly be said to survive disembodied, then nothing has been said which gives purchase to the sort of objection which we are presently considering. But if the intention really was to deny that Subject Assessment and the notions peculiar to it have any proper application to any of these very complex organisms; then it will once more be relevant, fair, and decisive to object that this denial itself was and had to be expressed through the utterance of a proposition which, were that denial well founded, could not properly be said to be either known or not known, either true or false, either probable or improbable. Is the physiologist not himself a human being?

(c) If we assume that at least in the present limited area a Co-existence Thesis is correct, then there are certain analogies which may illuminate the relations, or lack of relations, between the physical and the musical consideration of a particular musical performance or between an engineering and a logical interest in a particular Turing machine. In the former case, investigations of the sort described by Sir James Jeans in *Science and Music* do not in any way prejudice a concern with the distinctively musical characteristics of musical performances. It would be quite wrong to insist that physics has shown, or might show, that music is *merely* so many phons and decibels of acoustic disturbance; at least if that particular '*merely*' is to be interpreted, as it presumably is, as denying that there is any room for some consideration of the same ongoings introducing such terms as 'harmony', 'con brio', 'counterpoint', and so on. It would be equally wrong to urge that the possibility and necessity of a Musical Assessment of these ongoings showed that even in their purely physical aspects they could not be comprehended within the terms of a natural science. And it would be downright fantastic to suggest that a logical irreducibility of musical to physical concepts meant that musical characteristics must belong to some incorporeal, though nevertheless substantial, musical soul!

In the other case, a Turing machine might be specified as one which fulfils a certain logical programme. But the engineers might be able to meet this specification in radically different ways: there could, for instance, be both electronic Turing machines as well as others which were, in the narrower sense, purely mechanical (Putnam, 1961).

(3) The Conflict Thesis at Large

Both Winch and MacIntyre affirm their allegiance to the Conflict Thesis in comprehensive forms. Where Winch emphasizes the sociological, MacIntyre is more concerned with individual psychology. Neither tells us precisely which nor how many concepts on either side of the great divide are supposed to be logically incompatible with which and how many on the other. It is, however, possible to make some worthwhile remarks without demanding any preliminary restatements. Indeed we shall see more of the nature and the number of the concepts involved as we discover what are the suggested grounds of incompatibility. It will also emerge that at least some of those who have put their names to a Conflict Thesis appear really to want to be committed only to something much weaker.

(i) Had we hoped to find reasons for accepting his own

version of the Conflict Thesis in Winch we shall, I think, be disappointed. This lacuna is the more surprising after his announcement: 'I want to show that the notion of a human society involves a scheme of concepts which is logically incompatible with the kinds of explanation offered in the natural sciences.' Unfortunately the arguments which he then proceeds to offer do not in fact support any Conflict Thesis; and, more seriously from our point of view, when it comes down to detail Winch does not even try to show that they do. What he really does try to show is that purposive and rational concepts are fundamentally different from the mechanical notions of the natural sciences; that the former are both characteristic of and essential to social and human studies; and that Mill was wrong in thinking 'that there can be no fundamental logical difference between the principles according to which we explain social changes' (Winch, 1958, p. 71).

But now to show, as Winch tries to do, that there could be no sufficient account of any social phenomenon in exclusively natural scientific terms, and without any reference to the plans and purposes of the people concerned; or even to show that no rational and purposive notion can be either derived from or reduced to the purely mechanical; is not at all the same thing as demonstrating that explanations involving concepts of these two different categories must be logically incompatible. To show that A is incomplete without B, or that B is neither logically derivable from nor reducible to A, is scarcely even to begin to show that A and B are logically incompatible. And, furthermore, supposing that Winch had actually been hoping to demonstrate so drastic a conclusion it surely would have been irresponsible not to have attempted at least a sketch-map of the true ontological divisions, and a diagram of the appropriate disciplinary frontiers. If we are to be told that 'the notion of a human society involves a scheme of concepts which is logically incompatible with the kinds of explanation offered in the natural sciences', then we are entitled to ask how and how far a natural science of human physiology can be possible.

(ii) MacIntyre on the other hand, although explicitly disclaiming any present attempt to develop a case for the Conflict Thesis as he chooses to formulate it, does in fact indicate what he takes to be the basis of the incompatibility. Thus he begins by affirming 'that human behaviour can only be understood in terms of such distinctive concepts as purpose, intention, consciousness, rationality, and language. And these concepts rule out the possibility of causal explanation, in the sense in which, for instance, mechanical explanations are causal explanations'. He then adds: 'In the space available to me I can only assert this. I cannot argue for it.'

It is nevertheless quite clear that the heart of the matter for MacIntyre, now expressed with some help from earlier chapters of the present book, is that the notions of a law of nature (descriptive) and of a cause (physical) carry implications of contingent necessity and of unavoidability, and hence that, wherever explanation in these terms is possible, explanation in terms of notions presupposing that—in the fundamental sense—an agent could have done otherwise must be precluded; and the other way about. In this I shall argue, as I have by implication argued already, that MacIntyre is substantially correct. But I shall start by contending that he is mistaken in trying to involve far too many notions in his great confrontation. Afterwards I shall go on to suggest that the truth in what MacIntyre is suggesting does not, as might be feared, saddle us with an excruciating choice between intolerable restraints upon the ambitions of the physiologists or denying the inexpugnable realities of human agency.

(a) First, he seems to have no warrant for urging that consciousness as such must be beyond the possibility of causal explanations. For consciousness, in the sense in which we speak of someone losing or recovering consciousness through or after anaesthetization, by no means presupposes any ideas of choice, or being able to do otherwise. There is nothing either unintelligible or self-contradictory in Edgar Allan Poe's nightmare tales of people seemingly dead, motionless and incapable of moving, yet fully aware of first being about to be and then being buried alive. Nor can we say that it is a priori impossible for the causally sufficient conditions of states of consciousness to be mechanical: 'It is only experience which teaches us the nature and bounds of cause and effect, and enables us to infer the existence of one object from that of another' (Hume, 1748, XII(iii), p. 172).

(b) Second, MacIntyre is altogether too quick to conclude that every notion of rationality and language must involve and be involved with choice, and with being able to do otherwise. Some at least of the concepts characteristic of Subject Assessment do not have this involvement. Certainly we cannot speak of his reason or of my reason for acting without presupposing some alternative possibility of action or inaction. But there surely could be evidencing reasons for the truth of assertions, and assertions could be understood and the evidencing reasons for their truth could be recognized as good, even in a world in which no one was ever in a position to choose what if any assertions they made or refrained from making. Again, what we now believe or disbelieve, and what we now see as good or bad evidencing reasons for believing this or that, is no more a matter for our own immediate choice than what we now want or do not want, like or dislike. This is so, notwithstanding that we can now or at any other time either choose or refuse to begin to impose on ourselves disciplines of inquiry which would in due course result in changes both in our beliefs and in our assessments of evidence. For instance: perhaps I cannot now help believing that my daughters could not have done such a thing; but I can now start to attend more carefully and less wishfully to the evidence—with maybe and eventually results naught for my comfort!

(4) *The Implications of MacIntyre's Conflict Thesis*

Having explained that he has no space to argue his extreme version of the Conflict Thesis MacIntyre proceeds to bring out what he sees as the point of this contention, and some of its consequences: 'If I am right the concept of causing people to change their beliefs or to make moral choices, by brainwashing or drugs, for example, is not a possible concept. It is not, for part of our concept of having a belief or making a choice is that beliefs and choices cannot be produced or altered by non-rational means of such a kind. If one were to hypnotize someone so that he as a result of our hypnotic suggestion took one alternative rather than another, then the agent could simply not be said to have chosen. If one were to discover a drug as a result of which a man permanently became unable to say other than what he believed to be true, one would not be in a position to call the man truthful. For the essence of being truthful is that one could be a liar and isn't. Thus where human concepts such as those of morality or rationality have application, causal explanations of a physical kind have not' (MacIntyre, p. 91: footnote 4).

(i) Let us consider in turn the three claims made in the passage quoted. MacIntyre asserts, first: 'If I am right the concept of causing people to change their beliefs . . . by brainwashing or drugs . . . is not a possible concept . . . part of our concept of having a belief . . . is that beliefs . . . cannot be produced or altered by non-rational means of such a kind.' A thesis which has friends like this has no need of an enemy. Certainly he would be right to insist that his own comprehensive version of the Conflict Thesis must carry this consequence. For if all notions of 'rationality, and language', which must pre-sumably include belief, are indeed logically incompatible with those of mechanical explanation, then it must surely follow that no belief could ever be produced in a mechanical and non-rational way. But, since this consequence is false, the compre-hensive version of the Conflict Thesis from which it is thus validly derived must itself be false.

Were this consequence true, as MacIntyre himself believes it is, then all indoctrination by non-rational techniques would be by the same token impossible. The account of Pavlovian conditionings in Aldous Huxley's *Brave New World* would be not a nightmare fantasy but contradictory nonsense. We could know a priori, when William Sargant and his publishers presented *Battle for the Mind* as 'A Physiology of Conversion and Brain-washing', and as preliminary studies of 'The mechanics of indoctrination, brain-washing, and thought-control', that the book was at least being falsely advertised, since any such enterprise must be radically misconceived and aborted. These would indeed be rich and strange fruits of philosophy. How very odd that it seems never to have occurred to any of those labouring to defend either the Chinese treatment or prisoners taken in the Korean War, or the K.G.B.'s continuing opera-tions in the Serbsky Institute of Forensic Psychiatry, to urge that the charges levelled against the Communist clients of these apologists could not be true; because self-contradictory!

Again, if MacIntyre were right, one of the criteria for belief would have to be essentially backward-looking. Yet this is surely not the case. The actual criteria are concerned with the present and future dispositions of the putative believer; and not at all with how he may have been led, or misled, into his beliefs. You can perfectly well say that Murphy believes that it is better that the peoples of less happier lands should continue to be poor and hungry; rather than that they should pursue policies of restrictive population planning, without thereby implicitly denying either that this is something which Murphy wishes to believe, or that his belief results from early indoctrination. Still less are you committing yourself by this straightforward reporting of Murphy's lamentable views to the even more rash denial that there are, in a limited sense to be explained in (ii)(b) below, physiological sufficient conditions of his conviction. Indeed if the statement that someone believes something really carried the negative implication which MacIntyre is claiming that it does carry, it would be difficult to see how anyone could ever be in a position to know that anyone believed anything.

(ii) MacIntyre asserts, second: 'If one were to hypnotize someone so that he as a result of our hypnotic suggestion took one alternative rather than another, then the agent could simply not be said to have chosen.'

(a) The crucial question with this central thesis is whether this 'result' is to be construed in terms of what in Section 4 of Chapter Four we distinguished as the physical sense of the word 'cause'. If that is MacIntyre's intention, then this second assertion is as true as it is important. Indeed it is, if anything, too weak. For, unless some being could be said to be able to do otherwise, in the most fundamental sense, it would be scarcely proper to describe it as a true agent, doing.

But suppose MacIntyre wishes that 'as a result of' to be construed in the other sense of 'cause', and to imply only that the hypnotizing and suggesting brings it about that—although the subject was afterwards still an agent, able in the most fundamental sense to do otherwise—he does in fact choose one alternative rather than any other. Then, surely, it is false to say that 'the agent could simply not be said to have chosen'? What would be true would be that the hypnotizer and the suggester, if he knew what he was doing, must by his post-hypnotic suggesting have become at least a sharer in responsibility for the choice suggested. He must be if not the prime mover at least an accessory before the fact!

If we are talking about causes (physical), then the conclusion which MacIntyre wishes us to draw does indeed follow. For such causes do necessitate their effects: given the sufficient cause or causes (physical), then the effect must be unstoppable by anything or anyone. But any choice to do this rather than that is paradigmatically stoppable. To be a chooser at all you must be able to do otherwise. You must be able to choose otherwise, that is, in the most fundamental sense; the sense which, as we have seen, can and surely has to be defined ostensively on lines indicated in that classic passage from Locke's *Essay*. (See Section 3(ii) of Chapter Two above.)

Because this key notion is thus ostensively definable there can be no room for any doubt but that we are often agents capable of doing other than we do, agents able and having to choose. What may still reasonably be disputed is not this basic and familiar fact of our nature and condition, but its implications. Yet one of these implications is this: whereas there could be sufficient causes (physical) of the existence of agents having a choice, and being therefore unable not to choose; it must be contradictory to speak of such causes for the actual making of a choice in one sense and not another.

(*b*) I have earlier entertained the possibility of there being physiological sufficient conditions for all those bodily states and movements which are on any particular occasion involved in the performing of some action. Two explanations are called for.

First, the insertion of qualifications like 'on any particular occasion' is intended to provide for the fact that what should be in question is the action token not the action type. The action type is the class of performances and non-performances which, in different contexts and on different occasions, could correctly be described as actions of such and such a sort. The action token is any of these particular sets of performances and non-performances in one particular context and on one particular occasion (Flew, 1971, pp. 249 and 352). The reason for introducing this complication is to allow for the fact that, on some of the various occasions on which it will be proper to describe someone as, for instance, making a will, physiologically very different states and movements will be involved.

Second, where there is talk of possible physiological sufficient conditions of someone's acting or choosing to act in one sense and not another the expression 'sufficient condition' is on no account to be construed as equivalent to 'sufficient cause (physical)'. Sufficient causes (physical) are, for the reasons expounded in sub-subsection (a) immediately above, precluded. Sufficient conditions in this special context have to be sufficient conditions in the third and weakest established sense of that expression.

The first and strongest of these senses refers to logical necessity. To be married and to be a man are the two together logically sufficient conditions of being a husband. The second and weaker refers to a contingent necessity: in this sense a sufficient condition is a sufficient cause; and our present concern is only with those cases where this cause is a cause (physical). This sort of condition, like its causal equivalent, contingently necessitates. That is why there could not be, in this sense, contingently sufficient conditions of anyone's acting or choosing to act in one way and not another.

The third sense carries no implications of any necessity, whether logical or contingent. It is defined in terms of material implication—not-as-a-matter-of-fact-this-and-not-that. It is, therefore, entirely possible without self-contradiction to say that such and such are, in this third and weakest sense, the sufficient conditions for people to choose to act in one way and not another. For in saying that sufficient conditions, of this sort, have been met or provided you are not implying that, in the most fundamental sense, these people cannot do other than they do do. It is a matter only of what they will in fact choose to do, and do. On this sort of basis, and with this sort of implication, we are in fact often able to predict such things as the outcome even of a genuine and contested election. So, as we shall be seeing in Section 5(v)(a) below, those neo-Humeans who hold that there is no such thing as contingent necessity, and hence that physical causation can be adequately analysed in terms of material implication, find no great difficulty in reconciling causation so understood with the presuppositions of human action.

(c) As a final point before passing to MacIntyre's third assertion, and even at the price of still further complicating the already complicated structure of the present chapter, we must notice and get on guard against a temptation to which many have succumbed. I will on this occasion name no other names, saying only that the common mistake is to argue: from the assumption that there are, in the third or material implication sense just explained, physiological sufficient conditions for our choosing as we in fact do choose; together with the observation that, if there are such conditions, then these always conceivably might be brought about either by another person or by a quasi-personal supreme Being; to the conclusion that, if indeed there always were such conditions, then we always must be in the situation in which we would be if these conditions actually were always brought about, with the intention of by these means manipulating our conduct, either by some other person or by some quasi-personal supreme Being.

This now obvious logical fallacy matters. It matters because questions about the nature and extent of the involvement of other people are generally somehow relevant, if not to questions about the true degree of credit or discredit due to us in respect of the choices which we make, then at least to the different issue of the burden of responsibility actually felt by us for those decisions. If we can show that there were others involved, then maybe we can push off part or all that burden on to them. Of course, as my former colleague Donald MacKay was fond of saying, there is no Law of the Conservation of Responsibility. You do not become any the less guilty of murder simply and solely because you are not the only but the Third Murderer (Smythies, p. 130). Nevertheless we can by thus involving others in a shared discredit make our own offences seem less egregious; as well as reduce the numbers of those felt to be in a position to cast stones.

So suppose that we take it to be, as it surely is, a logical consequence of traditional Mosaic Theism that God as the Creator and sustaining cause of the Universe provides the physiological and other sufficient conditions of our conduct. Provided that the expression 'sufficient conditions' is here read in the weak material implication sense, rather than as referring to full physical causes, this terrifying supposition is not inconsistent with the familiar, fundamental fact that we are agents, able to choose and unable to avoid choosing between alternative courses of conduct. We cannot, therefore, from this firm and undeniable fact immediately infer the comfortable conclusion that that 'terrifying supposition' must be false. Such depths are not to be plumbed by so short a line. (Compare Flew, 1976a, VII.)

Suppose next that it is added, as traditionally it usually has been added, that this God arranges that most of us will be eternally tortured, while a fortunate few are eternally rewarded, for what God himself thus arranges that we severally choose to do or not to do. Then many unreconstructed spirits will be inclined to protest that this God punishes—as his devotees themselves often assert that he rewards—for what is in truth more God's doing than that of us creatures. (MacIntyre is, I think, borrowing his here unfortunate post-hypnotic suggestion example from my own by now antique suggestion that the Divine 'justice' manifested in such traditional nightmares of judgement would be like nothing on earth so much as that of a person who tortures people for doing what he himself has, by post-hypnotic suggestion, induced them to do.)[24]

But now, even granted that if this were our situation then we could not justly be punished by God, still it does not follow that, if there are such sufficient conditions of our choosing as we do in fact choose, then it can never be just to punish us when we do choose to offend. For, from the fact that, if there are such physiological conditions, then it must be in principle possible to bring about conduct by bringing about these conditions, it still does not follow that any or all of our actual conduct is in fact thus brought about either by other persons or by some quasi-personal supreme Being. By choosing an example in which conduct is supposed to be in some sense 'a result of' the operations of another person MacIntyre is bound to suggest that the mere existence of any sufficient physiological conditions for conduct necessarily undermines the assurance that we do often have to bear the ultimate and undivided responsibility for what we do. But this is wrong.

(iii) MacIntyre asserts, third: 'If one were to discover a drug as a result of which a man permanently became unable to say other than what he believed to be true, one would not be in a position to call the man truthful.' MacIntyre's stated and good reason is that he is construing 'truthful' as a term referring to a disposition to behave in one particular sort of way on occasions when there is a choice between that and an alternative: 'the essence of being truthful is that one could be a liar and isn't.'

If this were all then it would be fine. Unfortunately he wants to draw too wide a conclusion: 'Thus where human concepts such as those of morality and rationality have application, causal explanations of a physical kind have not.' We have already seen how he takes the list of notions presupposing the idea of choice to be even longer than it is. And the third assertion itself seems to be offered as support for his wholly misguided doctrine that belief is essentially and immediately a matter of choice: 'If I am right the concept of causing people to change their beliefs, or to make moral choices, by brainwashing or drugs, for example, is not a possible concept. It is not, for part of our concept of having a belief or making a choice is that beliefs and choices cannot be produced or altered by non-rational means of such a kind.'

But although MacIntyre's third assertion is made in support of his peculiar doctrine or belief, and although that assertion is itself true, it does not in fact support what he supposes it to support. For if his hypothetical truth drug affects only the subject's ability to say what he does not believe, then it does not as such affect his beliefs. This makes the supposition irrelevant. Yet, if the truth drug were to be supposed to affect what the subject actually believes, then the supposition itself would contradict the thesis which it is introduced to support.

(5) The Limitations of Physiology as a Natural Science

Let us look back for a moment over the ground we have covered, in order to see more clearly where we now are. Section 1 presented two very general contentions, the Conflict Thesis, and the Co-existence Thesis. Section 2 considered an important special case. The upshot of that consideration was that the Physiological Approach is not incompatible with Subject Assessment—not, at any rate, until and unless the latter begins to involve the notion of choice. Just as we can consistently both provide an exhaustive account of the physics of the structure and behaviour of an Aldis lamp, and raise questions about the meaning and truth of the morse messages which it is employed to signal; so we can, equally consistently, both develop a complete physiological account of the mouth and throat movements which caused certain acoustic disturbances, and recognize those acoustic disturbances as the expressions of someone's beliefs. We may also recognize those or other disturbances as expressions of his, and perhaps the, reasons for holding those beliefs to be true. In Sections 3 and 4 we examined the Conflict Thesis in general. The main conclusion, implicit in much which had already been argued in earlier chapters, was that the fundamental notion of ability to do otherwise, which is absolutely essential to Action Assessment, really is incompatible with the notions both of cause (physical) and of law of nature (descriptive). These certainly are at the very least characteristic of the natural sciences, even if not perhaps today always and everywhere indispensable to them.

If this main conclusion is accepted then it becomes imperative to inquire what has to give, and how much, and where; or, alternatively, how what would appear to entail an irreconcilable conflict between any comprehensive accounts of man as an organism and man as an agent nevertheless involves no ultimate incompatibility. If we are to be told, as Winch has told us, that 'the notion of a human society involves a scheme of concepts which is logically incompatible with the kinds of explanation offered in the natural sciences', then we are not merely, as I said in Section 3(i), entitled, but also, I say now, required, to ask how and how far a natural science of human physiology can be possible.

(i) One response would be to urge that the Physiological Approach and Action Assessment deal with different aspects of the human being. This parallels the answer given in Section 2 to the parallel question about the relations between the Physiological Approach and Subject Assessment. In that case I contended that the notions of evidencing reason and of physical cause are too different to have any logical relations other than that of compatibility. A similar answer may be assayed in the present case. It is not precluded by the fact that the two key notions here are allowed to be logically incompatible. For it is not necessarily contradictory to say that a single object possesses in two different aspects properties which it would be contradictory to attribute to one and the same aspect of the same object.

This is the answer apparently favoured by many contemporary protagonists of the Co-existence thesis. Thus, in Melden's formulation this thesis reads: 'absolutely nothing about any matter of human conduct follows logically from any account of the physiological conditions of bodily movement'. He has just been saying 'that there is a radical disparity between these modes of explanation', although some 'psychologists are obsessed with their desire to establish their inquiry on a parallel footing with the natural sciences'. But, 'as bodily movements items of overt behaviour are physiological occurrences for which physiological occurrences would appear to be sufficient causal conditions'; and where this is what psychology has studied, its 'alleged explanations of human action have succeeded only in changing the subject, in substituting explanations of bodily movements for explanations of action' (Melden, pp. 200 and 201).

(*a*) Now it is one thing, and surely right, to urge that an action qua action would not have been either appropriately or sufficiently explained if what we had been given was a physiological account of all the relevant movements and structures of and in the organism. But it is quite another thing and, I shall try to show, wrong to maintain that from such an account no inferences at all could be drawn to consequences about conduct; or, for that matter, the other way about. It is also, as I shall also try to show, wrong to assume that a full physiological description of bodily movements could afford to overlook those differences which are crucial to the question whether those movements are, or part of, actions.

On the first of these two counts appeal is now commonly made to the distinction between action types and action tokens—a distinction explained earlier, in Section 4(ii)(*b*). Thus P. F. Strawson argued, in one of a series of broadcast talks and discussions later published as *Freedom and the Will*, that if 'every case of someone's telling a lie were an instance of one physically specifiable class of sets of physical movements (and vice versa), and every case of someone's jilting his girl-friend were an instance of another such class (and vice versa), then the reign of law in physical movements would mean that lying and jilting could be deterministically explained. There would, as far as lying and jilting were concerned, be physical laws of human action as well as physical laws of physical movement. But there is no question of any such correlations ever being established' (Pears, p. 66).

Again, in *The Concept of Motivation* R. S. Peters starts by agreeing with D. W. Hamlyn 'that we can never specify an action exhaustively in terms of the body or within the body'. He proceeds to give as his reason that a person performing on 'different occasions what would nevertheless be characterized as the same action would vary his movements in a great variety of ways' (Peters, pp. 12 and 15; and compare Hamlyn).

What is being said here about action types is true. We could not specify an action type as the class of one particular set of physical movements. I have also myself argued, in Chapter Three, that there could not be natural laws of human action. But I argued this for the different reason that the necessity proper to such laws precludes that very possibility of doing otherwise which is essential to the concept of human action. My objection now is to the complacent suggestion that, since 'A precise functional relationship could never be established' between ongoings described and explained in purely physio-logical terms and action types, therefore all physical move-ments could be subjected to natural law without prejudice to the reality of human action (Peters, p. 13).

In the original broadcast discussion, J. F. Thomson's response to Strawson took the inept form of an appeal to the populace: '. . . if we assume . . . unlimited success in physical explanation of physical movements, then it's by no means clear to me that people in general would find your point about absence of correlations an adequate defence against determin-ism.' Strawson then had his own short way with dissent: 'I can't help it if people are confused' (Pears, p. 67).

The apt reply is to point out that, from this general observa-tion about physical movements and action types, we are not even entitled to infer that there are no physiological necessary conditions for any particular action type, in either of the

contingent senses of 'necessary condition'. Nor, certainly, are
we by the same observation qualified to draw the far more
important conclusion that there can be no necessary or sufficient conditions—or no necessary and sufficient conditions—
for any action token. We are here a world away from anything
which might show that the Co-existence Thesis is true; that
'absolutely nothing about any matter of human conduct follows logically from any account of the physiological conditions
of bodily movement'.

In fact it is false; and this can even be known without
prejudice to any contentious questions about the putative
incompatibility between the notions of physical cause and
motivating reason. Later in the same book G. J. Warnock
argued that, even if it were impossible from any purely
physiological statement to deduce that some action has been
performed, it would nevertheless remain entirely possible to
draw from such statements conclusions about what had not
been done (ibid., p. 77). It is not hard, for example, to think
up physiological descriptions from which we could infer that
the person so described had not sat down in a chair, bowled an
over overarm, or committed adultery.

(*b*) Melden, as we have already seen, suggests that 'as bodily
movements items of overt behaviour are physiological occurrences for which physiological occurrences would appear to be
sufficient causal conditions', and he complains that too many
psychologists obscure 'the all important distinction between
bodily movements or happenings and actions' (Melden, p. 200).

But this misses two crucial points: first, that actions often
are, or at least involve, bodily movements; and, second, that
there is an enormously important difference between two sorts
of bodily movements. This difference is actually one of which
Melden himself elsewhere makes much. But I will develop the
distinction in my own way. The altogether familiar difference
is seen in the contrast: between, on the one hand, such cases
as those in which it is true to say that, although I did not move
it, my arm moved; and, on the other hand those on which
it is true to say that, with no outside means or mechanism,
I moved my arm. Let us pick out the former as motions and
the latter as movings—two species of the genus (bodily)
movements.

This is one distinction which must in some form find a place in both of the two worlds. Certainly it is in these terms alone that we can hope to understand and to define the nature and the scope of action. Yet it is, surely, equally clear that a human physiology with proper pretensions to completeness must both recognize and give some account of this most familiar and fundamental feature of the human condition? For a moving of an arm, which just is an action, is at the same time no less and no more a bodily movement than any reflex or other motion. And, furthermore, the difference between these two kinds of movement is clearly relevant to incontestably physiological questions about response to stimuli: movings can be encouraged or discouraged by stimuli which are impotent to affect motions; while motions may be produced by means which would have no or a very different effect in encouraging or discouraging movings.

(ii) In the previous subsection I considered, and rejected, a suggestion that philosophical diplomacy might remove the threatening conflict between Action Assessment and the Physiological Approach. The idea was that it might be shown that the crucial conflicting notions apply only to completely different aspects of people. If this were so, then Action Assessment could presumably cohabit as easily with the Physiological Approach as, as has been argued, the latter does with Subject Assessment. But that, it seems, is not how it is. So let us attend to the suggestion which, perhaps significantly, J. F. Thomson was careful not to make in his own person. Can we assume that physiologists might achieve 'unlimited success in physical explanation of physical movements'?

(a) It is obvious that the expression 'physical explanation' has in this context to be construed in terms of physical causes and laws of nature. Yet, given that interpretation, it is equally obvious that those 'people in general', whom Strawson put down with such contempt, would have been absolutely right to discern formidable deterministic implications. They are formidable because the word 'determinism' has to be construed correspondingly—in terms, that is, of physical causes and laws of nature. In this sense—though not, as we shall be seeing soon in the present chapter and again later in Chapter Eight, in every sense—determinism does entail unavoidability;

and about that 'people in general' have every right and reason to be worried.

Yet it is precisely this entailment which warrants us to insist that we already know the proposed assumption to be false. We know this because we know that there are not only bodily motions but also bodily movings, and we also know that a genuine moving cannot be explained in terms which are inconsistent with its really having been a moving. The crucial points are, that all the key notions and the key contrasts are inseparably linked together, and that these elements all are and can only be given in the basic baby business of learning to control ourselves, and to operate on and with other people and inanimate things. The notions of personal power and of impotence, of being able or not able to do something at will, are thus in effect defined ostensively; and, of course, where any terms either have been or can be so defined there is no question of anyone's discovering that there neither are nor have been any actual examples correctly so described (Flew, 1966b).

But Thomson's supposed 'unlimited success in physical explanation of physical movements' entails that all human bodily movements, past, present, and to come, must have been, must be, and must be going to be, motions rather than movings. The proposed assumption, therefore, is inconsistent with the most fundamental and universal human experience. If anything is or can be known, we know that this is false.

Much the same again applies, surely, to the notion of physical causing. It is and can be mastered only by a reference to the elementary and infantile experience of bringing things about by pushing and pulling (Black). But then, if this is right, the notion of contingent necessity itself is, and has to be, given by reference to an ultimate contrast between what is and is not subject to the will. It is a notion which we have, and can have, only through ourselves being 'both agents and spectators in the drama of existence' (Bohr, p. 318). We understand the claim that everything is fully determined by physical causes, that there are no such things as genuine movings, only on condition that it is not true (Hannaford).

(b) Certainly physiologists might discover in the future, what has often been discovered in the past, that some particular person's scope for action is either greater or less than that same person uninstructedly believes. You may be or become in a position to know that I cannot now move my leg, because you have learnt either that it was cut off in the operating theatre or that it has been afflicted with a sudden paralysis, while I am still taking it for granted that I can move it whenever I wish. Similarly, although this affirmative alternative has had less or no attention in the philosophical literature, you could also come to know, thanks to your advancing physiological expertise, that—since the operation perhaps—some part of me which I was assuming to be outwith my control is now again, or has for the first time become, subject to my will.

Certainly all this is possible. Indeed it actually happens. But what does that prove—except that mankind is, in these matters too, both teachable and fallible? Surely no one wants to suggest that the progress of physiology may, or might, or must, reveal that we all of us always have been, and still are, totally paralysed? From that conclusion it would indeed follow that we are not, and never were, in any way agents able to affect certain movings or abstentions from moving at will. But that is a conclusion which no science will ever demonstrate. Because it is not true.

A rather more promising line, and hence at first hearing more disturbing, would be to suggest that physiological investigations might reveal that everything perceived as a moving is really a motion. Certainly mistakes here are, as everywhere else, conceivable. But they neither are nor could be, as the hypothesis requires, the universal rule. For how is an error of the kind suggested to be identified as such? Sooner or later one of the people concerned has to attempt to inhibit the putative moving; and to find, to his surprise, that he fails. Yet neither they nor anyone else can understand either the point of this experiment, or the meaning of the instructions given to the subject, save in so far as they are, as of course every one of us is, familiar with both authentic movings and motions. And this contradicts the hypothesis.

(iii) The upshot is, therefore, that the threat described by J. F. Thomson cannot be realized. So I have now to make good the undertaking of Section 3(ii)—that we are not saddled with 'an excruciating choice between intolerable restraints upon the ambitions of the physiologists or denying the inexpugnable realities of human agency'. The promise is kept by showing, not that there is no limit, but that the limit there is is not intolerable.

(*a*) First, nothing has been said to suggest that those bodily movements which are movings cannot have necessary conditions, in the full causal sense, and sufficient conditions, in the weaker material implication sense distinguished in Section 4(ii)(*b*) above. Sufficient conditions of this sort can provide an adequate basis for rational prediction. But, of course, what is inferred from a statement of such conditions is: not that a certain moving will occur and that no one—not even the mover himself—*will be able to stop it*; but that a certain moving will occur and that no one—not even the mover himself, who could—*will in fact stop it.*

(*b*) Second, nothing has been said to preclude the possibility of finding physical causes for our being in a bodily state such that we cannot but choose either to move or not to move. For, as Locke long ago pointed out, in a passage already quoted in Section 2(ii) of Chapter Four, no one who is in such a state has any choice but to choose between those alternatives between which he has to choose.

(*c*) Third, nothing has been said to preclude the possibility— which is surely being ever more abundantly realized—of finding physical causes for most of what goes on when a moving occurs. The only thing which it is contradictory to suggest— The scandal comes out at last!—is that there might be a complete explanation in terms of physical causes, all in their turn fully so caused, of the moving itself. Thus, when I move the little finger of my right hand there may be—there surely are— ongoings within the right arm which contingently necessitate appropriate contractions in the muscles of that finger. But what there certainly cannot be, if the moving is truly a moving and not a motion, is an unbroken chain of sufficient physical causes stretching back indefinitely. It would therefore seem that the central nervous system must either be or contain an apparatus of which the total input does not contingently necessitate every element of total output.

(iv) Such conclusions have, of course, been reached before.

Thus in Section 2(iii) of Chapter Four we saw Sartre, for no good reason given, shying away from the *clinamina*. (These are those occasional unpredictable swerves which Epicurus introduced into the original Classical atomic theory of Democritus in order, it was hoped, to accommodate the reality of choice.) The nature and peculiarity of the present more tentative and rather less determinate suggestion will come out best in short reviews of two recent treatments.

(*a*) J. J. C. Smart has a final chapter in *Between Science and Philosophy* on 'Determinism, free will, and intelligence'. He starts from a definition of 'determinism' which is as he says, essentially that given by Laplace: 'To say that determinism is true is to say that from a knowledge of the positions and motions of all particles in the universe at a certain time . . . a sufficiently powerful calculator could deduce the positions and motions of all particles of the universe at any earlier or later time' (Smart, 1968, pp. 291 and 292).

But this, as I have argued in Section 1 of Chapter Three and elsewhere, is much too weak to capture the ideas of a physical cause and of a descriptive law of nature. It makes no room for the crucial notion of contingent necessity. Employing only this definition Smart naturally does not even see the problem which has led us to conclusions which are, in our much stronger sense of 'determinism', indeterministic. He proceeds to argue that there is no incompatibility between prediction and choice; or as he prefers to say, regrettably, 'free will'. On the contrary: 'so far from free will and determinism being incompatible with one another, a close approximation to determinism on the macro-level is required for free will' (ibid., p. 298). This is no doubt all very well. (Certainly I have argued it often enough myself!) But it is not immediately relevant to our present conclusion. For, as has been emphasized yet again just now in (iii)(*a*), it would not be inconsistent to reject determinism in our stronger sense while happily accepting it in Smart's.

Smart considers a suggestion from the Nobel Prizewinning neurophysiologist Sir John Eccles. Smart begins: 'A good many philosophers have held that the indeterministic nature of quantum mechanics leaves a loophole for free will.' He comments: 'We must not entirely discount the possibility of

very small events, possibly below the level of quantum mechanical uncertainty, which occur in synaptic knobs of single
neurons, being amplified by neuronal mechanisms so as to
produce behavioural effects . . . Eccles thinks that in this way
events in an immaterial mind can have effects on the brain'
(ibid., p. 304).

Note well what Eccles is after. He is both a devout Roman
Catholic and an unabashed Cartesian. So, unlike most of the
anonymous contemporary philosophers aforementioned, he
wants: not some sort of break in the chain of physical causes
within a material system taken to be closed to any corporeal
intrusion; but a twentieth-century substitute for the pineal
gland, a substitute through which some minute material yet
immaterial force might trigger macroscopic bodily movements.
So Smart begins by objecting, in a way with which as far as it
goes I can only concur (Flew, 1976a III): both that 'the
postulation of an immaterial mind seems to raise difficulties
for the genetical theory of evolution by natural section'; and
that 'the postulation of an immaterial mind does not help to
illuminate the problem of free will' (ibid., p. 305). He goes on
at once to suggest that any supposition 'that the brain can
contain a mechanism which amplifies very small triggering
events' has to propose some answer to the question of 'how
such events are not masked by "noise" (in the informational
theory sense of the word)'. This objection too carries weight
against Eccles. Finally Smart adds: 'Moreover it is likely that
the behaviour of an animal depends on the mass behaviour of
very many neurons, and that what is important are the
statistical characteristics of very large ensembles of neurons
. . .' (ibid., p. 306). But now, whatever its force against
Eccles, this last point appears to open a door to us. For surely,
as was suggested in Section 1 (iii)(b) of Chapter Three,
statements of the purely 'statistical characteristics of the very
large ensembles' do not carry the fatal implication of contingent
necessity?

(b) A second treatment of contemporary ventures in this
Epicurean tradition is found in D. J. O'Connor's *Free Will*.
After referring back to Susan Stebbing's handling of Sir
Arthur Eddington and Sir James Jeans in her classic *Philosophy
and the Physicists*, O'Connor makes three demands of anyone

who maintains 'the thesis that the freedom of the will is supported by the findings of twentieth century physics'. First, 'it must be explained exactly how the occurrence of unpredictable events in the atoms making up a human brain can account for the brain events which correspond to human choices'. Second, 'it must be shown how the supposedly immaterial self or mind can connect with these unpredictable physical events . . .' Third, 'it must be shown how moral values and responsibility . . . are . . . safeguarded by supposing that the brain events corresponding to our choices are spontaneous and random rather than regular and lawlike (O'Connor, pp. 57 and 58).

This bombardment may well be enough to annihilate some intended target. But it should be clear that it scarcely engages at all with the conclusions of the present chapter. In the first place, I have not been looking to physics or to physiology or to any other natural science for support for what I see as a threatened and inherently disputatious conjecture. For, whatever may or may not be true of any factitious doctrines of philosophical libertarianism, there can be no doubt at all but that we all are often agents, that we do make choices, that we do have powers to do or to refrain from doing this or that, that some of our movements are motions and some are movings. The question is: not whether physics or any other science can provide us with any reason for believing that we can sometimes, in the fundamental sense, do other than we do; but, rather, what that sense is in which we know that we can; and how far, if at all, this knowledge forecloses on what we might otherwise have admitted as physiological possibilities.

Second, my reluctant suggestion 'that the central nervous system must either be or contain an apparatus of which the total input does not contingently necessitate every element of total output' involves no postulation of any 'supposedly immaterial self or mind' either connecting or not connecting with 'unpredictable physical events'. On the contrary, it is made as part of an attempt to develop and to defend an Aristotelian as opposed to a Platonic-Cartesian view of the nature of man.

Third, once these first two points are appreciated it becomes clear that it is not incumbent on me to explain 'exactly how the occurrence of unpredictable events in the atoms making up a human brain can account for . . . human choices'. On the contrary, the less precision from me the better. I am not, after all, in hopes of explaining a mechanism attempting to excogitate a Popperian 'bold conjecture'. I am instead, and somewhat shamefacedly, suggesting that a piece of classical clockwork is precisely what we cannot have.

Fourth, it should also be clear that, though I am saying that there are not and could not be true descriptive laws of nature explaining human actions, to say this is not to assert that actions cannot in fact conform to regular—even predictable—patterns.

Fifth, a page or so later O'Connor urges that 'on the account of free choice that we are now considering I am free only on a condition, namely, that the right kind of sub-atomic event occurs at the moment of my choice. Thus, to base the possibility of free choice on the findings of quantum mechanics is to introduce the concept of freedom that differs in an important respect from the standard concept' (ibid., p. 59). This is more subtle. Certainly if we were so to define 'choice' that we had no choice save where the causal ancestry of the chosen course of conduct included a quantum jump, then we should indeed have something 'that differs in an important respect from the standard concept'. But our general denial that the sense of any choice can have been fully determined by necessitating physical causes is not on all fours with any assertion that there must have been some particular kind of ongoing in its causal ancestry. Certainly movings are not members of 'a class which we could, so to speak, pick out by eye' (Lucas, p. 12). There is, therefore, always a theoretical possibility of misidentifying a motion as a moving. It is always conceivable that when I think I can truly say 'I am moving my arm' I may be wrong. Yet, if I have been for some time moving and checking that same arm both on my own initiative and in response to the suggestions of others, then it really is out of the question that these operations have all along been entirely outwith my control. In that case they cannot have been physically necessitated. They must have been not motions but movings.

Finally, whatever is said about physiological mechanisms, or the lack of them, it is never those but only persons who act or choose. To say, therefore, that part or the whole of the central nervous system could or did decide to act or not to act would be as much a solecism, though not so nicely calculated, as Philip Marlowe's remark in *Trouble is my Business*: 'I had a couple of short drinks . . . and sat down to interview my brains' (Chandler, p. 145).

6

MIND/BRAIN IDENTITY AND THE
CARTESIAN FRAMEWORK

A PLATONIC-CARTESIAN understanding of human nature insists that our most distinctive characteristics cannot belong to creatures of flesh and blood: the true me and the true you must be things essentially incorporeal. These things, these Platonic-Cartesian souls or minds, are conceived always as logical substances. The crux is that logical substances are defined as whatever can significantly be said to exist separately and in its own right. Plato's soul, as he argues in *Phaedo* §§ 85E ff., is not a kind of harmony, which could not sensibly be said to outlast the elements of which it is composed. It is, rather, something which can and does exist both before and after our present bodily lives. Descartes, in the second paragraph of Part IV of his *Discourse on the Method*, hastens to the conclusion 'that I was a substance the whole essence or nature of which is to think, and that for its existence there is no need of any place, nor does it depend on any material thing; so that this "me", that is to say, the soul by which I am what I am, is entirely distinct from body . . . ; and even if body were not, the soul would not cease to be what it is' (Descartes, 1637, Vol. I, p. 101). Plato and Descartes are both equally quick to see and to point out that it is only and precisely because they do conceive their souls in this way, as logical substances, that they can coherently proceed to develop doctrines of the immortality of the soul (ibid., p. 118; and compare Plato, loc. cit.). For had they thought of the soul not as the (true) person but as the personality, defined as 'That . . . assemblage of qualities which makes a person what he is as distinct from other persons', or of the mind as something all talk of which could be fully cashed in terms of personal dispositions and capacities; then it would have been as absurd for them to speak of the immortality of the mind or soul as it is for *Through the Looking Glass* to speak, for instance, of a dog's lost temper remaining after that dog's withdrawal (Flew, 1971, IV; and compare Flew, 1964, *passim*).

In Plato the emphasis is upon rationality, the rationality both of the practical agent and of the theoretical thinker. Descartes, though not of course abandoning this Platonic fundamental, introduced a new emphasis upon consciousness. Thus in the *Principles of Philosophy* he redefined the term 'thought' to include all and only modes of consciousness: 'By the word "thought" I understand all that of which we are conscious as operating in us. And that is why not alone understanding, willing, imagining, but also feeling, are here the same thing as thought. For if I say I see, or I walk, I therefore am, and if by "seeing" and "walking" I mean the action of my eyes or my legs, which is the work of my body, my conclusion is not absolutely certain . . . But if I mean only to talk of my sensation, or my consciously seeming to see or to walk, it becomes quite true because my assertion now refers only to my mind . . .' (Descartes, 1644, Vol. I, p. 222). In as much as the modern problem of mind and matter was set by Descartes the terms are to be construed as, on the one side, consciousness, and on the other, stuff.

It is to this problem, thus construed, that Two-way Interactionism, Psychophysical Parallelism, and Epiphenomenalism have been offered as rival candidate solutions. Since the end of World War II a further alternative has been developed, the Identity Thesis or the Identity Theory. This now has many resolute and well-girded defenders. The claim is that the advance of science can, and surely will, show that states of consciousness just are states of the brain or of the whole central nervous system. This claim is illustrated by citing the discoveries that the Morning Star and the Evening Star are one and the same planet Venus, and that lightning just is a certain sort of electrical discharge.

I shall not attempt either to establish or to overthrow this Identity Thesis. Yet I do hope by examining two hostile arguments deployed by Norman Malcolm to do my mite to advance the discussion. His paper on 'Scientific Materialism and the Identity Theory' was originally read at the Sixtieth Annual Meeting of the American Philosophical Association,

Eastern Division, in answer to a contribution by J. J. C. Smart, entitled simply 'Materialism'. My references to these and other articles in the present chapter will, however, be to their reprintings in C. V. Borst's *The Mind/Brain Identity Theory*. This is the best selected and the most helpfully edited of the three similar collections known to me at the time of writing, and is as such the handiest and most widely available source.

(1) *The Spatial Objection*

Malcolm begins with 'the claim that mental events or conscious experiences or inner experiences are brain processes'. But he proceeds forthwith to complain that 'These expressions are almost exclusively philosopher's terms, and I am not sure that I have got the hang of any of them'. So he chooses to 'concentrate on the particular example of *sudden thoughts*. Suddenly remembering an engagement would be an example . . . Suddenly realizing, in a chess game, that moving this pawn would endanger one's queen, would be another example of a sudden thought' (Borst, p. 171: italics original).

(i) Malcolm's first response to 'Smart's claim that a sudden thought is strictly identical with some brain process' is this: 'It is clear that a brain process has spatial location'; but *'as things are* the bodily location of thoughts is not a meaningful notion . . . We do say such a thing as "He can't get the thought out of his head"; but this is not taken as giving the location of a thought, any more than the remark "He still has that girl on the brain" is taken as giving the location of a girl' (ibid., p. 174: italics original).

I can only, yet must, commend Malcolm's further insistence upon the irrelevance to the philosophical discussion of thoughts, or of anything else, of speculations that the future progress of science will induce people to employ the word 'thought', or any other word, in some sense quite different from any in which these words are used today. Such speculations have no more direct relevance to the question whether pain, in the present English sense of 'pain', is a brain process than does the unspeculative, dull, present fact that already all francophones use that particular four-letter word 'pain' to mean not pain but bread.

Malcolm is also, and more centrally, right to urge that 'the bodily location of thoughts is not a meaningful notion'. With appropriate alterations the same applies to sensations. For, although it is true to say that the throbbing, or the tickle, or whatever, is wherever the subject ingenuously indicates that it is, this truth does not carry the implication that there is any thing in that position. A famous observation by Descartes drew the attention of philosophers to the fact that sensations may be felt as where some limb or part of a limb might have been had that limb not been amputated. In our own time Wittgenstein urged that a whole person, who had never suffered any amputation, might ingenuously and without any logical impropriety indicate as the felt position of some sensation a place outside his body. There is, therefore, no contradiction in saying that she has a stabbing pain in her leg, while simultaneously suggesting, either that the physiological basis of this sensation is to be found elsewhere, or even that it has no particular physiological basis at all.

But the most this shows is that to be viable an Identity Theory has to be more careful in stating precisely what the proposed identity is supposed to be between. Thomas Nagel took two of the steps necessary in a paper on 'Physicalism'. In this he said: 'But if the two sides of the identity are not a sensation and a brain process, but my *having* a certain sensation or thought and my body's *being* in a certain physical state, then they will both be going on in the same place—namely, wherever I (and my body) happen to be . . . even if a pain is located in my right shin, I am *having* that pain in my office at the university' (ibid., p. 218: italics original).

This proposal requires not just one but two amendments to the position often, whether rightly or wrongly, attributed to such leading hardline Identity Theorists as U. T. Place, J. J. C. Smart, and David Armstrong. In the first place, we have to be both explicit and consistent in maintaining that on the one side we have a person and that person's states of consciousness: 'the psychological term of the identity must be the person's having a pain in his shin rather than the pain itself, because although it is undeniable that pains exist and people have them, it is also clear that this describes a condition of one entity, the person, rather than the relation between two entities, a person and a pain. For pains to exist *is* for people to have them. This seems to me perfectly obvious, despite the innocent suggestions of our language to the contrary' (ibid., p. 216: italics original).

What seems so obvious to Nagel, and to me, was always, I believe, equally obvious to Descartes. But his contention that states of consciousness are not and could not be states of anything corporeal has provided, and continues to provide, indirect support for the notion that such Cartesian 'thoughts' are themselves logical substances; or, as Nagel would say, entities. Thus, while Descartes himself contended that all states of consciousness are and must be attributes of essentially incorporeal subjects, radicals within the same Cartesian traditions are apt to follow Hume in attempting to dispense with such metaphysical entities by arguing that people are 'logical constructions' out of loose and separate fragments of consciousness. It is indeed one of the most striking of all the many paradoxes of the history of ideas that that lifelong mortalist Hume, by accepting altogether without question that people are essentially incorporeal, followed in the steps of such establishment immortalists as Descartes and Berkeley and Butler. Hume here confined his ostentatiously radical challenge to the proposition that there are (incorporeal) logical substances for the activities and affections of people to be attributes of: 'There are some philosophers, who imagine we are every moment intimately conscious of what we call our SELF . . . But setting aside some metaphysicians of this kind, I may venture to affirm of the rest of mankind that they are nothing but a bundle or collection of different perceptions . . .' (Hume 1739–40, I(iv) 6, pp. 251 and 252).

The second amendment proposed by Nagel involves 'making the physical side of the identity a condition of the body rather than a condition of the brain'. His reason for proposing this is that he is 'doubtful that anything without a body of some conventional sort could be the subject of psychological states' (ibid., p. 217). He thus accepts Malcolm's objection against Smart: 'Could a *brain* have thoughts, illusions, or pains? The senselessness of the supposition seems so obvious that I find it hard to take it seriously. No experiment could establish this result for a brain. Why not? The fundamental reason is that a brain does not sufficiently resemble a human being' (ibid., pp. 179–80: italics original).

I do not in general dissent. But there is a very serious ground for unease in the particular case of pains. We cannot be too careful to avoid making a mistake such as was made by all those Cartesians who denied consciousness to any of the brutes. This mistake licensed, even if it did not in fact have the effect of encouraging, unlimited cruelty to non-human animals, on the formally decisive, but substantively erroneous, ground that it is impossible to be either cruel or kind to creatures incapable of any mode of consciousness. We must not by any philosophical argument weaken, however slightly, what may already be inadequate inhibitions on stimulating brains and other nervous tissues preserved *in vitro*; and be in fact, like the Cartesians about the brutes, wrong.

A second suggestion is that we ought to retain on the physical side of the alleged identity some reference to the brain and to the central nervous system in general. There are good philosophical reasons for abandoning the exclusive concentration upon these. But there are equally good scientific reasons both for mentioning them and for allowing that their functioning is contingently dependent on that of the rest of the organism. All these claims can be met by a formulation which speaks of the person's body (or, better, the person), and particularly his brain or central nervous system, being in such and such a (physical) condition. Whether we should specify particularly the brain or the whole central nervous system must, presumably, depend both on the findings of the physiologists and on which particular mode of consciousness is presently under discussion.

(ii) Once the mental and the physical sides of the alleged identity have both been adjusted along the lines suggested by Nagel, the first of the two objections presented by Malcolm loses its force. Yet nothing could show more clearly the strength and the durability of the Cartesian intellectual framework than the facts: first, that the supporters of an Identity Theory have so often exposed themselves to falsification by this objection; and, second, that their opponents seem just as often to have taken it for granted that the same objection must be equally decisive against every version of the theory.

(*a*) Under the first head consider, for example, in U. T. Place's landmark paper on 'Is consciousness a Brain Process?' his statement: 'The thesis that consciousness is a process in the brain is put forward as a reasonable scientific hypothesis, not to be dismissed on logical grounds alone' (Borst, p. 42). Again, in 'Mind-Body, not a Pseudo-Problem', Herbert Feigl writes: 'Certain neurophysiological terms denote (refer to) the very same events that are also denoted (referred to) by certain phenomenal terms. The identification of the object of this twofold reference is of course logically contingent . . .' (ibid., p. 38).

In his 'Sensations and Brain Processes' J. J. C. Smart does talk of people reporting that they have after-images and so on. Yet when he turns to meet the objection that 'The after-image is not in physical space. The brain process is,' Smart replies: 'This is an *ignoratio elenchi*. I am not arguing that the after-image is a brain process, but that the experience of having an after-image is a brain process' (ibid., p. 61). Smart's reply is as exposed to the spatial objection as the theses of Place and Feigl. For the word 'experience' is surely one of Feigl's 'phenomenal terms', while 'the experience of having an after-image' is certainly a mode of consciousness. It makes no sense to ask where the experience, the consciousness, is, as opposed to where the person is who either enjoys or suffers that experience, that consciousness.

(*b*) It is again easy, but also worthwhile, to provide further illustrations of the fact that opponents have often found it obvious that the spatial objection must be decisive. In 'Could Mental States be Brain Processes' Jerome Shaffer begins by distinguishing C(onsciousness)-states from B(rain)-processes. He concludes: 'The fact that it makes no sense to speak of C-states occurring in a volume occupied by a brain means that the Identity Theory cannot be correct' (ibid., p. 115).

Shaffer then proceeds to consider Smart's suggestion that 'We may easily adopt a convention . . . whereby it would make sense to talk of an experience in terms appropriate to a physical process' (ibid., p. 62). Shaffer on this point concludes: 'There is nothing in the way we teach the use of C-state expressions that rules out their having spatial location . . . So we can adopt an additional rule that would allow us to locate C-states in space' (ibid., p. 118). The interest of this conclusion for us is that Shaffer has overlooked that his C-states are not logical substances, not what Nagel would call entities. It surely cannot be right to substantialize C-states by trying to provide them with locations logically independent of the locations of the logical substances of which they are states. In essaying this Shaffer embarks upon an ill-starred neo-Humean 'bold attempt'. He is sufficiently the orthodox Cartesian not to attribute C-states to persons of flesh and blood, while he is at the same time enough of the Hymean radical to want to substantialize these states rather than to allow them to be states of incorporeal subjects.

Yet it is one of Shaffer's critics, Robert Coburn, in 'Shaffer on the Identity of Mental States and Brain Processes', who provides a still more bizarre illustration of the strength and persistence of the Cartesian framework. For Coburn objects against the Smart–Shaffer proposal: that 'the idea that something should be going on in such and such a place, and yet that one person should occupy an intrinsically privileged epistemological position *vis-à-vis* that occurrence, is *prima facie* absurd' (ibid., p. 132).

It is important not to confound this objection to the idea that C-states might be spatially located with another urged against Smart, by Kurt Baier, in 'Smart on Sensations'. Baier's contention bears directly not on the idea of spatial location in C-states but on Smart's fundamental identification: 'Smart is . . . wrong in thinking that introspective reports leave open the question whether they are reports of something private or of something public; hence in thinking that they leave open the question whether or not they are reports of something irreducibly psychic; hence in thinking that there is room for the "metaphysical discovery" that sensations are identical with brain processes' (ibid., p. 105).

It is, therefore, Coburn and not Baier who has exposed himself to devastating rejoinders. Not merely is it not the case that 'the idea that something should be going on in such and such a place, and yet that one person should occupy an intrinsically privileged epistemological position *vis-à-vis* that occurrence, is *prima facie* absurd', but it is the case that everything about which anyone could be said to 'occupy an intrinsically privileged epistemological position' is something which goes on in such and such a place. For such epistemological privilege is, by common consent, if it exists at all, the prerogative of people having sensations, and so on. And someone's having sensations, and so on, is something which goes on, and could go on, only wherever that person happens to be situated. That Coburn should thus insist that what appears to constitute a truth of logic 'is *prima facie* absurd' can be explained only in terms of a deep though tacit Cartesian conviction that modes of consciousness cannot ever be attributed—as in fact they always are and must be—to beings which are essentially corporeal, and hence essentially spatial.

(2) *The Circumstantial Objection*

This runs: 'A thought requires circumstances or, in Wittgenstein's word, "surroundings" (Umgebung). Putting a crown on a man's head is a coronation only in certain circumstances. The behaviour of exclaiming "Oh, I have not put out the milk bottles," or the behaviour of suddenly jumping up, rushing to the kitchen, collecting the bottles and carrying them outside—such behaviour expresses the thought that one has not put out the milk bottles *only in certain circumstances*' (ibid., p. 176: italics original).

This too is, I think, a decisive objection against the thesis that particular thoughts, in the present everyday and quite untechnical sense of the word 'thought', might be identified with particular ongoings in the brain. But, once again, it is not the whole story. Malcolm, it will be remembered, started to take issue with 'the claim that mental events or conscious experiences or inner experiences are brain processes'. He then complained: 'These expressions are almost exclusively philosophers' terms, and I am not sure that I have got the hang of any of them.' So he chose to 'concentrate on the particular example of *sudden thoughts*'.

I will not resist the temptation to mention that the Master himself apparently was not afflicted with this insufficiency of understanding when he wrote, in the *Investigations*: 'The feeling of an unbridgeable gulf between consciousness and brain-process: how does it come about that this does not come into considerations of our ordinary life' (Wittgenstein 1953,

§412, p. 124). But what has to be noticed is the present relevance of the introduction by Descartes of his peculiar sense of
'thought', and the corresponding criterion of the mental.
(On the later rejection of this criterion by the psychoanalysts,
see Chapter Eight below.)

This new definition makes the word 'thought' embrace all
modes of consciousness; and the Cartesian criterion of the
mental is, consequently, consciousness. What, therefore,
Descartes officially means by 'thought' and 'mental events' is
just 'conscious experiences or inner experiences'. But, as we
ought to expect when someone prescribes a new usage which
goes so much against the grain of entrenched verbal habits,
he himself was among the first to mistake what is and is not
implied by the word in its new as opposed to its old meaning.
The most interesting example of such a lapse from his freshly
embraced principles is provided by the treatment in Part VI of
the *Discourse* of what we have learnt to call The Problem of
Other Minds. In this phrase we today construe the word 'mind'
in a strictly Cartesian way. It is for us the problem of how we
know that other people have 'conscious experiences or inner
experiences'. But when the fount and origin himself inquired
how, supposing we were to be confronted with 'machines which
bore a resemblance to our body and imitated our actions as
far as it was morally possible to do so', we could 'recognize
that, for all that, they were not real men', his 'two very certain
tests' for the controlling presence of minds were tests of rationality, with no explicit reference to the stipulated crux of consciousness (Descartes, 1637, Vol. I, p. 116).

The relevance of all this lies in the fact that the Identity
Theory was originally developed to serve as a solution to the
Cartesian psycho-physical problem; the problem, that is,
again, of the relations or lack of relations between consciousness
and stuff. It should, however, cause no surprise that both
proponents and opponents have from time to time forgotten
the limitations determined by the official Cartesian definition
of 'thought' and the official Cartesian criterion of the mental.
Malcolm as an opponent so lapses when, after announcing
that he has perhaps not 'got the hang of' talk about 'conscious
experiences of inner experiences', he chooses 'to concentrate on
the example of *sudden thoughts*'. And, as we shall see in a moment,

Smart as a proponent, especially when carried away by his own wider ideological aspirations, gives some occasion for Malcolm's misunderstanding.

But Malcolm is, as I have agreed already, absolutely right in urging that, in the ordinary as opposed to the Cartesian sense, 'A thought requires circumstances . . .'. And, just as in different circumstances 'the thought that one has not put out the milk bottles' involves different behaviour, so in different circumstances and in different people that same thought involves or is accompanied by different 'inner experiences', and maybe sometimes by none at all. The moral is that an Identity Theorist must not claim that a person's having such and such a thought just is that person's being in such and such a physiological condition, and in particular his brain's being in such and such a condition. That road is definitively closed by what Malcolm says. The Identity Theorist, as such, ought not to say anything directly about thoughts, in the ordinary sense of 'thought'. Instead he should attend to all but only conscious experiences, all but only what I have sometimes alternatively called modes of consciousness. This class will, of course, include all the 'inner experiences' which are for different people and in different circumstances involved in having thoughts, in that same ordinary but more complex sense of 'thought'.

Proponents of the Identity Theory usually start with and emphasize the Cartesian psycho-physical problem, narrowly construed. But then, like Descartes himself, they tend to move, without fully appreciating that they are making a move, and a very big move indeed, to a quite different and much more wide-ranging interpretation of 'thought' and 'the mental'. Feigl provides in a single sentence a textbook example showing how quickly and how innocently this enormous and unfortunate shift may be effected: 'The crucial and central puzzle of the mind-body problem, at least since Descartes, has consisted in the challenge to render an adequate account of the relation of the "raw feels" as well as of other mental facts (intentions, thoughts, volitions, desires, etc.) to the corresponding neuro-physiological processes' (ibid., p. 35).

Both Place and Smart begin in the same place, as is indicated by the titles of their first statements of the Identity Theory.

These were, respectively, 'Is Consciousness a Brain Process?' and 'Sensations and Brain Processes'. But Smart is also, very explicitly and very properly, concerned with issues of world-outlook: the debate over the Identity Theory is for him a vital battle on the ideological front. (I suspect that this is true also of Malcolm, although he is much less forthcoming about such matters.) It will be helpful to distinguish, as perhaps Smart himself does not always do, two different ideological aspirations. One is materialism, specified by Smart as 'the theory that there is nothing in the world over and above those entities which are postulated by Physics' (ibid., p. 159). The other is something which, sympathetically parodying Chinese denunciations of 'the New Tsars', I label 'Great Physicist imperialism'.

For anyone who accepts the anti-Cartesian principles of the present book the only immediately relevant difficulty about the former is likely to be that arising from Smart's insistence upon specifying materialism in terms of 'those entities which are postulated by Physics'. Will the fact that persons and other possible subjects of consciousness are seen to be essentially corporeal be sufficient to satisfy Smart's ontological requirements? If so, then his materialism will be of the straightforward and unqualified sort so classically specified by Thomas Hobbes in Chapter Forty-Six of *Leviathan*: 'The World (I mean not the Earth onely, that denominates the Lovers of it *Worldly men*, but the *Universe*, that is, the whole masse of all things that are) is Corporeall, that is to say, Body; and hath the dimensions of Magnitude, namely, Length, Breadth, and Depth: also every part of Body, is likewise Body, and hath the like dimensions; and consequently every part of the Universe, is Body, and that which is not Body, is no part of the Universe: And because the Universe is All, that which is no part of it, is *Nothing*; and consequently *no where*' (Hobbes, p. 689). But if a Hobbist insistence that persons and all other possible subjects of consciousness must be corporeal is still not enough for Smart, then his dissatisfaction must surely be a manifestation of what I have been characterizing as Great Physicist imperialism.

What this is, is: not only the demand that our ontology must provide no houseroom for any entities other than those acceptable to the complete Hobbist; but also the insistence that all explanations and even all concepts are, or ought to be, ultimately physical. I fear that this more stringent interpretation of Smart's materialism is correct. For he writes: 'I am concerned to deny that in the world there are non-physical entities and non-physical laws. In particular I wish to deny the doctrine of psycho-physical dualism. (I also want to deny any theory of "emergent properties" since irreducibly non-physical properties are just about as repugnant to me as are irreducibly non-physical entities.' A footnote to the second sentence quoted remarks: 'That Strawson's view is essentially dualistic can be seen from the fact that he admits that disembodied existence is logically compatible with it' (Borst, p. 160).

This note is significant. For the truth is that Strawson is most categorically committed to a monistic position: persons are tokens of 'a type of entity such that *both* predicates ascribing states of consciousness *and* predicates ascribing corporeal characteristics . . . are equally applicable to a single individual of that single type'. The admission to which Smart refers, which occurs only in the final section of the relevant chapter in *Individuals* and has no predecessor in the first published version of this material, should, I think, be seen rather as an aberrant and inconsistent postscript than as the ultimate revelation of a basic ontological dualism (Strawson, 1959, III; and compare Flew, 1976a, pp. 153–4 and Strawson, 1958). That Smart sees this Strawsonian backsliding as he does suggests that he shares the Cartesian inability to accept that one and the same subject may carry two fundamentally different kinds of predicate. The consequent fear of ontological inflation if he admits such different kinds of predicate is, presumably, one of the reasons why for Smart—as has often been remarked—one of the two terms of the alleged identity appears to disappear in favour of the other. Experiences are really a special class of brain processes. Yet even these special brain processes are not really experiences.

Equally—as has not been noticed so often—it is in part because of this vicarious imperialism on behalf of the physicists that the first term of the identity is taken to embrace a whole lot more than 'inner experiences'. Thus Smart affirms: '. . . even though love may elude test-tubes, it does not elude materialistic metaphysics, since it can be analysed as a pattern of bodily behaviour or, perhaps better, as the internal state of the human organism that accounts for this behaviour' (Borst, p. 160).

Yet even when all this has been said about Smart's wider concerns, and about how his Great Physicist imperialism constitutes one motive for over-extending the scope of the Identity Theory, I still remain a little perplexed about just what is the sort of reduction to physics which he hopes to achieve, and why. For he seems at least part of the time to concede that talk about 'inner experiences' (and presumably also talk about motives and purposes and intentions) is legitimate, and is not logically reducible to talk about the behaviour of organisms—much less the behaviour of 'those entities which are postulated by Physics'. But, conceding this legitimacy, and if such logical reduction is impossible, then the explanation of conduct in terms of the motives of agents must be other than physical explanation and not logically reducible to it.

On the other hand Smart apparently cannot rest content with the sort of ontological reduction which is manifested when we insist that 'there cannot be . . . nations without nationals' (ibid., p. 167). Yet we can certainly allow, and allow without making any reckless claims on behalf of physics: both that people have emergent characteristics, in the sense that things can significantly and truly be said about people which could neither be significantly said, nor logically reduced to what could significantly be said, either about the organs in a human organism, or even about any other whole organism at a substantially lower evolutionary level; and that there could no more be instantiations of these various emergent characteristics without there being the appropriate flesh and blood organisms for them to characterize, than there could be football or cricket teams and displays of teamwork and team spirit without any corporeal players.

(3) *The Collapse of the Psycho-physical Problem*

So far in the present Chapter Six I have eschewed any ambition either to establish or to refute an Identity Theory. I have not even tried to dispose of all the objections actually mentioned: that of Baier, for instance, was cited only in order to contrast it with another offered by Coburn. But the upshot is to throw

light, not on one presently prominent candidate solution only,
but also on the whole Psycho-physical Problem as well. For
the reformulations which Malcolm's objections have shown
to be required cannot be restricted to the Identity Theory.
Every other solution suggested, and the problem itself, will
have to be similarly reconsidered and, if possible, represented.
It is not easy to discern what will survive such necessary
restructuring. So the remainder of this chapter is put forward
with much hesitation.

Certainly it makes no sense to talk of consciousness as if
experiences were things occurring loose and separate. It is,
for instance, absurd to talk as if you could first identify a pain
and then set about inquiring who, if anyone, happens to be its
owner. We have, therefore, to think of all modes of consciousness as always and essentially conditions of organisms. We
cannot start with loose and separate atomic pains; we have to
begin with flesh-and-blood people, suffering. But, given that
this is right, then there is no deep, perhaps unbridgeable
Cartesian gulf between consciousness and stuff. Consciousness
just is a very special characteristic of a very special kind of
physical structure—that of (higher) organisms. Nor does there
seem to be any room, again given that we are on the right lines,
for Cartesian speculations about the possible operations of
consciousness as a separate causal factor. For how could this
separate causal factor be identified as such? And how could
we put or pursue any question about the biological functions
of consciousness as such; as opposed to those of the capacities
by which it is manifested, or which it characterizes or
accompanies?

What can still be asked—what constantly is asked—is
whether when someone is enjoying or suffering some particular
kind of consciousness, their enjoyment or their suffering has
some more particular basis, in the internal condition and constitution of the organism, than that provided by whatever
more general and external features entitle us to say that the
subject is indeed enjoying or suffering in whatever way it may
be. It was such clearly answerable and often answered questions which I had in mind when I wrote, in Section 1 (i) above:
'There is, therefore, no contradiction in saying that she has a
stabbing pain in her leg, while simultaneously suggesting,

either that the physiological basis of this suggestion is to be found elsewhere, or even that it has no particular physiological basis at all.' It is scientific discoveries in this area, revealing the particular physiological bases of particular forms of consciousness, which its protagonists hope will, if the philosophical objections can be overcome, overwhelmingly vindicate the Identity Theory. (See, for instance, M. Williams.)

But we must appreciate the crucial importance here of the difference between particular and general. Certainly we can sensibly ask about the particular physiological bases of particular forms of consciousness; and our scientists may find, for instance, that it is a contingently necessary condition of the having of visual experience that the 'visual' area in the cortex should be in such and such a state, being stimulated thus and thus. Yet the enjoying or suffering of any form of consciousness is essentially an attribute of the organism as a whole: it makes no sense to say that the cortex or part of a cortex either enjoys or suffers anything. It is this fundamental logical fact—the fact that consciousness essentially is an attribute of an organism as a whole, an attribute which can only be identified by reference to the general condition and behaviour of that organism—which inhibits the identification and even the theoretical isolation of consciousness as a separate causal factor. We simply cannot first isolate the particular state of consciousness of some organism, and then contrast it with the whole general material state of that organism when it is thus conscious; asking whether the former affects the latter. The immediate moral seems to be that Two-way Interactionism, conceived as requiring that sort of impact of consciousness on stuff, has to be ruled out as a nonsense.

The Identity Thesis survives, however, and in it a kind of Epiphenomenalism. For suppose we find, in the sense indicated above, particular physiological bases for various forms of consciousness. Then it will surely be tempting, and not by the same token necessarily wrong, to say: not only that it is because their central nervous systems, or some parts of them, are in such and such a state that they are suffering in this way; but also that their suffering in this way has been discovered to be the fact that their central nervous systems, or these parts of them, are in that particular state.

To the Baierian suggestion that this equation is incoherent because each person has privileged access to their own 'inner experience', whereas there is no such privilege with regard to the corresponding internal states of the organism, may we not reply: 'But of course the person who is actually enjoying or suffering, and of course no one else, can actually enjoy those enjoyments or suffer those sufferings; but this does not prevent that person being the same one, who others with no such privileged access know to be having these experiences?' To the objection that Epiphenomenalism cannot consist with an Identity Thesis, since what being in a particular state of consciousness is by the latter equated with must be allowed to possess the causal efficacy denied by the former, may the Identity Theorist not reply that, though perhaps equally paradoxical, it is no less idiomatically correct to say that lightning both is and is produced by, but does not produce, appropriate electrical discharges?

7
HUMAN PSYCHOLOGY AND
SKINNERIAN BEHAVIOURISM

BACK in Chapter Four we noticed Sartre concluding: 'Thus the notion of conduct is itself destroyed with Janet and with the Behaviourists. The existence of the act implies its autonomy.' This very serious charge can be illustrated and, as far as we go, supported by considering the apologia of one who has for many years been a leader in experimental psychology. This work, by Professor B. F. Skinner of Harvard, has a title which to any friend of mankind must appear sinister, *Beyond Freedom and Dignity*. Described by its original New York publishers as 'his definitive statement about man and society', it very quickly received the accolade of republication as a Pelican.

The book is not, however, what Skinner's first London publishers said that it was: 'the summary of his life's work in the scientific analysis of human behaviour'. It cannot be that, whatever else it is. For it neither contains summaries of any actual scientific work, nor references to original papers reporting such work, nor even—like that mischievous slim volume *The Thought of Chairman Harold*—blank pages. The writer of the New York dust-jacket was more careful; revealing perhaps that he had at least riffled through the book. That original dust-jacket said of Skinner: 'Basing his arguments on the massive results of the experimental analysis of behaviour in which he pioneered, he rejects traditional explanations of behaviour in terms of states of mind, feelings, and other mental attributes, in favour of other explanations to be sought in the individual's genetic endowment and personal history.'

Certainly Skinner throughout writes as if Skinnerian psychology had already achieved 'massive results', just raring to be applied. Yet he never particularizes, either directly or indirectly. So nothing is done to allay the reader's well-founded suspicion that the 'explanations to be sought' are also—at least in the detail sufficient to generate new possibilities of human application—still to be found. Instead what Skinner actually does is: first, to indicate what he, and presumably the throng of his younger followers too, believe that the scientific study of human psychology must presuppose and imply; and, second, to appeal for the systematic application of the unspecified but supposedly massive results of such Skinnerian inquiries to 'the terrifying problems that face us in the world today' (Skinner 1971, p. 3).

I want in this present chapter to examine Skinner's 'definitive statement'; and to bring out that he is attempting, like many others before, to develop a comprehensive science of man without coming to terms with the recalcitrant peculiarities of human beings. In particular he thinks that he has to deny the reality of choice. He thus becomes committed to dismissing all explanations of conduct as conduct; all explanations, that is to say, which refer to the agents' own reasons for acting, or not acting, as they did. With Skinner and his followers 'the notion of conduct' is indeed 'destroyed'; and that precisely because, as we saw in Chapter Three and Chapter Four, action does essentially involve possible alternatives.

(1) Skinner's Presuppositions of Psychological Inquiry

His most catastrophic misguiding principle is that to be scientific any study of man must eschew all anthropomorphic notions. The explicit and authoritative statement of this grotesque assumption is possibly more important than anything else in the entire book. For Skinner is saying outright what others more cautious leave implicit. He begins: 'We have used the instruments of science; we have counted and measured and compared; but something essential to scientific practice is missing in almost all current discussions of human behaviour' (ibid., p. 7).

It appears that what is missing is, awkwardly, the absence of certain notions which Skinner insists can have no place in any truly scientific discourse. For, he continues, 'Although physics soon stopped personifying things . . . it continued for a long time to speak as if they had wills, impulses, feelings, purposes and other fragmentary attributes of an indwelling agent. . . . All this was eventually abandoned, and to good effect . . .' Nevertheless, deplorably, what should be 'the behavioural sciences still appeal to comparable internal states . . .' (ibid., p. 8). We are, therefore, supposed to regret that 'Almost everyone who is concerned with human affairs— as political scientist, philosopher, man of letters, economist, psychologist, linguist, sociologist, theologian, educator, or psychotherapist—continues to talk about human behaviour in this prescientific way' (ibid., p. 9).

(i) Certainly such discourse about people is prescientific, in the obvious but purely temporal sense that it was going on long before there was anything which deserved to be called science. Yet Skinner clearly takes it to be not only, innocuously, pre-scientific, but also, damagingly, unscientific. He takes it that it must be as much a superstitious mistake thus to try to explain the actions of an actual person by reference to his will, impulses, feelings, and purposes; as it undoubtedly would be to personify some inanimate object, and then to undertake to explain its movements in the same sort of way. The reason why the latter enterprise would be superstitious and a mistake is, simply, that inanimate objects are not people or even animals; and hence do not and cannot have wills, impulses, feelings, purposes, or any other such attributes. But the former under-taking is, by the same token, neither superstitious nor a mistake. So any psychological programme committed to maintaining the contrary is, by that preposterous commitment alone, sufficiently discredited.

The first and obvious reason why Skinner believes that he has to embrace this absurdity is that he misconstrues the expulsion of such notions from physics as the repudiation of essentially superstitious ideas, rather than as the rejection of misapplications of ideas in themselves proper and indispens-able. He supplements this first misconception with two other less obvious but equally inadequate considerations.

(a) Of these the first is: 'we do not feel the things that have been invented to explain behaviour. The possessed man does not feel the possessing demon and may even deny that he exists . . . The intelligent man does not feel his intelligence or the introvert his introversion' (ibid., 15–16). Certainly, if we confine ourselves to those examples, there is something in what Skinner says. But this something does nothing to destroy the obvious truth. The man, for instance, who confesses, 'I am determined to make it with Cyn', very obviously does have, and knows without inference that he has, a will, impulses, feelings, and—definitely—a purpose in life; and it was 'wills, impulses, feelings, purposes', not intelligence and introversion, which Skinner wanted to dismiss as prescientific fictions.

(*b*) The second of the supporting reasons is more subtle. Skinner writes: 'If we ask someone, "Why did you go to the theatre?", and he says, "Because I felt like going", we are apt to take his reply as a kind of explanation' (ibid., pp. 12–13). We are indeed. For that 'I wanted to go to the theatre', or that 'I am determined to make it with Cyn', may fully explain conduct previously puzzling. What of course these responses will not do is answer as well as set the further questions: why I have a taste, and this particular taste, for the theatre; and why I find girls, and in particular Cynthia, so powerfully attractive. But these are the questions which Skinner wants to press: 'It would be much more to the point to know what has happened when he has gone to the theatre in the past, what he heard or read about the play he went to see, and what other things in his past or present environments induced him to go . . .' (ibid., p. 13).

(ii) That Skinner finds these further questions so much more interesting, and that he wants to suggest that explanations at the first level are not explanations at all, are in part consequences of another of his misguiding doctrines about what it is to be truly scientific: 'A scientific analysis shifts both the responsibility and the achievement to the environment' (ibid., p. 25). It is therefore, according to Skinner, unscientific to claim that anyone ever effected anything. Hence certain unnamed Freudians are rebuked for recklessly 'assuring their patients that they are free to choose among different courses of action and are in the long run the architects of their own destinies' (ibid., pp. 20–1). For Skinner the true causes of all human behaviour are, and can only be, environmental.

This curious but common doctrine is actually inconsistent with the presupposition of universal causality, from which by many it is thought to follow. For if everything that has a cause is by that fact disqualified from itself being a cause in its turn, then there can be no causal chains. Every discovery of the cause of some cause must be sufficient to show that the original cause was not, after all, a cause. All true causes must be themselves uncaused.

(iii) Perhaps the main reason why Skinner holds that the explanation of human behaviour is to be sought always and only outside the agent, is that he sees any alternative as involving the black beast notion of 'autonomous man'. This he believes to be the main basis of the to him equally repugnant concepts of human freedom and dignity. Let Skinner explain himself: 'Two features of autonomous man are particularly troublesome. In the traditional view, a person is free. He is autonomous in the sense that his behaviour is uncaused. He can therefore be held responsible for what he does, and justly punished if he offends' (ibid., p. 19).

In order to appreciate more fully the grounds of Skinner's opposition to all these notions it is helpful to look back at his earlier utopian novel *Walden Two*, in which many of the ideas of *Beyond Freedom and Dignity* were put into the mouth of Frazier. ('*Frazier*' is Skinner's middle name.) In Chapter XXIX Frazier says: '"I deny that freedom exists at all. I must deny it—or my programme would be absurd. You can't have a science about a subject matter which hops capriciously about."'

If what has been argued in earlier chapters is right, then the behaviour of a human being, in so far as it is the conduct of an agent, cannot indeed have causes (physical). For causes (physical) necessitate: given such causes there can be no alternative but that their effects will occur. So, in as much as Skinner is committed to the construction of a para-physical science of man, he is absolutely correct to see the idea of the person as an agent ('autonomous man') as the obstacle in his path. But he is just as totally wrong to go on to infer that there can be no sort of regular and disciplined science concerned with such subjects. For to say that someone was on this occasion and in these respects an agent, having and giving reasons for acting not in that way but in this, and hence to say that there could not have been causes (physical) of this conduct, is not to say but rather to deny that the agent hopped capriciously about. So obviously there is room for explanations; and hence for something which can be rated, albeit not perhaps in the narrowest physical sense, science. Nor has anything been said to preclude the possibility of prediction, whether by reference to the known characters of the agents, or whether by inference from physiological or other preconditions guaranteeing, not that this is how it must be, but only that this is how it will be.

(2) Skinner's Principles of Application

So far we have attended only to what Skinner takes to be the necessary presuppositions of a science of psychology. But his main concern both here and in *Walden Two* is with the application of that science; which nowadays he writes as if we already have—or, at any rate, as if he already has. Thus *Beyond Freedom and Dignity* begins with a review of 'the terrifying problems that face us in the world today'. It then proceeds to argue that to solve these 'we need to make vast changes in human behaviour'; so that 'what we need is a technology of behaviour'. He eventually concludes, 'A scientific view of man offers exciting possibilities. We have not yet seen what man can make of man' (ibid., pp. 3, 4, 5, 215).

(i) We should recognize, what is not immediately obvious from this latest statement, that Skinner's programme is both elitist and authoritarian; although it is among such programmes in our time unusual in owing nothing to Lenin. The crux is to appreciate that the words 'we' and 'man', upon which so much depends, are not always used to refer to exactly the same collections of individuals. Earlier, in Chapter XXXI of *Walden Two*, Frazier made exactly this point with characteristic frankness: ' "When we ask what Man can make of Man, we don't mean the same thing by 'Man' in both instances. We mean to ask what a few men can make of mankind. And that's the all-absorbing question of the twentieth century. What kind of world can we build—those of us who understand the science of behaviour?" '

(a) Once this is appreciated it becomes wryly interesting to notice Skinner's trendy dismissal of one supposedly irrelevant old-timer: 'Greek physics and biology are now of historical interest only . . . but the dialogues of Plato are still assigned to students and cited as if they threw light on human behaviour' (ibid., pp. 5–6). Although insight into the eternal and immaterial Forms, which was to give Plato's philosopher kings their right to absolute power, would have been very different from 'the science of behaviour', from which Frazier and Skinner claim their title; still Plato remains the first and most brilliant forefather of everyone who has wished to secure all power for some Guardian élite, united and justified by its alleged special knowledge of the most fundamental realities. It is a point which in respect of the collective absolutism of the Bolshevik directorate in Russia was well and early taken by Bertrand Russell. In that case, of course, the legitimating expertise is a putative Marxist understanding of class structures and historical necessities. Russell summed up his observations after a study tour of the U.S.S.R.: 'Far closer than any actual historical parallel is the parallel of Plato's *Republic*' (Russell, 1920, pp. 28–9).

(*b*) Any environmentally introjected liberal inhibitions on the implementation of so authoritarian a programme are in Skinner removed by assailing all the crucial distinctions. The bases of his general offensive are two assumptions. The first, which he does nothing to warrant, is that we already have that para-physical science of psychology, to the construction of which he has devoted his whole professional life. The second, which we saw in Section 1 to be correct, is that the presuppositions of Skinner's supposed new science are incompatible with all notions of choice, and hence with traditional ideas of human freedom and dignity. Since distinctions which refer to any of these must be unscientific, they have to be swept away in the name both of the science and of the application of that science.

Thus Skinner refuses to recognize any significant difference between a set-up in which abortion is illegal and one in which it is not. In the latter case, he says with a perverse sneer: 'The individual is "permitted" to decide the issue for himself, simply in the sense that he will act because of consequences to which legal punishment is no longer to be added' (ibid., p. 97). Well yes, I suppose, precisely in that sense; and exactly that is what it is all about. Skinner has already shown the same doctrinally determined scotoma with regard to the difference between having or not having criminal laws forbidding people to 'gamble, drink, or go to prostitutes' (ibid., p. 91).

Again, he considers 'the practice of inviting prisoners to volunteer for possibly dangerous experiments—for example, on new drugs—in return for better living conditions or shorter sentences'. He asks, rhetorically, 'but are they really free when positively reinforced . . .?' (ibid., p. 39.) Since positive reinforcement is precisely and only his fancy way of referring to the promised rewards, the correct answer is, clearly, 'Yes'. The contrast is, for instance, with those prisoners in Belsen and Dachau who were made subjects for medical experimentation willy nilly.

Again, 'A person never becomes truly self-reliant. Even though he deals effectively with things, he is necessarily dependent upon those who have taught him to do so' (ibid., p. 91). But what self-reliance excludes is helplessness, not having been educated to be self-reliant. It is disturbing to reflect that a great many of those employed to teach and practice educational psychology in the U.S.A. belong to this strange, blinkered, illiberal, Harvard school.

Yet again, Skinner refuses to allow any important difference between persuasion by the giving of reasons and forcible methods of mind-bending: '"Brain-washing" is proscribed by those who otherwise condone the changing of minds, simply because the control is obvious' (ibid., p. 96). But the issue does not concern what is overt and what is covert. It is, rather, a matter of giving or not giving what are, or are thought to be good reasons; and the receiving and considering of reasons can scarcely proceed without at least the receiver being aware of what is going on. (No doubt the whole business is out of place and unfamiliar in and around the rat cages and pigeon lofts of a Skinnerian psychology laboratory.)

(ii) Politically libertarian hopes rise a little when we read: 'Permissive practices have many advantages.' Such hopes are soon dashed: 'Permissiveness is not, however, a policy; it is the abandonment of policy, and its apparent advantages are illusory. To refuse to control is to leave control not to the person himself, but to other parts of the social and non-social environments' (ibid., p. 84). This statement is on two counts obnoxious.

(a) First, even if I have got to be controlled either by a person or by impersonal forces, still the difference between these alternatives matters enormously. If, for instance, I suffer something painful I am much less upset if I believe this to be the result of blind forces than if I believe it to be someone's intention to do this to me. (This is one reason why a moment's thought makes the ideal of a totally planned society so repellent to all but those who see themselves as the total planners; and, correspondingly, so endlessly enchanting to actual or aspiring members of that power élite.)

(b) Second, Skinner's contention that leaving control to the person himself is an illusion is supported only by his insistence that the true causes of human behaviour are, and can only be, environmental. This popular misconception was demolished in Section 2(b) above. It is, furthermore, altogether incongruous with the present proposal, that the unenlightened laity should be controlled by the psychologically illuminated élite. For how, upon Skinnerian principles, can it be right to say that in Skinner's utopia it would be Skinner's Controllers who would be controlling the lesser breeds; rather than the environment of the Controllers which would be ultimately controlling everybody?

(iii) Not only is Skinner uninhibited by any liberal scruples, he is also untroubled by questions about the values which ought to direct his programme for total control. His various statements about value could, and hopefully will, do yeoman service as exercise material in elementary ethics courses. But they are additionally remarkable as revealing once again Skinner's ineptitude in the handling of any concepts having a distinctively human application.

Thus, for instance, Skinner writes: 'If a scientific analysis can tell us how to change behaviour, can it tell us what changes to make? This is a question about the behaviour of those who do in fact propose and make changes' (ibid., p. 103). But, of course, it is nothing of the kind. A question about what changes ought to be made is precisely not a question about what some controllers or would-be controllers are in fact proposing to do, or actually doing. Again Skinner tells us, cheerful, innocent, and unabashed: 'To make a value judgement by calling something good or bad is to classify it in terms of its reinforcing effects' (ibid., p. 103). But, of course, it is not. For to classify things in terms of their reinforcing effects is to classify them by reference to the effects which it is believed that they will in fact have; while to make a value judgement is not to make an assertion about what is or will be the case. It is, rather, to prescribe what ought to be.

A third and slightly more subtle example begins when Skinner quotes Sir Karl Popper: 'It is impossible to derive a sentence stating a norm or a decision from a sentence stating a fact . . .'. Skinner comments: 'The conclusion is valid only if indeed it is "possible to adopt a norm or its opposite". Here is autonomous man playing his most awe-inspiring role, but whether or not a person obeys the norm "Thou shalt not steal" depends upon supporting contingencies, which must not be overlooked' (ibid., p. 14).

There is indeed something awe-inspiring here. But it is the naïve audacity with which Skinner rushes forward to challenge a logical contention, which he has not even begun to understand, armed only with weapons inherently incapable of ranging on to the target proposed. For Popper's thesis is one about what can and cannot be validly deduced from what. It is, therefore, wholly beside the point to tell us what in fact leads people actually to adopt one norm or another.

(3) New Science on an Old Continent

Earlier in the present chapter I suggested that we would see in Skinner some of the consequences of attempting 'to develop a comprehensive science of man without coming to terms with the recalcitrant peculiarities of human beings'. That Skinner has been attempting precisely this became absolutely clear from the moment when in Section 1 we first attended to his bizarre insistence that the nature of science precludes any admission that people—unlike inanimate things—really do have 'wills, impulses, feelings, purposes'.

Skinner—believing that this is required by his scientific cloth—refuses to recognize either the reality of choice and the inexpugnable difference between movings and motions, or the legitimacy of the explanations of conduct which presuppose and come to terms with these realities. He is thus committed to denying the most fundamental difference between the natural and the peculiarly human sciences. Another consequential difference arises from the fact that the subject-matters of the former cannot, while the subject-matter of the latter can, and regularly does, offer explanations of at least some parts and aspects of its own behaviour. The aspiring human scientist has, therefore, always to find his scope not in virgin but in already partly settled territory. Either he must try to drive some, or all, the earlier occupants off their land; or else he must discover his own new niche where no predecessor had ever before contrived to establish himself. For him it can never be as it was for Adam and Eve in Milton's *Paradise Lost*: 'The world was all before them, where to choose' (XII, 646).

Skinner meets this problem by essaying a clean clearance. The titles of all established explanations of conduct as conduct are bogus. They presuppose an idea of 'autonomous man' for which a para-physical psychology can allow no room: 'What my nets will not catch is not fish!' But this is no way to behave. Science requires that we recognize all facts, however disturbing to our own proclivities and preconceptions. No method is scientific except in so far as it is suited to the investigation of the particular and sometimes peculiar subject to which it is directed.

So what is to be done? We have, surely, to abandon the hope of developing a single comprehensive science of man, containing a unified theory providing explanations of only one type. The Skinnerian psychologist, who wants to employ nothing but the physical notion of cause, must find—as of course he can find—questions which refer only to those bits or aspects of our behaviour which cannot be explained as, because they are not, conduct. The human psychologist, the psychologist who is able and willing to come to terms with the peculiarities of human subjects, must find—as of course he too can find—questions about conduct which the layman either has not asked or has answered wrongly. And maybe, as we shall see in Chapter Eight, there is a third possibility. Maybe it will prove somehow possible greatly to extend the range of application of the notions employed in the explanation of conduct, those notions which are to many paradigmatically psychological.

8 .

MOTIVES AND FREUD'S
UNCONSCIOUS

THIS chapter has two main objects: first, to reformulate, to explain, and, as far as is then necessary, to defend a thesis about the logical status of the discovery of the unconscious mind; and, second, to point two or three morals which are implicit in this thesis. It is, without any refinements of qualification, that the kernel of Freud's discovery was this. If you are prepared so to extend such notions as motive, intention, purpose, wish, and desire—the notions, that is, involved in the explanation of conduct as conduct—that is becomes proper to speak of motives and so forth which are not known to, and the behaviour resulting from which is not under the immediate control of, the person who harbours them; then you can interpret, and even guide or change, far more in terms of concepts of this category than any of Freud's predecessors had realized. The morals of this thesis all arise from the peculiarities of the notions thus extended. These peculiarities are such as to ensure that the central and basic place of these notions in psychoanalysis must give this discipline a logical status different from, although not for that reason either superior or inferior to, that of studies concerned with subjects other than the distinctively human aspects of human beings, and in particular that of the psychology which aspires to become a para-physical science.

Most of the evidence for the main thesis will be drawn from some of Freud's own works, works which are both classical and fundamental. It may be objected that these are all out of date, that even psychoanalysis has moved on. But, first, this is not in the relevant respects true: both because these texts are still prescribed as essential in the training of analysts; and because there are, as I have found myself, plenty of parallel passages in recent works by orthodox Freudians. Second, even if these

Freudian classics did represent a closed incident in the history of thought, his stature is in itself sufficient to justify study of his ideas in their own right.

These two answers, the second even more than the first, are also apt to the rebuke which one austere colleague delivered to me after the publication of the first forefather of the present chapter: 'One should no more do philosophy of science on psychoanalysis than on astrology!' Certainly I accept, and would on another occasion press, the point that, starting with Freud himself, psychoanalysis has been and remains marked and marred by a pervasive and systematic evasiveness in its response to whatever obstreperous facts may seem to falsify its cherished hypotheses (Popper, 1953; and compare Eysenck, XII, Cioffi, 1970 and 1972, and Cioffi, 1973, pp. 1–24). Nevertheless it is also true, as Ryle said in *The Concept of Mind*, that Freud was 'psychology's one man of genius' (Ryle, p. 324).

(1) *The Stretching of the Concepts of Conduct*

Freud was, of course, himself the first to recognize and to emphasize how far his development of a notion of the unconscious mind has been anticipated by poets, novelists, biographers, and plain men. But I shall continue to speak without qualification of Freud's discovery: first, because always to insert such awkward qualifications is unnecessary and tiresome; and, second, because Freud surely was the person mainly responsible for developing and systematizing insights which had previously been isolated.

(i) The degree of that extension required to permit us to speak of motives or intentions and the like, when these are either unrecognized or even ingenuously repudiated by those to whom they are attributed, varies from case to case. It is perhaps least of a stretch with motives and with wishes. For people without benefit of Freud, and with no egregious claims to psychological insight, have often come to admit underlying motives which were at first unnoticed or denied; while it is everywhere notorious that some are as slow to recognize as others are swift to mistake themselves to be in love. The collector of ideas might like to add to the list of anticipations provided in Freud's own writings another from a very different tradition. In an important letter to Franz Mehring, Friedrich

Engels wrote: 'Ideology is a process accomplished by the so-called thinker consciously, indeed, but with a false consciousness. The real motives impelling him remain unknown to him, otherwise it would not be an ideological process at all. Hence he imagines false or apparent motives' (Torr, No. 227: 14.vii.'93).

The extension in this first and apparently more obvious direction seems to be greatest with intentions. For surely before Freud, and perhaps not only before Freud, we should have been, or perhaps should be, at the very least uneasy about talk of intentions never consciously formulated and even honestly denied after careful reflection? But the Freudian enterprise also requires extensions in another dimension. This is more disturbing, and much less often appreciated. Let us put it in the terminology introduced in our earlier chapters. Whereas traditionally only movings and abstentions from movings are explained in terms of the motives, intentions, and so on of the agent; Freud proposes to provide similar explanations of some motions too, but in terms of his own stretched concepts—unconscious motives, unconscious intentions, and unconscious whatever else it may be.

So when, for instance, we explain that this elector voted for that lot because he believed that 'the gentlemen in Whitehall know best' or because he wanted the then Shadow Chancellor and his party comrades to satisfy their longing 'to make the rich howl in agony', we presuppose that the elector in question, in the most fundamental sense, could have either voted for some other lot, or abstained. But when Freud claims to be uncovering the unconscious sources of paradoxes, dreams, and obsessive actions, these are not, and are not thought to be, all performances which the subject could put on or shut off at will.

Certainly there are differences between these three sorts of cases; and maybe the differences between movings and motions is—like most such humanly crucial contrasts—a matter of degree; in the sense that the clear-cut, defining extremes are, or could be, linked by a series of actual or theoretically possible instances such that the amount of dissimilarity between each member and the next becomes vanishingly small. Yet we must never allow marginal or disputed instances to distract our attention from the fundamentals which these are marginal or disputed between (Flew 1975, §§7.14–7.24).

Even if we were to accept, what Thomas Szasz seems frequently to suggest, if never quite to say, that all Freud's favourite case-studies were in fact studies of malingerers, still we should have to admit that his theorizings assumed the contrary, that they could not turn on or shut off their symptoms at will: 'This is a mad disease, surely . . . such a patient . . . simply cannot help himself; the actions performed in an obsessional condition are supported by a kind of energy which probably has no counterpart in normal mental life' (Freud 1933, p. 220; and compare Szasz, Book One). A truly compulsive obsessive action is not, therefore, an action done under compulsion; because it is, or is supposed to be, no more a genuine action than any of those motions which we characterize idiomatically as 'reflex actions'.

(ii) The most cursory examination of the basic texts makes it quite clear, both that it is with these essential conduct-explaining notions that Freud and his followers are engaged, and that these notions are here being extended in the two ways indicated in the previous subsection. Take, for example, a by now oft-told tale from the *Introductory Lectures*. (Do not, by the way, be deceived: these are in every way superior to the *New Introductory Lectures*.) The heroine, 'A lady of nearly thirty years of age suffered from very severe obsessional symptoms . . . In the course of a day she would perform . . . several times over. She would run out of the room . . . take up a certain position at the table in the centre of the room, ring for her maid, give her a trivial order . . . and then run back again.'

All became intelligible after Freud had been shown 'a great mark on the table cover', and told of the lady's disappointing and traumatic wedding night: 'More than ten years previously she had married a man very much older than herself, who had proved impotent . . . Innumerable times on that night he had run out of his room into hers in order to make the attempt, but had failed every time. In the morning he said angrily: "It's enough to disgrace one in the eyes of the maid who does the beds," and seizing a bottle of red ink . . . he poured it on the sheet, but not exactly in the place where such a mark might have been.'

The interpretation of these fragmentary leaves from a de Maupassant apocrypha is, 'that the patient identified herself with her husband . . . the purpose of the obsessive act . . . evidently lies in the calling of the maid, to whom she displays the mark . . . In this way he, whose part she is playing, is *not* ashamed before the servant, the stain is where it ought to have been . . . The obsessive act thus says: "No, it is not true . . . he was not impotent." . . . The deepest secret of her illness was that it enabled her to shield him from a malicious gossip, to justify her separation from him, and to make a comfortable existence apart from her possible for him' (Freud 1933a, pp. 221, 222, and 223).

This official interpretation explains the curious ongoings as if they were the outcome of a consciously thought-out plan, and as if these bell-ringings had been as much deliberate and controllable as the lady's normal summonings of her breakfast or of her carriage. But, of course, neither of these two conditions was at the beginning satisfied. The unconscious plan and purpose was not known to anyone until the moment when all 'was discovered by the patient herself in a flash' (ibid., p. 223). Regrettably we are never told: either that, as the theory demands, she became in that moment of illumination capable of abstaining from these domestic dramatics; or whether, if so, she decided to continue ostensibly as before.

(iii) Freud himself did show signs of recognizing the nature and justification of his conceptual innovations; although he never, I think, put his finger sharply on what I have distinguished as the second of two dimensions of extension. Thus, in writing of 'the psycho-analytical definition of the mind', he defends himself against the charge that his moves were emptily or perversely verbal: 'It seems like an empty wrangle over words to argue whether mental life is to be regarded as co-extensive with consciousness or whether it may be said to stretch beyond this limit, and yet I can assure you that the acceptance of unconscious mental processes represents a decisive step towards a new orientation of the world and of science' (ibid., pp. 17 and 18).

Indeed it does: 'We have widened the domain of mental phenomena to a very considerable extent and have won for psychology phenomena which were never previously accredited to it' (ibid., p. 47). And psychology for Freud is without doubt, though I can find no neat nutshell statement, understood as the area of application of such basic conduct-explaining notions as motive, wish, plan, purpose, and intention.

What Freud is doing, and what, if dimly, he sees that he is doing, is: first, to replace a Cartesian by an entirely different criterion of the mental; and, second, by vastly extending the range of application of the key terms involved in that new criterion, correspondingly extending the territories open to psychological study. Thus, in the 1915 essay on 'The Unconscious', he writes of the identification 'of conscious and mental. This identification . . . is a matter of convention, of nomenclature . . . it is of course no more open to refutation than any other convention. The only question that remains is whether it proves so useful that we must needs adopt it. To this we may reply that the conventional identification of the mental with the conscious is thoroughly unpractical. It breaks up a mental continuity, plunges us into the insoluble difficulties of psycho-physical parallelism . . . and finally it forces us to retire from the territory of psychological research without being able to offer us any compensation' (Freud, 1948–50, Vol. IV, p. 100). Again: 'All these conscious acts remain disconnected and unintelligible if we are determined to hold fast to the claim that every single mental act performed within us must be consciously experienced . . .': and, furthermore, 'the assumption of the unconscious helps us to construct a highly successful practical method . . .' (ibid., Vol. IV, p. 99).

(iv) In the light of what has been said already in the present Section 1, it is clear that the most obvious and natural interpretation of substantial talk about the unconscious, or the unconscious mind, takes these expressions as referring to what used to be called a logical construction; or—in the terminology made popular by Paul Meehl and Kenneth MacCorquodale—'an intervening variable'. The paradigm case of a logical construction is the average man. For talk about this unfleshed not-particular is a function of talk about those flesh and blood individuals whose actual characteristics have supposedly been measured and averaged. Thus, if in a given group of twenty women the average of the heights of all the twenty is—say—5 feet, 8 inches, then in that group our average woman must

necessarily be of exactly that height: notwithstanding that
perhaps not one of the twenty is in fact even roughly 5 feet,
8 inches; and notwithstanding that there certainly is not a
mystic twenty-first member who is, and must be. (I am, of
course, quite conventionally in this case, construing the average
to be not the median but the arithmetic mean.)

The point is, that, if and in so far as the unconscious mind is a
logical construction, in the sense just explained, then to talk
about the unconscious mind is a shorthand way of talking
about unconscious motives, purposes, and so on. The contrast
is with interpretations which would make it a hypothetical
construct, presumably a logical substance. In our everyday
discourse the word 'mind' is certainly to be construed in the
first, rather than the second of these two ways: to say that
someone possesses a first-class mind, or a third-class mind, is to
say nothing more than that they are endowed with certain
capacities, or incapacities; while to say that Ethiopia's win in
the marathon was a triumph of mind over matter is to say only,
albeit in slightly more flowery language, that the Ethiopian
victor displayed enormous determination.

Thinkers in the Platonic-Cartesian tradition, however, at
least in their more self-conscious moments, propose to construe the word 'mind'—or, more usually, 'soul'—as referring
to a kind of logical substance. In this second interpretation
minds, or souls, would be exceptionally elusive, 'offstage',
hypothetical, entities, the presence and activities of which
might be called upon to assist in the explanation of familiar
and visible ongoings 'onstage'. Precisely this is what Descartes
himself was doing when he insisted, in Part V of the *Discourse*,
that two sorts of intellectual performance constituted 'two
very certain tests' by which to establish the presence and activity
within a human body of a rational Cartesian soul (Descartes,
1637, Vol. I, p. 116). But to try to employ the other sort of
concept of mind for such a purpose would be absurd. If my
enthusiastic written appreciation of her first-class mind simply
is a description of certain intellectual capacities and qualities
of character, then I cannot, by referring to that first-class mind,
explain how she comes to be so fortunately endowed. For,
for me, that would be to offer only a more or less equivalent
redescription of the phenomena to be explained.

The present relevance of all this is that we need always to be on the alert for shifts between the first kind of interpretation of talk about the unconscious mind, and the second. Only where the fundamental difference between the two is recognized shall we be ready to demand, whenever that shift occurs, that we be now provided: both with an adequate sketch of the nature of the entity being thus hypothesized; and with some sufficient reason for believing that, in this new interpretation, there are unconscious minds. So long as the expression 'unconscious mind' is definable in terms of unconscious motives, desires, and so on, there is no doubt but that the reality of these guarantees the reality of the unconscious mind. But the moment that that expression comes to be construed as referring to some putative and hypothetical further entity, then we urgently need to be informed how such entities might be identified, and what reason we may be thought to have for believing in their existence.

Here I can and will say little more than that, although Freud was always making this shift, he seems to me never to have done anything like enough to meet the two consequent demands. Yet notice how in the *Introductory Lectures* he seems to want to deny any meatless suggestion that the unconscious mind is nothing but a logical construction: '. . . we are accustomed to deal with it as something actual and tangible' (Freud, 1933a, p. 235); and, 'when anyone objects that in a scientific sense the unconscious has no reality, that it is a mere makeshift, *une façon de parler*, we must resign ourselves with a shrug to rejecting his statement as incomprehensible. Something unreal which can nevertheless produce something so real and palpable as an obsessive action!' (ibid., pp. 234–5).

This 'real and palpable unconscious' then becomes a region of the mind, the scene of many colourful but at the same time mysterious proceedings. It becomes a country in diplomatic and topographical relations with others, such as the preconscious; which was early separated from it. Both to elucidate the nature of the new hypothetical construct thus entertained, and to discover what reason we may have for accepting any of the hypotheses consequently proposed, we urgently need, but never seem to get, down-to-earth and theory-free answers to pedestrian questions: such as, 'How does a woman patient exhibit to her analyst the fact that her unconscious experienced intense disappointment at her lack of a penis, and that she blamed the mother for this deficiency?'; or 'How does a man patient similarly manifest the fact that there were in his unconscious passive sexual wishes directed at the father, notwithstanding that he was intimidated from indulging these by castration fears?'

(v) In the first subsection of this Section 1 I emphasized that the introduction of the original Freudian notion of the unconscious involved a second and less obvious extension of the scope for applying certain terms typically employed in the explanation of conduct as conduct. This extension calls for two remarks.

(a) First, it is obviously important for assessing ethical implications. Take dreams, for instance. At one point in the *Introductory Lectures* Freud makes so bold as to stipulate 'that exactly what the dreamer tells us is to count as the dream . . .' (ibid., p. 68). Nevertheless, as we ought to expect, he fails in practice consistently to observe a stipulation which goes flat against the entrenched force of established verbal habit. So it is in the ordinary non-behaviourist sense of 'dream' that he concludes, in his paper on 'Moral Responsibility for the Content of Dreams', that 'the problem of responsibility for the immoral content of dreams no longer exists for us as it formerly did for writers who knew nothing of the latent dream thoughts and the repressed part of our mental life. Obviously one must hold oneself responsible for the evil impulses of one's dreams' (Freud, 1948–50, Vol. V, p. 156).

So long as this means no more than that, if we accept Freudian theory, then we must accept that the unconscious desires and so on revealed in our dreams, like the recognized wishes of our waking hours, provide indications of the sort of people we are, Freud's conclusion is, no doubt, all very well. The connoisseur of ideas will again savour a comparison: 'Several moralists have recommended it as an excellent method of becoming acquainted with our own hearts, and knowing our progress in virtue, to recollect our dreams in the morning, and examine them with the same rigour, that we wou'd our most serious and most deliberate actions. (Hume, 1739–40, I(iv) 3, p. 219).

But it is another thing altogether, and surely altogether unacceptable, if this supposedly obvious conclusion is to be construed as meaning that the content of our dreams is just as much part of our conduct as the activities of our waking lives. Freud has by extending the range of application of certain key words done nothing to alter any facts; and the fact is that the contents of our dreams cannot, whereas the activities of our waking lives can, be determined at will. This crucial difference may be obscured here by Freud's concentration on our wishes. For indeed these, like the contents of our dreams, are not under our short-run control. Neither, therefore, falls into the same category as the dream reports which he once thought to substitute for dreams. I cannot, at least in the short run, help devoutly wishing for some consummation. But I can abstain from any conscious attempt to realize that wish. In the same way, although I cannot help dreaming of the consummation aforesaid, I can abstain from telling anyone about my dream.

Suppose someone now quotes Jesus bar Joseph: 'Everyone that looketh on a woman to lust after her hath committed adultery already with her in his heart' (Matthew 5:28). Then let no one be misled to overlook the commonplace but vital distinctions: between what a person cannot and what they can do, or abstain from doing, immediately and at will; and between thinking, however longingly, of doing something, and actually doing it. On another occasion Freud himself cites a would-be practical lawgiver, not Jesus but Plato: Plato said, 'that the good are those who content themselves with dreaming of what others, the wicked, actually do' (Quoted Freud, 1933a, p. 122).

(b) Second, contemplation of the second of the two conceptual moves noticed in Section 1(i), above, may help us to formulate some questions about psychoanalytic cures, if not their answers. I start from a rash claim made nearly thirty years ago by Stephen Toulmin: 'There need be nothing mysterious . . . about the therapeutic success of psychoanalysis . . . if a fully fledged analytic explanation is not part of a successful cure, we do not regard it as a "correct" explanation in psycho-analysis: a therapeutic failure is as fatal to an explanation in psycho-analysis as predictive failure is to explanation in physics' (Toulmin, 1954, p. 138).

It was early objected, by among others the present writer, that Toulmin's claim did not correspond with either the theory or the practice of Freud himself. In *Totem and Taboo* Freud was prepared to tell us about those who were not ill, and whom he had never met; while in *Leonardo* and in *Moses and Monotheism* Freud offered what, presumably, he took to be correct psychoanalytic accounts of the psychology of men who had been centuries dead before he was born. When he discussed these issues as a question of theory he was emphatic against Toulmin's claim. In an encyclopedia article in 1922, for instance, Freud maintained that 'the narcissistic disorders . . . are scarcely accessible to analytic theory. But their therapeutic inaccessibility has not prevented analysis from making the most fruitful beginnings in the deeper study of these illnesses, which are counted among the psychoses'. And he continues: 'After the analyst's curiosity had, as it were, been gratified by the elaboration of the technique of interpretation, it was inevitable that interest should turn to the most effective way of influencing the patient' (Freud, 1948–50, Vol. V, p. 124).

Two possibly useful suggestions may be picked up from this refutation of Toulmin's overbold conjecture. First, some external assessor of psychoanalytic proceedings, unable perhaps to discern much truth or even sense in a lot of the theoretical discourse of analysts, might well choose to value this discourse solely by reference to its practical therapeutic success or failure, rather than to receive it as it is offered, as a contribution to theoretical knowledge. Second, although it is quite wrong to identify correct psychoanalytic explanations as all and only those instrumental in effecting cures, still there may be better grounds for saying that it is the acceptance by the patient of the correct explanation as correct which brings about or is the cure.

To appreciate this second suggestion we need to appreciate how badly Toulmin distorted Freud's own picture of his activities. Toulmin said: 'Freud . . . discovered that, by revealing to the mentally ill the contents of the unconscious minds, he could often cure them of their distresses' (Toulmin, 1954, p. 133). But it is, Freud insists, not merely not sufficient but even positive harmful simply to tell the patient that the troubles arise from unconscious Oedipal cravings, anal eroticism, or what have you. Thus, in his 1910 'Observations on "Wild" Psychoanalysis', Freud writes: 'The pathological factor is not his ignorance in itself, but the root of this ignorance in his *inner resistances* . . . If knowledge about his unconscious were as important for the patient as the inexperienced in psycho-analysis imagine, it would be sufficient to cure him for him to go to lectures or to read books . . . however . . . describing his unconscious to be patient is regularly followed by intensification of the conflict in him and exacerbation of his symptoms' (Freud, 1948–50, Vol. II, p. 302: italics original).

Granting thus that there is something more to the effecting of cures than simply telling patients about their unconsciouses, it now becomes natural to make the effecting of a cure the criterion for the achievement of this rather mysterious something more. And it is equally natural to see the achievement of this essential as the laborious acquisition of a real, deep recognition and understanding of what was previously unconscious. But although this leaves us better able to formulate, it scarcely begins to provide any answers to, the problems indicated by the original question: 'Why do psycho-analytic cures work at all?' (Toulmin, 1954, p. 133).

I have to say, what may of course be no more than a confession of my own inadequacy, that I have found here little help in Freud. In the 1904 lecture 'On Psychotherapy', for instance, he writes: 'This therapy, then, is based on the recognition that . . . the unconsciousness of certain mental processes constitutes the direct cause of morbid symptoms . . . The transformation of this unconscious material in the mind of the patient into conscious material must have the result of . . . lifting the compulsion . . . For conscious will-power governs only the conscious mental processes, and every mental compulsion is rooted in the unconscious' (Freud, 1948–50, Vol. I, pp. 260–1).

Even if it were true that conscious will-power governs not only but all conscious mental processes—and this is, surely, not true unless it is construed most artificially as true by definition—still that would merely state and not explain the correlation. Elsewhere Freud asserts without qualification: 'The proposition that symptoms vanish when their unconscious antecedents have been made conscious has been borne out by all subsequent research.' He adds: 'This discovery of Breuer's was not the result of any speculation . . . but you must recognize in it a fundamentally new fact, by means of which much else becomes explicable' (Freud, 1933a, pp. 237 and 236).

The first of these two statements in Freud, again providing that nothing is done to make it true by definition, is blankly inconsistent both with the 'Observations on "Wild" Psychoanalysis' quoted in the last paragraph but two, and with all the case studies which insist that curing neither is nor is thought to be the almost automatic consequence of discovering the true psychoanalytic explanation. The same statement is also wrong, surely, to say simply 'that symptoms vanish'. What we are supposed to be talking about is the relations or lack of relations between the recognition of the unconscious motivation of compulsive behaviour and the attaining of control over this. But this leaves open the logical possibility that a cured patient might choose to continue to indulge in behaviour which had previously been outwith his control. The Lady of the Pseudo-Bloodstain, for instance, might when cured still see no alternative and better way of protecting her husband's cherished self-respect. In that event the symptoms would not vanish, but would continue not as compulsive 'actions' but as the faked manifestations of a loyal malingerer. Or, at a more complex and equivocal level, consider the theme of Arthur Koestler's novel *Arrival and Departure*.

Certainly it would be easy to make it true by definition that symptoms referred to unconscious motivation become controllable as soon as the patient really recognizes these to be the outcome of such unconscious motivation. All we need to do is to specify controllability as a criterion of a new made-to-measure sense of 'real recognition'. Yet such manœuvres can do nothing to reduce our proper perplexities about the acquiring of control. Nor can we, for the reasons given, accept even an amended version of Breuer's Law as one of the most fundamental facts which can help to explain but cannot be themselves explained (Flew, 1971, pp. 197–8). What we need, and what Freud never surely attempts, is an account of the acquisition of controllability through psychoanalytic cure, in which this is seen as a special case within the still wanting general story of such acquisitions.

(2) *The Character of the Concepts Stretched*

Already at the beginning of the present Chapter Eight I suggested that the ideas that Freud was stretching are such 'as to ensure that the central and basic place of these notions in psychoanalysis must give this discipline a logical status different from . . . that of studies concerned with subjects other than the distinctively human aspects of human beings, and in particular that of the psychology which aspires to become a para-physical science'. It is time to develop this point a little.

(i) The first thing to emphasize is that these are notions which, typically if not altogether uniquely, apply to language-using creatures. Certainly we cannot, for instance, attribute even such not very sophisticated desires as the desire to get married, or to become a soldier, to any creature not seized of the concepts of a marriage, or of an army. Again, a decision, or an intention, to do this or that today week can be compassed only by a being which has first become master of the relevant temporal concepts. In general, it can be correct to specify some possible motive as his reason for so acting only if he is himself capable of the appropriate articulation. Nor, surely, can she be said to be moved by any exotic and unconscious cravings unless she is herself capable of the corresponding formulations, at least 'in her unconscious'? But now, since semantic ideas of language and meaning are essential both to the ordinary explanation of conduct as conduct, and to psychoanalytic extensions of this form of explanation, there can be no question of a logical reduction of the psychoanalytic to the physical or the physiological. However wayward and undisciplined the discipline of psychoanalysis may be, it must, for better or for worse, belong to quite a different world from that of rat-orientated, para-physical psychology.

Consider, as a spokesman for the latter, B. F. Skinner again, writing this time in 1938 in *The Behavior of Organisms*: 'We can neither assert nor deny discontinuity between the human and subhuman fields so long as we know so little about either. If, nevertheless, the author of a book of this sort is expected to hazard a guess publicly, I may say that the only differences I expect to see revealed between the behavior of a rat and a man (aside from enormous differences of complexity) lie in the field of verbal behavior' (Skinner, 1938, p. 442).[25] No doubt experiments on rats do have their place and their importance. But to limit yourself to work on rats, or pigeons, or any other temptingly handy species, which you see as just happening not to be endowed with elaborate linguistic powers, is by that token to disqualify your psychology as a human science. On another occasion Skinner revealed that as an undergraduate he had an enthusiasm for dramatics. Did he in those good old days labour to produce *Hamlet* without providing for that awkwardly demanding role of the Prince of Denmark?

(ii) Second, the fact that these teleological notions are, as I have argued, central and fundamental in psychoanalysis should encourage a search for illuminating comparisons with other disciplines concerned with men and their motives, above all with historiography—The Queen of the Human Sciences. Such comparisons may bring out, for instance, where and how far 'psychical reality' is crucial. Certainly the fact that the squadron commander led his tanks straight into an ambush becomes intelligible when and only when we learn he was told by his usually reliable intelligence that here is the weak spot in the defences: given his reasonable but wrong beliefs about the situation—given, that is, his 'psychical reality'—his disastrous decision was quite sensible. So, similarly, the psychoanalyst who wants to understand a patient's present conduct will labour to discover what that patient now believes, whether consciously or unconsciously, both about his present situation, and about any portions of the past which he sees as having present relevance. But that this or that is now for the patient a 'psychic reality', and one which is clearly crucial in determining his present conduct, is by no means a sufficient reason for concluding that in reality things are, or were, as the patient has come to believe. In order to warrant conclusions about reality, as opposed to 'psychical reality', and in order to justify recommendations based upon these conclusions, evidence of how things actually are, or of what actually happened, must be sought outside the analytic hour. I forbear to deploy embarrassing instances to show how often and how disastrously some analysts have overlooked this by now and to us obvious methodological truth!

(iii) Third, to say that psychoanalysis deals with men and their motives, and especially their unconscious motives, to say that these are its fundamental notions and that it tries to provide explanations in these terms, and to say that they are not logically reducible to physiology or to anything else acceptable to physicalism; all this is certainly not to deny either the possibility or the need sometimes to push beyond, or below, explanations of this sort. Once we reach the limit of such teleological explanation we can and should go on to ask why—in another sense of 'why'—people have the basic desires which they do have; and perhaps why these seem to have in different people different relative strengths. The answers will presumably have to be physiological, telling us what are the physiological preconditions and mechanics of desire and its satisfaction, and what are the genetic determinants of any relevant physiological differences; and at this level, and after, nothing more will be said about purposes, except by theologians. Freud himself, having been reared in the tough-minded epiphenomenalism of the Vienna medical school, always expected that 'all our provisional ideas in psychology will some day be based on an organic substructure' (Freud, 1948–50, Vol. IV, p. 36).

(iv) Fourth, it is wrong to present 'Freud's doctrine of "psychic determinism"', as it so often is presented, as contending 'simply that *mental phenomena are causally determined*' (McKellar, p. 229: italics his). Nor will it do to cite—as if this were either equivalent to, or at least sufficient to establish, the thesis that 'all behaviour is motivated'—the claim that 'everyday activities are all causally determined' (Young, p. 1). Contrast these unfortunate statements with another, more careful, assessment, offered in a *Survey of Objective Studies of Psychoanalytic Concepts*. Significantly, and aptly, this project was sponsored by the Subcommittee on Motivation of the (American) Social Science Research Council: 'Boiled down to an acceptable terminology the wish-fulfillment hypothesis becomes a statement that dreams are motivated' (Sears, p. 129; and compare p. vii).

The now rather ancient textbooks containing the first phrases quoted in the previous paragraph fail to do justice to the originality of Freud. For long before his day, and most certainly in that Vienna medical school of his own youth, it was in certain circles a commonplace to maintain that—in the broadest sense—all behaviour, and hence presumably parapraxes, dreams and obsessive actions, must ultimately be explicable in terms of physiological causes; and, though this distinction would never have been made in those times, these were certainly construed not as causes (personal) but as causes (physical). The new, or at any rate newer, move was to suggest, and to develop the suggestion, that they are 'explainable through purposive ideas' (Freud, 1904, p. 148); in terms, that is, of ideas such as motive, desire, purpose, intention, decision, plan, and so forth—suitably extended.

Psychic determinism is, therefore, not to be understood as the physiological special case of universal causal (physical) determinism. On the contrary, as will be argued more fully below in Chapter Nine, psychic determinism, at least in so far as it refers to conscious rather than unconscious motives, would appear to be, not a case of, but incompatible with, a completely universal causal (physical) determinism. For, given always the qualification just made, the only kind of causes promised by psychic determinism are causes (personal). And these surely have to be defined in terms of precisely those alternative possibilities which causes (physical) preclude.

(v) Fifth, at the beginning of the first subsection of the present Section 2, I emphasized 'that these are notions which, typically if not altogether uniquely, apply to language-using creatures'. There and elsewhere it was, and is, difficult to find formulations which do simultaneous justice both to the peculiarities of the distinctively human and to the continuities between mankind and non-human animals. Certainly I am not confident that I have always succeeded. In that particular subsection the object was to insist upon one relevant aspect of the enormous and differentiating importance of our various and sophisticated linguistic capacities. But even there there had to be a qualifying clause to allow for the truths urged by Darwin in *The Descent of Man*, and since supported with so much further evidence by the findings of our contemporary ethologists. 'We have seen in the last two chapters,' Darwin wrote at the beginning of Chapter Three of that book, 'that man bears in his bodily structure clear traces of his descent from some lower form . . .'; and 'My object in this chapter is to show that there is no fundamental difference between man and the higher animals in their mental faculties'. Certainly, he concludes in the Summary at the end of Chapter IV, 'the difference between the mind of the lowest man and that of the highest animal is immense . . . Nevertheless . . . the difference is one of degree and not of kind'. And, furthermore, the immense differences which certainly do subsist are 'mainly the result of the continued use of a perfect language'.

There is a danger here that we shall by tripping over our own terminology blind ourselves to one or other of the two sets of facts, trying to ignore or even to deny either the peculiarities or even the continuities. For instance, perhaps for the best of reasons, we may insist that certain words—at least in the full sense—be applied only to human beings. The temptation then is to construe the conceptual barrier thus created as marking a difference in kind, a gulf which we now come to see as unbridged by similarities and uncrossable by any evolutionary development. Alternatively we may prefer to stress the reality of evolution. In that case our temptation will be not to maximize but to minimize the actual differences. Even if we avoid the curiously seductive fallacy, noticed above in the final subsection of Chapter One, of arguing that everything must really be whatever it evolved from, we may still be inclined to mis-take it that the differences, because differences of degree, must therefore be ultimately inconsiderable.

No doubt the differences between human beings and other animals are all differences of degree; in the sense that it would be possible to construct spectra of actual or possible cases stretching between the distinctively human and the distinctively non-human, with no sharp breaks at which a dividing line has naturally and inevitably to be drawn. Nevertheless the enormous development of language, and all the other developments which this alone makes possible, when they are considered together, justify us in speaking of 'distinctively human prerogatives' and even of 'the uniqueness of man'.

First, it is in general quite wrong to dismiss or to depreciate differences of degree as necessarily *mere* differences of degree. On the contrary: most of the humanly most important differences are, in the sense just now explicated, differences of degree. Consider, for instance, the oppositions between poverty and wealth, between age and youth, between sanity and insanity, between a free society and one in which everything which is not forbidden is compulsory. Second, in the present particular case we are taking account not of one single difference of degree, however massive, but of an accumulation of very many such differences. It is this accumulation of very many substantial differences of degree, rather than the possession of one special component of a unique kind, which warrants our talk of human distinctiveness, even uniqueness; and it is a justification which has no difficulty in marrying with an unreservedly evolutionary view of the origins of our species.

In this it is in complete contrast with the account of human uniqueness given by Descartes, and the very similar official Roman Catholic statement quoted already in Section 4 of Chapter One. The latter assured us that 'the teaching of the Church leaves the doctrine of evolution an open question, as long as it confines its speculations to the development, from other living matter already in existence, of the human body', but then ruled: 'That souls are immediately created by God is a view the Catholic faith imposes on us.' Descartes begins by deploying 'two very certain tests' which, if they elicit a manifestation of what he believes to be distinctively human capacities, guarantee the presence of an incorporeal soul: 'By these two methods we may also recognize the difference that exists between men and brutes.' He goes on to assure us that such a rational soul 'could not be in any way derived from the power of matter . . . but that it must be expressly created' (Descartes, 1637, V, Vol. I, pp. 116 and 118).

(vi) The final point of the chapter again starts from something said in the first subsection of the present Section 2, that the key ideas which Freud uses and stretches 'are notions which, typically if not altogether uniquely, apply to language-using creatures'. These ideas are at the same time essentially involved in the concept of a rational agent. The expression 'rational agent' is here, of course, to be understood in a capability rather than an actuality sense of 'rational': unless someone is a rational agent (capable) it would not make sense either to commend them as rational (actual) or to deplore their (actual) irrationality. To be a rational agent in this primary sense is to be capable of deciding to do, and doing, this rather than that, and of having reasons for deciding, and doing, what you do so decide.

The aim of psychoanalysis as a therapy can thus be seen as being to extend the scope of the patient's rational agency, again in a capability rather than an actuality sense of 'rational'. The object is to educate the patient to become able both to recognize formerly unconscious desires, and so on, and to choose whether to express them or not: 'To strengthen the ego, to make it more independent of the superego, to widen its field of vision and so to extend its field of vision that it can take over new portions of the id. *Where id was, ego shall be*' (Freud, 1933b, p. 106: italics supplied).

That last, though often quoted, is a dark and abstract passage, typical of the *New Introductory Lectures*. But it can be illuminated, and lowered a little towards the concrete, by calling in aid some less famous statements: 'The labour of overcoming the resistances is the essential achievement of the analytic treatment; the patient has to accomplish it and the physician makes it possible for him to do this by suggestions which are in the nature of an *education*. It has been truly said, therefore, that psycho-analytic treatment is a kind of re-education' (Freud, 1933a, p. 377); 'The making conscious of repressed sexual desires in analysis makes it possible . . . to obtain a mastery over them which the previous repression had been unable to achieve. It can more truly be said that analysis sets the neurotic free from the chains of his sexuality' (Freud, 1948–50, Vol. V, p. 128); 'But above all, all the energies which are today consumed in the production of neurotic symptoms . . . will, even if they cannot at once be put to uses in life, help to strengthen the outcry for those changes in our civilization from which alone we can hope for better things from our descendants' (Freud, 1948–50, Vol. II, p. 295). Finally here is a statement not from Freud but from a leading and faithful disciple: 'The aim of the psychoanalytical method is to achieve permanent eradication of the very root of the illness, and at the same time to put its psychic energies at the disposal of the ego or reason' (Berg, 1944, p. 229).

In so far as the aim of psychoanalytic therapy was, and

remains, as I have described it, then it must be essentially an essay in liberation, in education, in enlightenment. This observation about intentions can be made without prejudice to all disputed questions of verifiability and falsifiability. For it carries no implications that the therapy actually is effective or any of the theory true.

9
PSYCHOANALYSIS AND FREEWILL

AT the end of Chapter Eight I concluded that the aim of psychoanalytic therapy and, in so far as that therapy is in fact successful, its result is to extend the area of the patient's self-understanding and the scope of the patient's will. It should, therefore, be seen as paradoxical that most psychoanalysts and most students of their writings appear to feel bound to believe that it is both a presupposition and a finding of their work—and indeed of all the other psychological and psychiatric disciplines too—that really there is no such thing as genuine choice.

Consider two examples, picked more or less at random. The first comes from Freud's American translator A. A. Brill. Writing on *Psychoanalytic Psychiatry* Brill maintains: 'The rank and file of psychiatrists believe in absolute determinism.' This Brill takes to be antithetical to the belief of 'most persons' that 'they can do what they want, and regardless of motives' (Brill, p. 87). The second comes from the same leading British Freudian who was quoted at the end of the previous chapter as saying that the aim of the therapy is to put the 'psychic energies' now invested in the mental disease 'at the disposal of the ego or reason'. Having incontinently blurted it out Berg rushes forward to explain: 'I am using the word "blame" rather loosely, for psychology does not *blame* anyone; it recognizes that a person's acts, like the acts of any organism or *organ*, are predetermined by heredity, development, and environment' (Berg, 1944, p. 36: italics original).

It is distracting to see in the first of these two passages a reference to motives, which seems to be making the curious assumption that 'most persons' believe that they could be doing what they wanted to do even if—perhaps only if—they had no motive for doing whatever it was that they were doing. But despite, or because of, this odd reference to motives it is surely clear that both writers construe the word 'determinism' as carrying the implications of what we have distinguished as the physical causal kind rather than those of the personal or psychical type. And in the second passage the assimilation of the actions of persons to the 'acts [*sic*] of any . . . *organ*' seems to go much further than an often-quoted statement by Thomas Hobbes in Chapter I of *de Cive*. For, without reference to what anyone actually does, Hobbes was saying there only that it is inevitable that we should have certain desires and concerns: 'Among so many dangers therefore as the natural lusts of men do daily threaten each other withal, to have a care of one's self is not a matter to be so scornfully looked upon, as if so be there had been a power and will left in one to have done otherwise. For every man *is desirous of* what is good for him, and shuns what is evil, but chiefly the chiefest of all natural evils, which is death; and this he doth, by a certain impulsion of nature, no less than that whereby a stone moves downward' (Hobbes, 1641, p. 26: italics supplied).

Sometimes the extreme thesis to which Brill and Berg felt they had to commit themselves is replaced by something a little weaker and a little more plausible. Perhaps sometimes people, in some sense, could have done otherwise. Genuine choice is, nevertheless, an illusion; and, even if it would perhaps be going too far to say 'Tout comprendre, c'est tout pardonner', still the psychologist is almost always able to provide abundant extenuation. So in *Crime and the Mind* Dr. Walter Bromberg tells us: 'Many psychiatrists feel that no man can really "choose" a course of conduct, because "free choice" is determined by each individual's cultural and psychological background, his unconscious impulses, identifications, predetermined wishes and drives. Thus a criminal offender cannot be considered psychologically "free" in any absolute sense.' Clearly this conclusion cannot be maintained as an exclusive criminal privilege. It must be extended to everyone.

Unfortunately, we are not supplied with any positive account of what for Bromberg it would be to be psychologically free in some absolute sense. But even from the few lines quoted we can infer that he is presupposing an impossible monster. Bromberg's free man would have to be: both a creature without a past (no 'cultural and psychological background'); and one able now to decide, not only what it shall now do, but also what desires it shall now have (no 'predetermined wishes and drives'). Bromberg concludes: 'It is understandable that psychiatrists can look with greater ease on partial responsibility as a defence against criminal responsibility, since the traditional view of absolute freewill cannot be supported clinically' (Bromberg, p. 50). In all these psychoanalysts—the 'extremists' and the 'moderates' both—we see the same assumptions. They are, with no sense of the incongruity involved, taking it that psychoanalysis both presupposes and proves that there cannot really be any such thing as what it is in fact the main aim of psychoanalytic therapy to promote. The paradox is as entrenched as it is damaging. So it will be well worthwhile now, notwithstanding that many of the necessary distinctions have been made earlier, to devote a whole chapter to 'Psychoanalysis and Freewill'. I shall proceed by examining two representative treatments.

(1) Psychoanalytic Determinism: Ernest Jones

The first spokesman to stand forward was an original member of Freud's Fellowship of the Ring. Ernest Jones later became Freud's biographer. He was also unusual among his colleagues in his declared interest in some philosophical questions seen as such. Our first quotation is, however, more relevant to the general theme of the present book than to the particular concern of this chapter.

(i) In his autobiography Jones proclaimed his own main metaphysical commitment: 'I should not hesitate . . . to describe myself as a philosophical materialist . . . I would say that in the realms of both thought and action the distinction between men who believe that mental processes, or beings, can exist independently of the physical world and those who reject this belief is to me the most significant of all human classifications; and I should measure any hope of future evolutionary progress by the passage of men from the one class to the other more than by any other single criterion' (Jones, 1959, p. 59). He thus ranged himself, and indirectly psychoanalysis also, in the tradition of those who see people as corporeal and mortal—in the tradition of Aristotle as opposed to Plato, of Ryle as opposed to Descartes.

In this association of psychoanalysis with an Aristotelian rather than with a Platonic-Cartesian view of man, Freud's biographer was, as always, faithful to the spirit and to the fundamental insights of the Master. For Freud surely was an unwavering and lifelong mortalist and, in the last if not the first analysis, a philosophical materialist too. Nevertheless, to balance the picture, one must also notice two things.

(*a*) First, Freud and Jones also insist repeatedly on talking of 'regions of the mind', of 'the psychic apparatus', and so on, in ways which must suggest to themselves and to others that the substantives 'mind' and 'psyche' ought to be construed as words for substances; and, since there are no suitable corporeal substances available, as words for presumably incorporeal and as such essentially mysterious substances. Yet to precisely the extent that they do this, they are seeing their psychoanalytic work through incongruously Cartesian spectacles, hinting that the mind in general and the unconscious mind in particular is after all something which could significantly be said to exist apart from the person whose mind it is. For to say in this philosophical context that the mind is a substance just is to say that it is something which could significantly be said to exist separately, and apart from the person whose mind it is. But if it is once granted that we (or our minds) are incorporeal substances, it begins to seem sensible to propose that we (or our minds) might survive what might otherwise and uninstructedly have been thought of as our deaths and dissolutions.

Jones, for instance, in a radio talk on Freud's achievement asked himself: 'What did Freud really do? That can most shortly be answered by saying that he discovered a previously inaccessible region of the mind which we now call the unconscious' (Jones, 1956, p. 589). In a passage which has been mentioned here once before Freud complained: '. . . when anyone objects that in a scientific sense the unconscious has no reality, that it is a mere makeshift, *une façon de parler*, we must resign ourselves with a shrug to rejecting his statement as incomprehensible. Something unreal, which can nevertheless produce something so real and palpable as an obsessive action!' (Freud, 1933a, pp. 234–5.)

Such talk must suggest that unconscious minds are freshly

discovered, incorporeal, logical substances; or, at any rate, newly recognized aspects of a well-known sort of such substances. It is significant that Freud continues, later on the same page, to reiterate claims: 'that always and everywhere the meaning of the symptoms is unknown to the sufferer; that analysis invariably shows that these symptoms are derived from unconscious mental processes which can . . . become conscious. You will then understand that we cannot dispense with the unconscious part of the mind in psychoanalysis, and that we are accustomed to deal with it as something actual and tangible. Perhaps you will also be able to realize how unfitted all those who only know the unconscious as a phrase, who have never analysed, never interpreted dreams, or translated neurotic symptoms into their meaning and intention, are to form an opinion on this matter' (ibid., pp. 235–6).

Certainly evidence of the kind to which Freud refers is sufficient to establish the reality of the unconscious mind; to establish, that is to say, that affirmative and true things can be said in sentences in which 'the unconscious mind', or equivalent expressions, play the role of grammatical subject. But it would by no means be sufficient to prove that unconscious minds are logical substances; a conclusion which must surely imply that talk about the unconscious mind of—say—Mr. J. G. Reeder cannot be reduced without remainder to talk about the categorical or hypothetical sayings and doings and silences of that Edgar Wallace character.

It is, perhaps, a temptation here to try to think of the unconscious mind as a kind of unconscious consciousness; occurring at times or in places when or where there is no conscious consciousness. Yet if once we become firmly seized of the point that to talk of someone's (conscious) mind is to talk in a particular idiomatic way of that person's (conscious) capacities, feelings, and inclinations, then we shall have no difficulty in realizing that parallel statements about the corresponding unconscious mind have a similar ultimate reference to the same flesh and blood person. There is, therefore, no call to postulate some unheard-of and unseeable agency to serve as the cause of all these indisputably real neurotic symptoms. We already have the organism, and above all its central nervous system. These are as corporeal and substantial as the most materialist heart could desire.

However, until and unless we either abandon this incongruously Cartesian way of writing, which is so persistent in Freud and Jones, and other analysts, or take care to cash it into concrete terms, psychoanalysis is bound often to be misinterpreted as inconsistent with that philosophical materialism to which certainly both Freud and Jones were ultimately and fundamentally committed. I recommend an excellent essay in such cashing, *Eliminating the Unconscious*. In his Preface T. R. Miles describes, with feeling, 'the reactions of an experimentalist . . . plunged into the analytically oriented atmosphere of the Tavistock Clinic . . . In particular the theoretical concepts . . . bore no very clear relationship to the clinical findings, and in lieu of high-flown speculation one longed for a simple narrative of what was actually said and done by patient and analyst during their sessions together' (Miles, p. xvi).

(*b*) The second possible objection to the claim that in his philosophical materialism Jones was true to the spirit of Freud arises from the fact that Freud several times publicly expressed sympathy with the case for the occurrence of genuine telepathy. Certainly this was a sympathy which his biographer made it quite clear that he could not approve. Nevertheless Freud seems never to have committed himself to what would in the present context be the decisive step of concluding that the power of telepathy is a power of communication between incorporeal substances; which, at any particular time, may or may not happen to be embodied. For notwithstanding that Freud wrote of telepathy that 'the custodian used to remark: "*Dans des cas pareils, ce n'est que le premier pas qui coûte*" [In such cases it is only the first step which counts]. The rest is easy', any following here is not a matter of logical necessity but of psychological association (Freud, 1921, p. 193). It is a point which Freud had perhaps taken himself when he wrote of the spiritualists: 'Unfortunately [*sic*] they have not succeeded in disproving the fact that the appearances and utterances of their spirits are merely the productions of their own mental activity' (Freud, 1928, p. 48: and compare Dodds and Flew, 1953).

(ii) Jones, in order to indicate the ideas and ideals which

Freud imbibed in Brücke's Institute, quotes in his chapter on 'The Medical Student' from a manifesto by one of the leaders of the Helmholtz school of physiology: 'No other forces than the common physical and chemical ones are active within the organism. In those cases which cannot at the time be explained by these forces one has either to find the specific way or form of their action . . . or to assume new forces equal in dignity to the chemical-physical forces inherent in matter, reducible to the force of attraction and repulsion . . . Yet Brücke would have been astonished . . . had he known that one of his favourite pupils, one apparently a convert to the strict faith, was later, in his famous wish theory of the mind, to bring back into science the ideas of "purpose", "intention", and "aim" which had just been abolished from the universe' (Jones, 1953–7, Vol. I, p. 45).

So far, except perhaps for the final clause, so good. But Jones continues: 'We know, however, that when Freud did bring them back he was able to reconcile them with the principles in which he had been brought up; he never abandoned determinism for teleology' (ibid., p. 50). This further comment is unsatisfactory. By insisting that Freud never abandoned determinism for teleology, and still more by allowing that physiological work such as that done in Brücke's Institute could abolish from the universe 'the ideas of "purpose", "intention", and "aim"', Jones appears to suggest, what no psychoanalyst can afford to say, that determinism and teleology are incompatible.

Given the distinction between physical causal, and psychic determinism, and if the word 'determinism' is construed in the former sense, then maybe this would pass. But Jones like Freud, and many others, makes no such distinction. For him the word covers both senses indiscriminately. So he cannot afford to say that determinism and teleology are incompatible. For psychoanalysis essentially is both teleological and deterministic. It is teleological in as much as it seeks and offers explanations in terms of such notions as (conscious and unconscious) motive, purpose, and intention. Yet it is also—in so far as it insists that there always must be such a motive, purpose or intention—deterministic. Precisely this is Freud's 'psychic determinism'; and this—unless it is internally incoherent, which it is not—cannot be incompatible with teleological notions, since these are those in terms of which it is defined.

(*a*) There are two final comments to be made before we pass to the third subsection. First, notice how important it is in any account of psychic determinism to insert some phrase like that 'in so far as'. The reason is that no one seems to have got clear exactly how wide a scope they want to claim for this doctrine. Exactly how much behaviour is to be taken as motivated, at any rate unconsciously? So long as it is appreciated by one and all that there is a question here, the most prudent policy may be to leave that question open to be settled by the progress of the research. If we do want to draw a provisional and rather indeterminate line, then this might perhaps best be done by urging that psychoanalysis presupposes, and also aspires to show, that there is either an analytic or a non-analytic teleological explanation of whatever can be directly subjected to the will; deliberately leaving the meaning of this 'can' to be specified later.

(*b*) Second, especially when we recall what we saw of Skinner in Chapter Seven, we must emphasize that to have expelled teleological notions from the universe of discourse of physiologists is not at all the same thing as to have shown that there is no place in a scientific account of the world for the ideas of purpose, intention, and aim. As we saw in that earlier chapter, the fact that such notions do indeed have no place in sciences not dealing with human beings is no reason for denying that they have proper and indispensable applications on what is, so to speak, their own home ground. What is wrong with animistic projections, and with the Pathetic Fallacy in general, is not any employment of purposive ideas, but their unwarranted imposition on to things which must be constitutionally incapable of the desiring and the planning thus attributed.

(iii) We come now at rather long last to a statement bearing directly upon questions about freewill: 'One of the psychological arguments against the belief in a complete mental determinism is the intense feeling of conviction that we have a perfectly free choice in the performance of many acts. . . . It only means that the person is not aware of any conscious motive. When, however, conscious motivation is distinguished from unconscious motivation, this feeling of conviction teaches us that the former does not extend over all our motor resolutions. What is left free from the one side receives its motive from the other—from the unconscious—and so the psychical determinism is flawlessly carried through. A knowledge of unconscious motivation is indispensable, even for philosophical discussion of determinism' (Jones, 1920, pp. 77–8).

(a) This passage can be used to bring out that psychoanalysis may be relevant to two different sorts of discussion, both referring to the philosophical problems of freewill. The nature of one of these two sorts, which is in fact logically secondary to the other, will come out clearly if we consider a remark made very much in passing. Jones records an example of Freud's anti-Americanism and, without any thought of deep analysis, makes the comment: 'He was so obviously unfair . . . that one is bound to seek some explanation of his attitude' (Jones, 1953–7, Vol. II, p. 66).

The making of this remark indicates one kind of context in which even non-sociologists, non-psychologists, and non-psychoanalysts are apt to ask for some sociological, or psychological, or even psychoanalytic explanation. For such questions are very typically raised where it is thought that there has been some deviation from a norm, usually but not always a falling below. In the present case it appears that Freud was in uncharacteristic ways or to an uncharacteristic extent being unfair, getting the facts wrong, arguing invalidly. So, while taking these conclusions about the original and primary subject of discussion for granted, it is natural to drop the subject of America. Instead of asking about the truth of falsity of propositions and the validity or invalidity of arguments about that subject, we now raise quite different issues, about Freud. It was with cases of this kind in mind that Gilbert Ryle gave his magisterial ruling: 'Let the psychologist tell us why we are deceived; but we can tell ourselves and him why we are not deceived' (Ryle, p. 326).

In the passage quoted at the beginning of the present subsection, Jones starts by taking it for granted that it is simply a popular misconception 'that we have a perfectly free choice in the performance of many acts'. He therefore proceeds from that first order issue, which he assumes to be settled, to the logically secondary psychological question of how it is that so many of us come to be in error on the primary matter. His answer is that, although 'the person is not aware of any conscious motive', still there always is a motive even if only an unconscious motive, and this is what it is so easy not to notice: 'What is left free from the one side receives its motive from the other—from the unconscious—and so the psychical determinism is flawlessly carried through.' But Jones also sees, and says, that the findings of psychoanalysis are relevant to the primary discussion: 'A knowledge of unconscious motivation is indispensable, even for philosophical discussion of determinism.' It is relevant because, as I should say, psycho-analytic work and findings, whether correctly or incorrectly understood, help to generate the problems.

(b) Where Jones begins to go wrong is in his perception of what the philosophical problems are. I shall in the next few paragraphs be retraversing some ground already broken earlier, especially in Section 1(i) of Chapter Four. But the points repeated are all such as will bear—indeed demand—repetition.

Like most philosophical laymen, and like far too many professionals paid to know better, Jones thinks always in terms of a profound and insurmountable antithesis between Freewill and Determinism. Certainly there are commonly accepted in interpretations in which these two terms must be antithetical. If, for instance, you construe 'freewill' as necessarily implying uncaused causes, and your determinism is a physical causal determinism, then it is indeed obvious that universal deter-minism cannot leave room for any freewill. But it is quite wrong to proceed as if there were one and only one accepted interpretation of each of these two key words, and as if these were they.

Furthermore, suppose we were to waive this first point; which an older generation may think of as tiresomely Joadian. Suppose we were to allow that in the only relevant senses it must be obvious that freewill and determinism just are incompatible. Then what would the remaining problem be, and however would it be accounted philosophical? For, granted the incompatibility, the most urgent questions are, obviously, whether the universe is completely deterministic, or whether there is any room for freewill and, if so, how much. But these are clearly factual rather than philosophical problems. The only philosophical problems remaining—the only problems, that is, of logical analysis, of presupposition, or of implication—would be problems of what is implied for notions of responsibility, blame, choice, and so on, by—on the one hand—the fact of universal determinism or—as the case might be—the facts of some measure of freewill.

The misinterpretation of the philosophical problems which we find in Jones, and in so many others, must leave anyone who accepts it altogether at a loss to understand how so many of the great philosophers and philosopher-theologians could have been—as they were—Compatibilists. The right way to approach these questions is to see, and to say, how they arise. It is because there appears to be, and perhaps is, an incompatibility between the presuppositions and the implications of two ranges of notions and activities, neither of which could we easily or even perhaps possibly abandon. On the one hand are the sciences both natural and human, together with various associated technologies. These seem both to assume and to imply that everything which happens comes about as the result of antecedent causes: if ever and wherever we know enough, it is suggested, we are bound to realize that whatever happens could not but happen. On the other hand all of us, including the scientists and the technologists, act and think in most of our lives in accordance with the at least ostensibly incompatible assumption that everyone sometimes—indeed most of the time—in some important sense, and perhaps in more than one sense, could do other than they do.

One traditionally most important special case is that in which some system of religious beliefs and practice takes the place filled in the previous paragraph by science and technology. Thus the central and fundamental doctrine of theism, that the universe is the wholly dependent creation of its Divine Creator, may at first sight seem to leave no room for genuinely responsible agency on the part of that God's creatures—and perhaps does. As Mahalia Jackson so magnificently sings: 'He's got the whole world in His hands.' In this special case Predestination, with its misleading temporal implications, takes the place of Determinism in the proposed and supposed fundamental antithesis. (For a discussion of this special case see Flew, 1976a, VII.)

Having now appreciated how the philosophical problems arise it is also easy to see that they are essentially logical rather than factual. The questions are all whether this or that idea or activity really does presuppose or imply what it may too easily and perhaps mistakenly have been thought to presuppose or imply. The function of the philosopher here is diplomatic. Those who conclude that reconciliation is possible are nowadays coming to be labelled Compatibilist. Those who go into the opposite lobby are called, correspondingly, Incompatibilist. Incompatibilists incur an obligation avoided by their Compatibilist opponents. For if the Incompatibilists are right then we have to discover which of the two incompatible positions is in fact true, and how we are to get along without making assumptions which have turned out to be false. (It is that obligation which I endeavoured to discharge at the end of Chapter Five.)

(c) In the passage quoted at the beginning of the present subsection Jones provides, both his explanation of why we are so inclined to fall into what he believes to be an error, and his reason for thinking that this actually is an error. But the popular conception is, surely, correct and not a misconception. Certainly his reason for thinking that we are wrong is itself mistaken. He says, as his reason for thinking that we do not 'have a perfectly free choice in the performance of many acts', that: 'What is left free from the one side receives its motive from the other—from the unconscious—and so the psychical determinism is flawlessly carried through.' Compare with this some of Freud's statements in *The Psychopathology of Everyday Life*. In arguing for 'the assumption of an absolute psychic determinism' he believes that he has to deny that anyone ever acts 'of his own freewill and without motives'. So he asserts: 'for some time I have been aware that it is impossible to think of a number, or even of a name, of one's own freewill' (Freud, 1904, pp. 162 and 148). Compare too Brill's assumption, noticed in the second paragraph of the present Chapter Nine, that 'absolute determinism' is incompatible with the belief of 'most persons' that 'they can do what they want, and regardless of motives' (Brill, p. 87).

There are two mistakes here, both persistent and obviously seductive. First, it is wrong to contrast acting of one's own freewill with acting with motives. In the ordinary, non-technical sense the opposite of to act of your own freewill is to act under compulsion. Typically, both the people who do something of their own freewill, and the people who do the same thing only under compulsion, have their reasons for doing what they do. But these will be different reasons. A person who freely chooses to join a trades union does so because he wants to be a member. A person who joins only under compulsion typically does so, in Britain today, because he wants to avoid being sacked—by an employer who is in turn under almost irresistible pressure from tyrannical socialist unions backed in their determination to enforce a closed shop by a tyrannical socialist legislature. More happily, a couple who of their own freewill choose to get married thereby indicate not that they have no desire to do so, but that this is a thing which they very strongly want.

Second, it is not only freewill but also desire which is being misconstrued. It is this misconstruction which prevents Jones and other analysts from recognizing that psychic determinism cannot be the psychological special case of universal causal determinism. They see desires as physical causes. So, they assume, if a desire determined a particular action token, then it must have made that action token something which happened necessarily and unavoidably. Yet this is as incongruous with the concept of desire as it is with the concept of action. The crux is that, given the sufficient physical cause, it becomes contingently necessary that its effect will occur; whereas, given the desire, there always remains the question whether the agent will choose to act in a way psychically determined by that desire. As every reader of detective stories knows, it is one thing to discover that all these characters had a motive, but quite another to establish which was the one who did actually commit the murder.

Again, since the misunderstanding of the nature and implications of psychic determinism is so pervasive and destructive, consider the difference between saying that every event has a cause and saying that every event has a motive. If in the former proposition the 'cause' is construed as physical while 'event' is extended to include human action, then, for reasons which have been thoroughly reviewed in previous chapters, it must be false. The primitive and animistic doctrine that every event has a motive must imply—unless it is qualified by some sophisticated proviso about unconscious motives expressing themselves in symptoms not subject to the will—that everything that happens must have been avoidable, at least by the agent in question. It is a doctrine which was surely seen at work, in a form perhaps better described as atavistic rather than primitive, in Stalin's dominions during the Great Terror. For, as has often been remarked, nothing was then allowed to have been outwith human control. Everything good was the intended achievement of the party and the government; under, of course, the inspired leadership of the genial Stalin. Everything bad had to be seen—and punished—as the work of black-hearted treacherous enemies of socialism.[26]

Notice finally the word 'drive'. This is a favourite with experimental psychologists, rather than with psychoanalysts. The attraction seems to be precisely that it does so powerfully suggest, what is manifestly not true, that the desires so described are external forces throwing the agent about like some helpless missile. It can thus appear to the aficionados of an almost deliberately misleading term that they and their colleagues are on their way to producing a new para-physical science, strictly on all fours with classical mechanics. Yet they neither are nor could be. For choice, as preceding chapters must sufficiently have reminded us, is an inescapable reality of the human condition: we are, in the Existentialist sense, abandoned. Nor can any system begin to deserve the diploma title 'science' until and unless it becomes able and willing to come to terms with this fact.

(iv) Jones begins a paper on 'Free Will and Determinism' by raising two questions, both of which he characterizes as psychological: the first is that of how it comes about that 'this problem has possessed such an extraordinary interest for the thinkers of all ages'; and, on the following page, 'A second consideration that calls for psychological inquiry is the ambivalence so often to be noted among those expressing opinions on the matter' (Jones, 1924, Vol. I, pp. 178 and 179).

Now it is not impossible to raise such psychological questions without presupposing any particular view either about the whole complex of problems or about any particular issue within that complex. But this very essay on 'Free Will and Determinism' would be enough to show, if any demonstration were needed, that it must be extremely difficult. We are so used to raising such questions where we believe something to be deviant or untoward that we are inclined to assume that any psychological account, and perhaps especially any psycho-analytic account, must be of something which has somehow gone wrong.[27] Neither reader nor writer is likely to pay enough heed to the caveat: 'There are of course rational and philosophical grounds for believing in one or the other . . .' It is more probable that they will latch on to the statement 'that even philosophers may be influenced by unconscious motives', and construe this as necessarily discrediting (ibid., Vol. I, p. 186).

It is easy to suggest answers to the two initial questions set by Jones, answers which seem to require no reinforcement from unconscious resources. Of course, even if they are both correct as far as they go and apparently adequate to their explanatory tasks, there may still in fact be room for something more. For we are here on part of the home ground of over-determination. People conceivably can and often do have several reasons for acting or wanting, any one of which would have been sufficient; and we certainly cannot dismiss a priori the suggestion that some of these are unconscious. But, once we realize the nature of the philosophical problems, and once we are seized of the obvious answers to the psychological questions, then we shall find no plausible basis for insisting, not that there may also be, but that there must also be, something unconscious. If and in so far as we have sufficient independent reason for saying that unconscious as well as conscious concerns are in fact engaged, then well and fine. But if the supposed disparity between the degree of concern actually shown and the objects of that concern is to be interpreted as a reason for saying, alternatively or additionally, that the interest must have an unconscious origin, then we must first make sure that justice has been done to the possible overt sources.

This is not, I think, a tribute which could be paid to the Jones treatment. Mainly because he has not realized what the philosophical problems are, and how they arise, he cannot grasp the importance of the issues at stake. Nor can he sympathize with the person who oscillates between what look like, and perhaps are, incompatible positions. If he had seen the apparent incompatibility obtaining between two constellations of ideas and activities neither of which would it be easy or even possible to abandon, then he could scarcely have thought it just obvious that 'the ambivalence so often to be noted among those expressing opinions' on this philosophical problem 'calls for psychological inquiry'. If he had been seized of the importance of the philosophical issues, then he could scarcely have taken their alleged irrelevance to practice as a premiss in an argument to other and unconscious concerns: 'All this is very odd . . . we cannot detect any difference it makes to his life or conduct according as he adheres to one answer or to its very opposite. Surely this remarkable fact calls for much consideration' (ibid., Vol. I, p. 181).

Even if 'this remarkable fact' was exactly as Jones thinks it is, it would of course still not be a sufficient reason for insisting that consciously declared desires and interests cannot adequately explain the concern of theoreticians with purely theoretical issues. For it is both unwarranted and philistine to dismiss unheard all claims to any disinterested fascination with purely philosophical problems. In the present particular case, however, you do not need to look very far to find people whose conduct has been, and is, substantially affected by some belief in a scientifically demonstrated inevitability. Reflect, for instance, how much both of dynamism and of inertia has been prompted by doctrines of historical inevitability, especially those thought to be trophies of 'scientific socialism'; and recall the Dedication of Popper's *Poverty of Historicism*.[28] Or think of the influence on all our penal institutions of a climate of opinion in which 'psychology has shown that there is no such thing as Freewill', and that no one—or at any rate no one outside an unfavoured few unconsidered groups—can ever really help doing what they do.[29] The sociologist to whom Jones appeals here must be, like so many actual sociologists, doctrinally blinkered and scotomatized. For he is brought in to make 'the curious observation that in practical daily life it does not seem to make any difference whether a given person, community, or religion adopt one or other belief, in free will or determinism' (Jones, 1924, Vol. I, p. 180).

(v) Jones says: '. . . man's belief in free will seems to be stronger in proportion to the unimportance of the decision. Everyone is convinced that he is free to choose whether to stand or to sit at a given moment, to cross his right leg over his left or vice versa "as he wishes". With vital decisions, on the other hand, it is characteristic that he feels irresistibly impelled towards one and one only, and that he really has no choice in the matter nor desires to have any. Luther's famous "Hier stehe ich. Ich kann nicht anders" . . . is a classical example' (Jones, 1924, Vol. II, pp. 181–2).

(a) It is indeed; and, as will be clear from what has been said before, especially in Section 3 of Chapter Three, it is being classically misunderstood. It is noteworthy that Freud himself once employed the same example, and misunderstood it in the same way (Freud, 1904, pp. 253–4). Certainly Luther's words were as truly spoken as they are magnificent. But it is absurd to read them as if they implied that he was somehow paralysed, literally unable to retreat. It is not as the victim of a general paralysis that anyone admires Luther, but rather as the dedicated incarnation of the protestant conscience. The point is not that he could not have done otherwise had he so chosen, but that he discounted all available alternative options as totally unacceptable. His defiant statement does not deny, it presupposes, that he was an agent; that, in what was in Section 2(ii) of the same Chapter Three distinguished as the fundamental sense, he could have done otherwise.

(b) Typically, when someone claims that he had no choice this is to be interpreted as meaning only that he had no tolerable alternative, not that he had no alternative at all. Even when we act under compulsion—in the ordinary as opposed to what seems to be the psychiatrist's sense of that term—we do have another choice. We have that choice the unacceptability of which is what we are claiming when we plead compulsion in the first place. Instead, for instance, of obediently and under compulsion joining a T.U.C. approved and Labour Party affiliated trades union, we can instead choose, as a handful of cross-grained or principled persons—or cross-grained and principled persons—have chosen, to accept the threatened alternative. We can choose, as enemies of socialism, ostracism and unemployment. The situation in which someone acts under compulsion is thus crucially different from that in which they are subject to an irresistible compulsion and do not, therefore, act at all. Any movements which result from such a psychiatric compulsion can only be, in terms of the distinction made in Section 4 of Chapter Five, not movings, but motions. Just as you do really have a choice when, truly and idiomatically, you say that you have no choice; so his compulsive actions, if they really are compulsive, like reflex actions, cannot be actions at all!

(c) It is quite wrong to assume that either the presence of strong motivation or possibility of prediction precludes either choice or freewill, in the ordinary senses of these words: 'With vital decisions . . . it is characteristic that he feels irresistibly impelled towards one and one only, and that he really has no choice in the matter nor desires to have any' (Jones, 1924, Vol. II, p. 182). But, that it is so easy to make a particular choice in a certain sense that there is no attendant anguish of decision, does not preclude the subsistence of alternatives for that particular choice to be a choice between. Nor does the fact that everyone knew which she was going to choose, show that she was not really going to choose at all; and hence, presumably, that they did not really know. I suggest, by the way, that it is because Jones believes that a predictable course of conduct cannot have been truly chosen, and because he is also concerned to show the unreality of true choice, that he insists that 'vital decisions' are, typically, made without stress of soul. Certainly this claim is not true to the experience of many, and it must undermine confidence to hear it made with unqualified assurance.

(vi) Jones also notices suggestions of the sort which we considered at the end of Chapter Five: '. . . recently some arguments derived from atomic physics have given a fresh turn to this ancient controversy and have illustrated once again how in the endeavour to sustain belief in the objectivity of free will support is sought in every possible direction. Starting from Planck's quantum theory and Heisenberg's uncertainty principle some physicists, notably Sir Arthur Eddington and in more ambiguous ways Sir James Jeans, hold that determinism is absent on the atomic plane and apparently present on the macrocosmic one only because of statistical averages' (Jones, 1924, Vol. II, pp. 187–8). Jones goes on to quote, with distaste, Eddington's statement: 'A complete determinism of the material universe cannot be divorced from determinism of the mind . . . Conversely if we wish to emancipate mind we must to some extent emancipate the material world also' (ibid., p. 188).

Jones has two main points to make, both correct. First, he insists that our present inability to discover determinants is not sufficient reason for postulating any measure of objective indeterminism. In this Jones ranges himself with Einstein and other critics against the Copenhagen School, refusing to concede that what no doubt is characteristic of one stage in the development of physics must therefore be a permanent and ultimate feature of the universe itself. The second Jones point is borrowed from Cassirer: 'To mistake the "choice" (*Auswahl*) which an electron has between different quantum orbits with a "choice" (*Wahl*) in the ethical sense of this word would signify becoming the victim of a purely linguistic equivocality. To speak of an ethical choice there must not be only different possibilities but also a conscious distinction between them and furthermore a conscious decision about them. To attribute such acts to an electron would be to relapse into a gross type of anthropomorphism' (ibid., pp. 189–90).

To these comments I have now only two points to add. First, that although references to quantum mechanics can indeed do nothing to establish the reality of choice—a phenomenon which is in any case well known—they can perhaps ease the pain of accepting that physiology cannot hope to discover sufficient causes for every bodily movement. For physicists are—rightly—regarded as the setters of the standards and the keepers of the conscience of the whole world of the natural sciences. So, if and in so far as they find that they have to abandon the idea of a universal determinism of physical causes, then it must be allowed to be no shame to the physiologists to be required to do the same in their own different and perhaps humbler sphere.

Second, one good objection to accepting merely statistical regularities as the last word is that this is bound to leave us with no answer to the question why these particular ones are among the x per cent which do this while those are among the $(100-x)$ per cent which do that. This is the point which Einstein seized in protesting: 'The Lord God does not play dice!' Of course, with all due respect to Einstein, there never is any a priori metaphysical guarantee that our cravings for explanations of contingent facts can or will be satisfied. But, allowing that such cravings are both proper to and definitive of the scientist, it should be some compensation to the physiologist to be assured that those movements which—being movings—cannot be the inexorable consequences of sufficient physical causes are at least alternatively explicable as (elements in) human action. It is more than can be said of the supposedly indeterministic phenomena of quantum mechanics!

(2) Psychoanalytic Determinism: John Hospers

The second spokesman is not a psychoanalyst but a philosopher. John Hospers published 'Freewill and Psychoanalysis' in *Philosophy and Phenomenological Research* back in 1950. But it still demands attention as typical because it has been reprinted in two widely circulating textbooks: *A Modern Introduction to Philosophy*, edited by Paul Edwards and Arthur Pap; and *Readings in Ethical Theory*, edited by John Hospers and Wilfred Sellars.

(i) Hospers, after seeming to accept that the opposite of acting of one's own freewill is acting under compulsion, immediately goes on to ask: 'Still, are we really free?' (Edwards and Pap, p. 75). It is only towards the end that he gives any explicit guidance on what he is proposing that the word 'free' should be made to mean, in order to permit this to be in the actual context a sensible fresh question: 'Of course, all depends on what you mean by "freedom" . . . When "free" means "uncompelled", and only external compulsion is admitted, there are countless free acts. But now we have extended the notion of compulsion to include determination by unconscious forces' (ibid., p. 84).

This extension is an ill-starred manœuvre; which consists extremely ill with the excellent advice of his own concluding paragraph: 'The facts are what they are, regardless of what words we choose for labelling them. But if we choose to label them in a way which is not in accord with what human beings have long had in mind in applying those labels . . . then we shall only be manipulating words to mislead our fellow creatures' (ibid., p. 85). Hospers himself goes contrary to all established usage. For when anyone is in his extended sense compelled there can be no question of offloading responsibility on to some other person. An unconscious mind 'compelling' is not any sort of person compelling; notwithstanding that Hospers persists in writing as if it were. Also it seems that the 'victims' here are not necessarily unwilling; while the determinations of the unconscious are, it appears, unlike the decisions of any flesh-and-blood coercer, entirely irresistible. Thus Hospers tells us what 'unconscious forces drive him into the wanting or not wanting to do the thing' (ibid., p. 80); while 'the unconscious is the master of every fate and the captain of every soul' (ibid., p. 82).

The analogy with the ordinary case of compulsion—the analogy which it is the declared purpose of Hospers to extend— seems, therefore, to collapse. But this collapse is more clarifying than destructive of his thesis. That thesis, I believe, behind all the unfortunate and uncomfortable expressions is: not that we (nearly) always act under compulsion; but that we never (or scarcely ever) act at all. What (almost) universal determination by the unconscious is supposed to show is that the person so determined could (almost) never, in the fundamental and strict sense, have done other than he did, that there is (as near as makes very little matter) no such thing as acting: that although our bodies move, and things happen to us or in us, we never (well scarcely ever) really do anything: 'the analogy of the puppet whose actions are manipulated from behind by invisible wires is a telling one at almost every point' (ibid., p. 80). From now on I omit the parenthetic qualifications. Since the only exceptions admitted are confined, apparently, to those rare and recent birds the successful graduates of a course of psychoanalysis they can for most purposes safely be ignored.

(ii) If this interpretation is correct, then, for all the familiar reasons cited in earlier chapters, the Hospers contention is simply not true. Nor are his supporting reasons good. I have already said enough against that contention. I will, therefore, now concentrate upon three bad reasons.

(a) Hospers remarks: 'we are not free with respect to the emotions that we feel—whom we love or hate, what types we admire, and the like' (ibid., p. 77). This is, of course, perfectly true. But it is not a discovery of psychoanalysis. In general and in the short run what we are free to choose is what we do, not what we feel, or what we want. But this truth has nothing to do with the contention that Hospers is labouring to make out, nor is it owed to Freud.

(b) Hospers protests: 'we say, for example, that a person is free to do so-and-so if he can do so if he wants to—and forget that his wanting is itself caught up in the stream of determinism, that unconscious forces drive him into wanting or not wanting to do the thing in question' (ibid., p. 80).

Certainly someone may set about acquiring a liking for beer or extinguishing a craving for tobacco; and in time, if only he persists intelligently, succeed. Yet it is absurd to presuppose as part of an ideal of responsibility that all likes and dislikes should have been in this sort of way achieved. For a being totally without preferences must be incapable of any choice at all, and hence incapable of setting himself to acquire preferred preferences. So, if and in so far as anyone entertains an ideal of authenticity in freedom and responsibility which requires that the authentic choices for which the chooser is thus responsible must somehow be the outcome only of desires all of which were ultimately self-chosen, then we have to say: not that that ideal is not as a matter of fact, as thanks to Freud we now know, realized in this world; but that it is, even as an ideal, internally incoherent.

(c) Allow that 'unconscious forces drive him into wanting or not wanting to do the thing in question'. It does not follow that his desire to do it or, as the case may be, not to do it, must be irresistible. We are neither required nor entitled to proceed forthwith, as Hospers does, to the conclusion: 'The analogy of the puppet whose motions are manipulated from behind by invisible wires . . . is telling at almost every point.' Nor does the same premiss warrant the earlier conclusions, that the conscious life of the human being is as 'merely a mouthpiece for the unconscious' (ibid., p. 76), and that 'our very acts of volition' are nothing 'but façades for the expression of unconscious wishes' (ibid., p. 77).

There are three objections to this. First, to produce an explanation why I have such and such a desire, whether that explanation be in terms of unconscious mental ongoings or physiological structure, is not at all to show that I do not authentically, sincerely, and deeply, want whatever it may be. The desire the origin of which is thus explained is not by that token a mere façade. On the contrary: thus to explain the source of my desire is, rather, to presuppose that I do genuinely want whatever it may be. Where could you find purchase for any explanation why I have a desire if I do not actually have it at all? (It is, by the way, extraordinarily common—and one of the intellectual faults which a first course in philosophy should help to cure—to offer or accept an explanation why something is the case as if it were some sort of demonstration that really it is not.)

Second, and more fundamentally, it is totally wrong to construe our desires as if they were irresistible external compulsions upon us. For they are strictly not either external or irresistible. Granted that I have a desire for Cynthia it is no more inevitable that I will set about trying to get her, than it follows necessarily that any attempts which I do make will succeed. Even supposing that someone can be in a position to know that I will and they will, still from this it follows only and uninterestingly that I will and they will; not that I will, inexorably, and they will, inevitably. It is one thing to say that he will win the election in a landslide, and quite another to say that those who will vote for him could not—in the strict sense—do otherwise.[30]

Third, it is, as we have already seen in discussing Jones, as misguided as it is common to misrepresent psychic determinism as if it were the psychological or psychoanalytic special case of universal physical causal determinism. For it is the essence of psychic determinism to claim that whatever is determined can be explained in terms of motives, plans, desires, purposes, intentions and so forth: if not conscious ones then unconscious. Yet—at least as regards the conscious—any explanation of this distinctively personal kind does not preclude but presupposes that those concerned, in the fundamental sense, could have done otherwise. If in truth they could not, then there was no true action; and all reference to their desires, their plans, their purposes, and so forth must be entirely beside the point. The perhaps still surprising moral is this. If the universal determinism of physical causes really is incompatible with the fundamental notion of an agent necessarily being able to do otherwise, as I have in the present book been arguing, then psychic determinism is not, as it sounds as if it must be, a special case of that first sort of universal determinism. And, furthermore, that first sort of determinism neither is nor could be the universal truth. For we know that we are in fact often agents; and, without this altogether familiar experience of agency, we could not have the notions either of agency (and the possibility of doing otherwise) or of contingent necessity (and the impossibility of alteration by human effort). Nor are we, nor could we be, puppets on the strings of our desires.

10
LENIN AND THE CARTESIAN
INHERITANCE

GILBERT Ryle as an Oxford examiner once set the question: 'What is the External World external to?' To this question, as later he privately agreed, the model answer must begin: 'The External World is external to the Ghost in the Machine.' The point is fundamental. For it was Descartes who introduced into modern philosophy what has since come to be labelled The Problem of the External World. This is construed as the problem of showing that, and how, anyone can ever have any knowledge of the universe around him; granted that all he is directly and immediately aware of must be his own private experience.

The expression 'private experience' has to be read in such a way that to say that she enjoyed a private experience, or had a sense-datum of—say—a cow precisely does not entail that she really saw, or otherwise perceived, a real, flesh-and-blood cow. This curious private interpretation of the word 'experience' is thus crucially different from the everyday, lay, public sense—the sense in which a would-be employer might advertise for people with experience of computers. For there the essential qualification for candidates is that they should have had dealings with actual, wires-and-transistors computers. It is the professional, private meaning which is characteristic, indeed almost perhaps definitive, of traditional philosophical empiricists; though of course the distinction between the two senses is in that area of discussion frequently overlooked. It is, after all, easy to succumb to the temptation of thinking, because it is obvious that all our knowledge of contingent fact must be based on our (public) experience, that the same must be true when the key word 'experience' is construed in the opposite, private meaning. (Compare, for instance, Flew, 1971, V§6, pp. 214–18.[31])

It is part of the constitutive framework of The Problem of
the External World that the Cartesian 'I', who is seeking
knowledge, is not the flesh-and-blood person of Aristotelian
common sense, but is, rather, an incorporeal substance. For
the Cartesian the external world does not begin, as for another
it would, outside the car he is driving; or outside the institution
in which he is confined; or beyond the national or imperial
frontiers; or with the very tangible Iron Curtain of barbed
wire and explosives bounding the present extension of the
Socialist bloc. For Descartes, and for every Cartesian, even his
own organism is itself part of the external world; and that
organism, like everything else in the material world, is to be
understood in purely mechanical terms. Hence the appro-
priateness of Ryle's mischievous epitome: man truly is for
Descartes 'the Ghost in the Machine'.

The main purpose of this final chapter is to bring out that,
and how, false assumptions embodied in The Problem of the
External World both presuppose and support what I contend
to be an equally erroneous view of the nature of man. The
chapter takes the form of a confrontation with Lenin. This is
because in 1908 Lenin took time off from his normal professional work as a revolutionary in order to write *Materialism and
Empirio-Criticism*. This book, like all the works of Lenin, is
polemic. His main enemies here were Russian disciples of the
British philosopher-scientist Karl Pearson and of the Austrians
Ernst Mach and Richard Avenarius. The Empirio-Criticism
of these thinkers was the immediate pre-World War I ancestor
of the old original Logical Positivism of the Vienna Circle of
the twenties and thirties. What particularly incited Lenin,
and what made him see the composition of this philosophical
polemic too as just another necessary party task, was that
people were trying to combine these other doctrines with
Marxism. He believed, I think correctly: both that they are in
truth idealistic in their implications and even solipsistic; and
that, this being so, they cannot by any means be made consistent with that faith. Following Engels, Lenin also believed
that what they both saw as the central party division in
philosophy must somehow either be or tend to become con-
gruent with other battle lines between the forces of light and
the powers of darkness.

Materialism and Empirio-Criticism has some significance quite apart from the fact that its author was to become by far the biggest single personal influence upon the development of our twentieth-century world; an influence which, it may already be evident, I myself judge to be almost entirely disastrous. Lenin had a very keen nose for heresy. He picks and points out with force and directness idealistic and solipsistic implications which were at the time generally ignored or denied; and very often still are. I myself well remember the exhilaration and illumination of my own first reading of the book as an undergraduate in the forties. Yet for all the force and fury of his polemic Lenin continues to accept without question those selfsame assumptions which lead so inexorably to the conclusions he exhorts us to reject. We could scarcely find a better example by which to display the fatal fascination of the Cartesian inheritance.

(*1*) *Lenin's Materialism Confronts Berkeley's Idealism*

Lenin starts by considering Berkeley; and offers two short definitions: 'Materialism is the recognition of "objects in themselves", or outside the mind; ideas and sensations are copies or images of those objects. The opposite doctrine (idealism) claims that objects do not exist "without the mind"; objects are "combinations of sensations" (Lenin, 1908, p. 17). This is an admirably brief and surely fair account of what mainly is at issue between Berkeley and his opponents; and, as Lenin at once goes on to note, it is materialism in this sense which Berkeley thinks is the 'foundation . . . of Atheism and Irreligion . . . How great a friend material substance has been to Atheists in all ages were needless to relate' (ibid., p. 19: the original is *Principles*, §92).

(i) But if this were all that was involved in the notions of materialism and idealism, then those critics who have complained that Marxists speak of materialism when they ought to be talking of realism would be right (Wetter, p. 46). Nor, on this limited interpretation of the two terms, is it immediately obvious why materialism is to be taken as necessarily irreligious and idealism as characteristically religious. The most which could reasonably be claimed on Berkeley's side is: not that materialism, in the present attenuated sense, necessarily commits us to atheism; but that atheism somehow requires or presupposes, in the same sense, materialism. Lenin, correspondingly, could scarcely maintain that this kind of materialism entails atheism. For most lay theists, and most theist philosophers also, have been, in this first unenriched interpretation, materialists; and it would be implausible indeed to suggest that they have been, in this respect, inconsistent.

It is, however, just worth remarking that controversialists of all parties are always under temptation to misrepresent opponents who have spoken only of necessary conditions to be saying what they said of sufficient conditions. Thus the socialist may have said only that in order to establish the New Jerusalem it is first necessary to enforce state monopolies of—to quote the original words of Clause IV of the constitution of the British Labour Party—'all the means of production, distribution, and exchange'. Opponents will nevertheless be inclined to attribute to him the even more unbelievable assertion that socialism is a sufficient and universal panacea. The liberal enemy of socialism may contend that both theory and experience have shown that economic is a necessary condition of political pluralism. He will certainly be told, if his opponents condescend to argue with him at all, that there are several economically pluralist societies in which there is almost as little scope for political dissent as in the fully socialist countries of the Socialist bloc; and he will then have to bear the chagrin of watching them celebrate what they will see as a triumphant routing of reactionary and—yes—divisive criticism.

(ii) The first complication to notice is that idealism, even as initially defined, can appear in different forms and with different emphases. Behaviourism is nowadays often distinguished as either metaphysical, analytical, or methodological: the metaphysical behaviourist by profession denies the reality of (private) experience; the analytical behaviourist contends that words and expressions which have been thought to refer wholly or partly to such experience are instead to be construed as involving nothing but overt behaviour, and dispositions to behave; while the methodological behaviourist recommends that to concentrate on overt behaviour and to abandon introspective inquiries is the right road for psychological science. Parallel distinctions need to be made with idealism. Where the emphasis is ontological or metaphysical, the idealist maintains that ideas or, in the Cartesian sense, thoughts are all there is, with .the exception—disallowed by Hume and by some neo-Humean radicals—of incorporeal, spiritual substances. (For an explanation of this sense of 'substance' see the first paragraph of Chapter Six, above; the word 'spiritual' here implies incorporeality, and is taken to cover both consciousness and all other psychological characteristics.)

Where the emphasis of the idealism is analytical, the idealist is a phenomenalist: both material things and minds (or 'selves') are logical constructions out of (private) experience; which, being translated, means that sentences about the former are analysable in terms of—are, that is, somehow ultimately reducible to—sentences about the latter. Where the emphasis is methodological or epistemological, the idealist contends only that such experience and its relations is all that we can really know. The philosopher who is in these analytical or epistemological understandings idealist may well, if he is himself thinking only of the metaphysical emphasis, repudiate the description.

(iii) Although he neither adds to nor alters the definition given Lenin soon makes it clear that he is himself reading more into the term. While his paradigm idealist Berkeley went so far as altogether to deny any material reality independent of mind, it now appears to be possible to qualify as an idealist by simply denying (not the reality but) the primacy of matter. Engels, says Lenin, divided philosophers into 'two great camps'. Engels, Lenin goes on, 'sees the fundamental distinction between them in the fact that while for the materialists nature is primary and spirit secondary, for the idealists the reverse is the case' (Lenin, 1908, p. 24). Given this it becomes easier to discern logical connections between idealism and theism: for, although the addition still does not make the former a sufficient condition of the latter, it does begin to make it look at least necessary.

To assert the primacy of matter over mind is to assert that mind is some sort of dependent function of matter: 'Materialism, in full agreement with natural science, takes consciousness, thought, sensation as secondary . . . associated only with the

higher forms of matter (organic matter) . . .' (ibid., p. 38).
Any general view of this kind clearly precludes suggestions
that people are or could be essentially incorporeal beings, or
that there might be an incorporeal yet somehow personal God;
while affirmations to the contrary must involve or otherwise
open the door to such suggestions. No wonder, therefore, that
Lenin fumed against Mach: 'That means that there are
"immediate experiences" *without* a physical body, *prior* to a
physical body! What a pity that this magnificent philosophy
has not yet found acceptance in our theological seminaries!
There its merits would have been fully appreciated' (ibid.,
p. 234: italics original).

Lenin's own version of this primacy thesis is logically
contingent: he takes it that scientists have discovered that, as
a matter of fact, consciousness and every other mental ongoing
does always have some sophisticated physiological foundation;
and presumably that it is also a matter of straightforward
scientific discovery that there are not, and that people are not,
incorporeal spiritual substances. In other and stronger ver-
sions the primacy thesis becomes necessary rather than
continent: the crux now is that it could make no sense to
attribute consciousness or any other mental characteristic to
anything but a creature of flesh and blood; or at any rate—
putting it into terms which are at the same time both more
general and more technical—anything but a corporeal
substance.

(iv) Again and again Lenin takes hold of some view—often
a view put forward as ultra hard-headed and scientific—and
insists: first, that it is in truth implicitly idealistic, and even
solipsistic; and, second, that these implications are inconsistent with known facts—and in particular known scientific
facts.

All this is salutary, splendid, and—I think—sound. Anyone
schooled in the traditions of twentieth-century British philosophy will compare Lenin's appeals to known facts with those
of G. E. Moore's 'Proof of an External World', and will
contrast Lenin's emphasis upon science with the apparent
indifference of Moore. Nevertheless, although Lenin's polemic
is, so far as it goes, excellent, it does not go far enough. It was
said of Francis Bacon that he wrote philosophy like a Lord

Chancellor; which, indeed, he was. It might similarly be said that Lenin wrote philosophy like a professional revolutionary; which, in fact, he was. The point is that Lenin was a dedicated and disciplined practical man, and when he discussed philosophical doctrines he was interested: first, in whether they were true; second, in how they fitted in with the ideas of his party; and, third, in what their social impact was or would be. So, having recognized that idealism must be false, he seems never to have gone on to ask himself what are the arguments which have in generation after generation misled acute and honest men to defend views which are not merely false but, one might have thought, obviously false.

Such neglect is in a practical man no doubt as excusable as it is natural. Yet it is unfortunate. For unless and until it is repaired no critique of idealism can be said to be complete, or even truly philosophical. And furthermore, as has already been suggested, Lenin's failure to inquire into the supporting arguments carried a heavy penalty. It enabled him to present as 'the materialist theory of knowledge' a structure incorporating components guaranteed to produce the same old, familiar fatal collapse into idealism (ibid., pp. 58–9).

(2) Beginning with Descartes

Lenin starts, as we saw in Section 1, with Berkeley. But the story of modern idealism, like the whole history of Modern Philosophy, begins with Descartes. It was he who, borrowing arguments from the recently revived Classical Pyrrhonian scepticism (Popkin, *passim*), proceeded systematically to doubt everything but his own present consciousness: '. . . since all the same thoughts which we have while awake may also come to us in sleep, without any of them being at that time true, I resolved to assume that everything that ever entered into my mind was no more true than the illusions of my dreams' (Descartes, 1637, IV, Vol. I, p. 101).

The problem therefore arises of how, if at all, Descartes can know that anything else exists in addition to, and as it were behind, his own 'thoughts'. Note the warning inverted commas surrounding that last word. They are put in as a reminder that for Descartes the term 'thought' officially covers all and only modes of consciousness. (This was explained and emphasized both in the second paragraph and at the beginning of Section 2 of Chapter Six, above.) In particular 'thought' here includes those private perceptual experiences which both Lenin and his contemporary opponents misleadingly described as sensations. These are what our contemporaries and immediate pre-decessors have labelled sense-data. Remember too what was said at the very beginning of the present chapter about what the Cartesian External World is external to.

With these reminders we are now in position to appreciate the decisive force of Lenin's terse yet relevantly reiterated objections: 'If bodies are "complexes of sensations", as Mach says, or "combinations of sensations", as Berkeley said, it inevitably follows that the whole world is but my idea. Starting from such a premiss it is impossible to arrive at the existence of other people besides oneself: it is the purest solipsism' (Lenin, 1908, p. 34).

A second example begins by quoting Mach: 'It is then correct that the world consists only of our sensations. In which case we have knowledge *only* of sensations . . .' Lenin comments: 'From which there is only one possible inference, namely, that the "world consists only of *my* sensations." The word *our* employed by Mach instead of *my* is employed illegitimately. By this word alone Mach betrays that "half-hearted-ness" of which he accuses others' (ibid., pp. 35–6: italics original).

Later, as he continues to hammer Mach's inconsistency, it emerges that, presumably because he began with Berkeley rather than with Descartes, Lenin is not fully seized of the crux that for any Cartesian the external world begins with his own body: '. . . if elements are sensations, you have no right even for a moment to accept the existence of "elements" *independent* of my nerves and my mind. But if you do admit physical objects that are independent of my nerves and my sensations and that cause sensation only by acting on my retina—you are disgracefully abandoning your "one-sided" idealism and adopting the standpoint of "one-sided" materialism' (ibid., p. 48: italics original). It should by now be obvious that the references to 'my nerves' and 'my retina' are out of place. (Compare the similar ineptitude in Schopenhauer, 1844, Vol. II, pp. 163–4; pointed out by Borges, pp. 49–50).

(i) In his general attack Lenin is doing no more than insist that Berkeley's premisses do yield the negative conclusions which Berkeley drew. Granted that our experience is and can be always and only experience in the sense just now distinguished as private, then it is not possible to justify any belief about an independently existing material world. What Berkeley called our sensible ideas must be essentially mind-dependent: it makes no more sense to talk of unowned, unsensed sense-data than of unowned, unfelt pains. And, if that is where we have to start, then there is indeed no escape from the 'dilemma' presented in *The Principles of Human Knowledge*: 'If there were external bodies, it is impossible that we should ever come to know it, and if there were not, we might have the very same reasons to think there were that we have now. Suppose, what no one can deny possible, an intelligence, without the help of external bodies, to be affected with the same train of sensations or ideas that you are, imprinted in the same order and with like vividness in his mind. I ask, whether that intelligence hath not all the reason to believe the existence of corporeal substances, represented by his ideas, and exciting them in his mind, that you can possibly have for believing the same thing?' (Berkeley, 1734, §20, p. 49.)

It is important to realize that this starting-point is part of the Cartesian inheritance; and that, despite some differences both of terminology and of surrounding belief, it is a fundamental shared with Descartes and Locke, with Hume and Kant. Precisely this is 'the new way of ideas', in its perceptual application. It was one of the fresh breezes stirring Oxford when Locke matriculated as an undergraduate. Fifty years later, embodied now in Locke's *Essay concerning Human Understanding*, it captivated the young Berkeley at Trinity College in Dublin. After another half-century Hume speaks of 'the obvious dictates of reason . . . that the existences which we consider when we say *this house* and *that tree* are nothing but perceptions in the mind . . .' (Hume, 1748, XII(i), p. 152: italics original).

The morals drawn by successive members of this apostolic succession of the great were, of course, various. Descartes as a philosophical rationalist believed that, by employing only 'means which are not derived from anywhere but from ourselves, and from the simple consideration of the nature of our own minds', he could validly deduce the existence of a good God, who, being no deceiver, guarantees that representations submitted by the senses with which he provides us are in general faithful to the realities outside (Descartes, 1641, Dedication, and Descartes, 1637, IV; Vol. I, pp. 134 and 100–6). Locke, without resort to any supernatural guarantees, and notwithstanding his readiness to argue against Malebranche that a creature never able actually to see things for itself could not know that its supposed representations do indeed correspond to something, appears typically to be sure that, at least as regards the primary qualities, this is in fact so. (Compare, for instance and accessibly, Woozley, p. 27 with Locke, II(viii) 15.)

Berkeley goes much further, by contending that the suggestion that there is some independently existing material reality behind our sensory ideas makes no sense. He then proceeds to argue that, since 'whatever power I may have over my own thoughts . . . the ideas actually perceived by sense have not a like dependence on my will', and, since the only sort of cause there can be is an active spiritual agency, 'There is therefore some other will or spirit that produces them'. Hence in every moment of sensory experience we immediately confront 'the goodness and wisdom of that governing spirit whose will constitutes the Laws of Nature' (Berkeley, §§23–4, 29, and 32; quotations at pp. 53 and 54).

The sceptical Hume makes short work of every version of The Representative Theory of Perception: 'This philosophical system . . . is the monstrous offspring of two principles . . . contrary to each other, which are both embraced by the mind, and which are unable mutually to destroy each other' (Hume, 1739–40, I(iv) 2, p. 215; and compare, for instance, Flew, 1971, §1, pp. 331–8). He has even less time for theological guarantees or for immediate confrontations with Divinity: 'To have recourse to the veracity of the Supreme Being in order to prove the veracity of our senses is surely making a very unexpected circuit. If his veracity were at all concerned in this matter, our senses would be entirely infallible . . . Not to mention that, if the external world be once called in question, we shall be at a loss to find arguments by which we may prove the existence of that Being or any of his attributes' (Hume, 1748, XII(i), p. 153).

At the end of the day Hume advocates reliance upon our senses as a matter of invincible and salutary natural belief. Nevertheless, he insists, this belief cannot be rationally vindicated: 'Thus the sceptic . . . must assent to . . . the existence of body, tho' he cannot pretend by any arguments of philosophy to maintain its veracity' (Hume, 1739–40, I(iv) 2, p. 187). The position of Kant is very similar. Although he is at pains to reject the label 'idealist' he nevertheless maintains that it is inherently impossible for us to know 'things-in-themselves' (Kant, 1783, p. 45). Both Hume and Kant therefore come under Lenin's lash for being, on the great dividing issue which requires every philosopher to stand up to be counted with either Ormuzd or Ahriman, 'agnostics'.

(ii) On his more particular point about solipsism, it is a pity that Lenin missed the brief references in *The Principles of Human Knowledge* to what has only fairly recently come to be labelled The Problem of Other Minds. With characteristically aggressive verve Berkeley puts it to his opponents that in his system 'God is known as certainly and immediately as any other mind or spirit whatsoever, distinct from ourselves. We may even assert that the existence of God is far more evidently perceived than the existence of men . . .' (Berkeley, 1734, §146, p. 108).

(*a*) Indeed we may. But then we must go further. For Berkeley provides no sufficient reason for believing in the existence of any spirits other than the Berkeleyan himself and his God. The true outcome of Berkeley's system is the most radical and total Protestantism: the lonely individual confronts his God, in a world in which he has no natural warrant for believing in the existence of anything beyond those two inordinately ill-matched minds, and their ideas.

Thus Berkeley says 'A human spirit or person is not perceived by sense, as not being an idea; when therefore we see the colour, size, figure, and motions of a man we perceive only certain sensations or ideas excited in our own minds: and these being exhibited to our view in sundry distinct collections, serve to mark out to us the existence of finite and created spirits like ourselves' (ibid., §148, p. 109). But now, as Berkeley himself has just urged, 'There is not any one mark that denotes a man, or affect produced by him, which doth not more strongly evince the being of that Spirit who is the Author of nature' (ibid., §147, p. 108: italics original). Suppose that I grant that an Author has to be postulated in order to explain the occurrence of those sensory ideas which are not creatures of my will. Then, I have to ask, what explanatory work can be found for further merely human spirits? This question seems never to have occurred, or been put, to Berkeley; and I can find no answer offered in his writings.

(b) Berkeley, however, like Descartes is most explicit and emphatic in asserting that people are incorporeal; and that this supposed fact provides a precondition or even a presumption of human immortality. Thus in his *Discourse on the Method* Descartes first argues that he is an incorporeal something whose whole essence 'to think', a soul 'entirely distinct from the body'; and then a few pages later proceeds to point the moral that such a being will not necessarily decay and dissolve with the body, but could be immortal (Descartes, 1637, IV and V, Vol. 1, pp. 101 and 118). Berkeley is equally insistent that people are not creatures of flesh and blood but incorporeal substances—though in his view it cannot even make sense to claim that there are independently existing material machines for those ghosts to inhabit: 'Hence it is plain, we do not see a man, if by *man* is meant that which lives, moves and perceives as we do: but only such a certain collection of ideas, as directs us to think that there is a distinct principle of thought and motion like to ourselves, accompanying and represented by it' (Berkeley, 1734, §148, p. 109: italics original).

It is in the present context worth underlining this commitment to the essentially incorporeal nature of man. For, although it can of course also be based on other grounds, or on none at all, this is an often unnoticed implication of the Cartesian fundamental distinguished in Section 2(i) immediately above.

Consider, for example, one of Hume's many statements of that fundamental: 'The only existences, of which we are certain, are perceptions, which being immediately present to us by consciousness, command our strongest assent, and are the first foundation of all our conclusions' (Hume, 1739–40, I(iv) 2, p. 212).

It is obvious that the 'we' here has to be construed as referring to our minds, which are in turn to be understood as incorporeal entities. The last word has to be the fastidiously non-committal 'entities' in order to allow for Hume's rejection of a substance in favour of a serial analysis: '. . . they are nothing but a bundle or collection of different perceptions, which succeed each other with an inconceivable rapidity, and are in a perpetual flux and movement' (ibid., I(iv) 6, p. 252).

Thus we find the radical young Hume, ever eager to challenge the pompous pretensions of metaphysicians, proceeding to speak of 'distinct . . . and separable experiences', in a way which, as we saw in the second paragraph of Section 3 of Chapter Six, is strictly nonsensical. He proceeds hence to develop an account of personal identity which very shortly afterwards elicits a confession of despair: 'I find myself involved in such a labyrinth, that . . . I neither know how to correct my former opinions, nor how to render them consistent' (ibid., Appendix, p. 633).

It is yet one more remarkable and salutary illustration of the enormous holding power of the Cartesian framework that even Hume—who had no immortal longings in him, and who had every other reason for cleaving to an Aristotelian view of man—should never have thought to challenge the ruinous assumption of personal incorporeality.

(3) An Impetuous Appeal to Practice

Lenin, as was said at the beginning of the chapter, is not interested in the intellectual sources of idealist error. He therefore never attempts to isolate and examine the Cartesian starting-point. Instead he is content to show that idealist or agnostic conclusions are false, while dismissing the theoretical difficulties of his opponents with a peremptory appeal to practice: 'The best refutation of Kantian and Humian agnosticism as well as of other philosophical fancies (*Schrullen*) is practice, repeats Engels. "The result of our action proves the conformity (*Uebereinstimmung*) of our perceptions with the objective nature of the things perceived", he says in reply to the agnostics' (Lenin, 1908, p. 136; and compare pp. 103ff.).

If this were nothing but the impatient dismissal by a practical man of troublesome theoretical difficulties then we might simply express our sympathy, and say no more about it: there is indeed—as Hume, for instance, always recognized—something far-fetched and fantastic about such 'philosophical fancies'. But this appeal to the criterion of practice is intended to be much more than this. For it is offered as an (if not *the*) essential element in what Lenin always calls (not an but) *the* materialist theory of knowledge: 'We have seen that Marx in 1845 and Engels in 1888 and 1892 placed the criterion of practice at the basis of the materialist theory of knowledge' (ibid., p. 136).

Now there are both true and extremely important things to be said on these lines. Certainly there can be no satisfactory account of scientific knowledge which does not centre upon the idea of practice, of testing by experiment. Again, and more relevantly, it is right to point out that Descartes's claim that he can doubt, and does doubt, various particular propositions about the external world is inconsistent with his behaviour. For it is false to say that a man is in doubt whether, for instance, a bridge is safe if he nevertheless entrusts what is dear to him to that bridge without hesitation and without anxiety. It is, too, significant that Descartes arranged to conduct his meditations in a room with a stove, isolated from all the demands of active, practical life.

Yet again, and, as we shall be seeing in the next Section 4, still more relevantly, it is only as flesh-and-blood doers acting upon other material things—and as doers in turn either being acted upon by those other material things which like us are agents, or as doers being otherwise subjected to the impact of those material things which are not themselves also agents— that we are able to acquire and to have the very notions in terms of which the present issues are discussed; or indeed any notions at all. Earlier, in Section 5(ii)(*a*) of Chapter Five, it was argued that we can only understand the rival claims that sometimes we could do otherwise, and that everything which happens happens inevitably, on condition that we know the former to be true and the latter false. Now in this Section 4 it will be similarly contended that the conflicting contentions of idealist and materialist can be understood only on condition that the one is known to be false and the other true. So, in a way, it is right to say that idealism is refuted and materialism proved by appealing to the (public) experience of practice.

However, the appeal, as Lenin puts it, cannot be allowed: 'The result of our action,' he says, again quoting Engels, 'proves the conformity of our perceptions with the objective nature of the things perceived'. If what was in question was a particular case, then this would be absolutely correct and to the point: 'Art thou not, fatal vision, sensible to feeling as to sight? Come, let me clutch thee . . .' But Macbeth's test is not similarly decisive, or even relevant, against a general and comprehensive scepticism about all perception.[32]

Descartes started by supposing 'that everything that ever entered into my mind was no more true than the illusions of my dreams' (Descartes, 1637, IV, Vol. I, p. 101). So he is committed to wondering whether the clutching may not be just another part of the dream; and so, similarly, with any and every other practical test which might be suggested. No wonder that, in another passage quoted by Lenin, the reluctant agnostic Helmholz cried: 'I do not see how one could refute a system of even the most extreme subjective idealism which chose to regard life as a dream' (Lenin, 1908, p. 241).

(4) The Primacy of the Public

There is, nevertheless, hope for Helmholz. For look now more closely at the suppositions of Descartes: 'Thus, because our senses sometimes deceive us, I wished to suppose that nothing is just as they cause us to imagine it to be. . . . And since all the same thoughts . . . which we have while awake may also come to us in sleep, without any of them being at that time true, I resolved to assume that everything that ever entered into my mind was no more true than the illusions of my dreams' (Descartes, 1637, IV, Vol. I, p. 101).

(i) We start with a comparatively minor point. If the systematic doubt of Descartes is to be genuinely doubt at all, then it has to be grounded. For suppose that I have in my hands *A Textbook of Comparative Phlebotomy*, and suppose that I, though very excusably knowing nothing whatsoever of what is to the best of my belief an entirely fictitious discipline, nevertheless

point to a statement on p. 397, and say: 'I doubt whether this
is true.' Then, surely, my claim to be in doubt can be at once
refuted by referring to my total ignorance of comparative
phlebotomy and everything connected with it.

Descartes however, and very properly, deploys grounds.
Unfortunately these grounds are inconsistent with the completely general doubts which he proposes to base upon them.
For he refers to what is, presumably, both his knowledge that
our senses sometimes deceive us, and his knowledge that
there is such a thing as, and that he has himself had, (public)
experience—'the same thoughts . . . which we have while
awake'.

If grounds are offered, as Descartes himself offers grounds,
then the proposed general doubt is contradicted by the
particular reasons deployed in its support. Yet a supposition
that it is perhaps all without exception just a dream, presented
with no evidencing reasons at all, must in the nature of the
case lack intellectual force. (For the distinction between
evidencing and motivating reasons compare the first paragraph of Chapter Five above.)

(ii) The first objection, in the previous subsection, was
purely epistemological. The second approaches an epistemological conclusion by way of a contention about semantic
priority. The initial contention is that all concepts of illusion
presuppose their correlative concepts of reality; in the sense
that, even to understand the former, you must first at least
understand the latter. The further, concluding point is that
some acquaintance with realities is a condition of possessing
any of these contrasting concepts.

(a) The purely semantic point is, surely, uncontentious. The
idea of dreaming, for instance, is essentially secondary and
derivative. To dream that you did, or saw, or heard, or smelt
something is a special sort of *not* doing, *not* seeing, *not* hearing,
or *not* smelling whatever it may be. Similarly too with every
sort of seeming: to seem to do or to seem to be is not something
primary and elementary; it is, rather, to *fail* actually to do or
to *fail* actually to be. The same indeed applies completely
generally to any and every contrast between appearance and
reality: the idea of the reality is the positive and primary one;
that of the appearance is negative and secondary. The relevant

consequence is that to understand any of these secondary ideas you must first understand the corresponding primary ones.

To say this, of course, is not to say, for example, what is obviously not true: either that no one can be in position to say that he dreamt of flying in a Concorde, unless he has first actually had a flight in one of those beautiful yet fabulously extravagant and environmentally obnoxious machines; or that no one could both properly and truly assert that this here is a forgery of a Vermeer, unless he had at some time himself seen a particular original of which he is now maintaining the present canvas to be a fraudulent imitation. The initial undisputatious point concerns understanding only: to be able to talk with understanding of any sort of failure actually to be anything you do need first to be able to understand what would be meant by the corresponding claim about not failure but success. So if Descartes is going to be able to wonder whether he really is in a room with a stove, then he does not actually have ever to have been in a real room with a real stove. But he does have to know what it means to say, simply, 'I am in a room with a stove.'

(*b*) But now, what about the absolutely general suppositions proposed by Descartes: that perhaps he has never actually perceived anything at all—never, in our terminology, had and known that he had any public as opposed to private experience; and that maybe he has never actually been awake at all, knowing that he was? Yet how could we say that Descartes understands what he is saying, how could Descartes himself claim to understand his own words, if in truth he never had actually perceived and was not now perceiving anything; and if he now shows himself to be completely unable to tell the difference between dreaming and waking, between illusion and reality? How, in a word, is anyone to grasp, and to know that he has succeeded in grasping the crucial concept of material things in a public world unless it is by in some way pointing at actual specimens truly perceived as such?

In the paragraph from which the first quotation of the present Section 4 is taken Descartes also suggests that, since he is—he falsely alleges—as apt as other men to be deceived by paralogisms 'even in the simplest matters of geometry', he must suppose that perhaps he never has correctly identified any argument as either valid or invalid; and cannot now. But grant that someone really was at a loss to identify any arguments, however simple and luminous, as either valid or invalid; and that there was no rhyme or reason in his persistent mis-identifications of the specimens provided for his attention. Then, surely, we could only conclude that we were confronted with a creature not seized of that crucial pair of correlative concepts; a conclusion in which that creature, if he could nevertheless be allowed to be so far rational, must himself concur.

(iii) Already, at the beginning of Section 2(i), we saw Berkeley presenting the Cartesian starting-point: 'Suppose, what no one can deny possible, an intelligence, without the help of external bodies, to be affected with the same train of sensations or ideas that you are, imprinted in the same order and with like vividness in the mind.'

It is indeed enormously tempting to believe that private experience is the one sure object of certainty, that it is upon this foundation that any knowledge of an external world will have to be based, and that if we are ever to get to material things we can start only from sense-data. Plausible though these suggestions may be, they are all wrong. In fact sense-data cannot even be identified without reference to material things; the only possible foundation for the structure of scientific knowledge is actual perception; and we cannot even give meaning to any descriptions of our elusive and floating private experience without in some way first referring to the public world.

(a) Take the claim of the third clause of that last sentence first. It seems that I must be in a perfectly and a uniquely privileged position to know my own private experience.

Certainly there is some privilege here. Such experience is after all necessarily mine and not yours, and the person who has—say—the pain is in the best position to know how it feels. True, but if we are to speak seriously of knowledge, then there has to be some articulation. This brings us face to face with the notorious difficulties of introspective knowledge—difficulties, that is to say, in knowing that assertions about private experience are true. These difficulties arise in part because such experience does as a matter of fact tend to be swiftly changing and elusive. But in the main what makes them as intractable as they are, precisely is the essential privacy; and the consequent facts that we cannot call upon other people or on instruments to confirm or disconfirm what the subject is inclined to say.

Anything which is to be said about private experience has to be given its meaning by reference to the public world. To appreciate that this is true consider the case of some descriptive word which I might wish to apply to some part of one of my fleeting and momentary sense-data. Let us make it, for example, the colour word 'blue'. Now, obviously, I cannot know whether you and I both use this word in the same way, with the same meaning, except in so far as I can compare the ways in which you apply it with the ways in which I apply it. Since it is necessarily impossible for me to observe your essentially private experience, I must, in order to make any such comparisons, be in a position to know about the relevant transactions between you as one public, material, thing and various other public, material, things.

So far, so good. But this rather obvious, yet often neglected, fact about the fundamental conditions of communication is not enough to show that I need to have, and to know that I have, access to material things if I am to know that I am using a language correctly in describing my own sense-data privately, to myself alone.

By the way: I should say here that I believe that it is only in the present Section 4(iii)(a) that I am developing what is said to be a thesis of the late Wittgenstein—that the notion of a language peculiar to one individual and able to compass assertions only about the private experience of that individual is incoherent. The more modest conclusion of Section 4(ii), immediately above, could survive the collapse of that most ambitious thesis.

To continue: in order to see that everyone does need to have this access to the public world, and to know that they have it, notice that to employ any word correctly is to follow the rules for its correct usage. So to know that you are using the word correctly you need to know that you are following these rules. Now, how is this to be done if we are not allowed to refer to material things or to call on the assistance of other people? It would seem that the whole weight of any claim to know would have to rest on the totally unchecked and unsupported memory of one person: 'Yes, it is blue, because it is the same colour as all the other sense-data which I have previously called blue; hence, I am using the word "blue" in the same way when I call this also blue.'

This may, at first sight, seem as if it were sufficient. For sometimes, and rightly, we do say that one man's unsupported memory claim is enough to establish that something did happen, and that he knows that it did. Yet this is deceptive. The two cases are not really parallel. For where we allow that a man's unsupported memory provides sufficient warrant for his claim to know, his memory is not unsupported in the sense in which memory would have to be unsupported in the supposed Cartesian situation. In the former case the unsupported memory is in fact supported, albeit indirectly, by whatever we know about the reliability of memory in general, about the reliability of the memory of the particular man in question, and about the probability of the event which he is reporting; and all this knowledge rests on all manner of tests and checks of and against the facts of the universe around us. In the latter case there could be no such checks or tests; and the memory claim could be backed by nothing more than an unverifiable and unfalsifiable conviction that a consistent usage was in fact being followed. To call this sort of conviction knowledge would surely be excessively flattering; and wrong.[33]

(b) The second claim of the present subsection, that 'the only possible foundation for the structure of scientific knowledge is actual perception' has, surely, already been sufficiently supported by the whole course of the preceding argument. Something more will, however, be added about sense-data in perception in the final Section 5. It remains to consider the first claim, that 'sense-data cannot even be identified without reference to material things'.

Certainly it must seem altogether reasonable for the epistemologically cautious philosopher, remembering the warning of that Berkeleyan challenge represented in the first paragraph of the present Section 4(iii), to try to confine himself to claims about his own immediate sense-data: here at last,

he muses, I have something which I can know, really know.
Yet wait. How is he to pick out specimens of this class of the
sole safe subjects of discourse? The author of the *Treatise* is
ready with the answer: 'To give a child an idea of scarlet or
orange of sweet or bitter, I present the objects, or in other words,
convey to him those impressions . . .' (Hume, 1739–40, I(i) 1,
p. 5: the ideas of Locke and Berkeley are by Hume proudly
distinguished into ideas and impressions; and that last word
can, for our purposes only, be taken as equivalent to 'sense-
data').

This splendid passage provides an excellent occasion for
applying my own favourite principle of Hume interpretation—
mischievous, yet always both respectful and affectionate:
'When Hume says "or in other words" expect that the two
expressions thus linked will be: not merely, as it happens, and
as a result of boring carelessness, not strictly equivalent; but
rather, to our great profit and instruction, crucially and
radically different in meaning' (compare Flew, 1961, pp. 129–
32). In order to provide the impression, and hence the corresponding idea, Hume boldly and explicitly recommends the
only thing he can recommend, that we 'present the objects'.
He might, I dare to suggest, have announced a little sooner
than he did his intention to collapse the crucial distinction
between objects and impressions or perceptions, between
material things and sense-data: 'I shall at first suppose that
there is only a single existence, which I shall call indifferently
object or *perception*, according as it shall seem best to suit my
purpose, understanding what any common man means by a
hat, or shoe, or stone, or any other impression, convey'd to
him by his senses. I shall be sure to give warning when I return
to a more philosophical way of speaking and thinking' (Hume,
1739–40, I(iv) 2, p. 202: italics original).

A second classical instance should fix the present second
point decisively. In a passage much quoted by the phenomen-
alistically inclined in succeeding centuries Berkeley is as
flagrantly inconsistent as any of them: 'The table I write on,
I say, exists, that is, I see and feel it; and if I were out of my
study I should say that it existed, meaning that if I was in my
study I might perceive it, or that some other spirit actually
does perceive it' (Berkeley, §3, p. 42). Come now, how are

incorporeal spirits, such as I am—and we are—supposed to be, supposed to move from one place to another among objects which are supposed to have no real existence 'without the mind'? It seems that for at least part of the time people must be known to be creatures of flesh and blood, moving among other things and other people themselves also known to exist 'in the External World'. A similarly inconsistent, but true, materialist assumption can be seen in the characteristically clear, but false, concluding sentences of *The Foundations of Empirical Knowledge*: 'The most that we can do is to elaborate a technique for predicting the course of our sensory experience, and to adhere to it as long as it is found to be reliable. And this is all that is essentially involved in our belief in the reality of the physical world' (Ayer, p. 274).

(iv) The moral of the last two whole subsections can be summed up in the sharp advice given to Petzolt by Lenin: '. . . you must replace the idealist line of your philosophy (from sensations to the external world) by the materialist line (from the external world to sensations)' (Lenin, 1908, p. 50). The idea of the primacy of the material, which was involved in Lenin's further understanding of the great confrontation between idealism and materialism, can now profitably be enriched by including the notions of the semantic and epistemological priority of the public, which have been outlined in these subsections. It is a proposal carrying the illuminating consequence that both *The Concept of Mind* and the *Philosophical Investigations* have to be recognized as major contributions to the development of a modern materialism—a consequence which is, I confess, appreciably the more agreeable to me because it is so obviously disagreeable to contemporary disciples of Lenin.

(5) *Finishing with Descartes*

In Section 3 we noticed how Lenin thought to dispose of idealism by impetuous appeals to practice, and to what he always insisted on calling not merely a but 'the materialist theory of knowledge'. It is time to examine this supposed absolute weapon. Lenin deploys it in the assurance that 'sensation . . . is regarded by all science which has not been "purified" by the disciples of Berkeley and Hume . . . as an *image of the external world'* (ibid., p. 58: italics original). Again: 'Matter is a philosophical category denoting the objective reality which is given to man by his sensations, and which is copied, photographed and reflected by our sensations, while existing independently of them' (ibid., p. 127: and compare Paul).

(i) The old Cartesian ghost is alive and well in Lenin's new machine of war. Certainly it is in terms of such analogies that working scientists, and in particular the physiologists of perception, are almost irresistibly inclined to think. Here it is to the point to notice that Descartes was, among so many other things, a physiologist; while Locke too, though never becoming in the formal sense medically qualified, underwent much of the training of a doctor. But, equally certainly, these same pictures both characterize and determine The Representative Theory of Perception. That must lead in philosophy to idealism or agnosticism, and solipsism too.

Has it really got to be said again? If all that I ever am or can be immediately aware of is my own private experience—my own sensations, my own ideas, my own Humean ideas and impressions, my own sense-data—then I am in no position to infer that there is an External World; much less that there are other people therein, involved with me in a common cognitive ruin. Nor—if we are always thus supposing that I can never actually inspect any public reality—it is a bit of good to suggest that I (or we!) could learn through action that my (or our!) sense-data are in fact faithful representations, copies, photographs, reflexions, or what have you, of what on that supposition must lie for ever hidden behind the necessarily impenetrable veil of mere appearances.

The truth is that there is in the end no substitute for a complete, consistent, and philosophically sophisticated rejection of the Cartesian starting point; and of the whole framework of which that forms a part. We have to begin by insisting that our own private experience is not the only sure or possible object of awareness. On the contrary: we are in fact all of us throughout all our waking hours able to see, or otherwise perceive, public objects; objects, that is to say, without the mind; objects logically independent of any observation or observer. From there we have to go on to reaffirm that we are indeed, as we always knew, creatures of flesh and blood; and hence that all perception is both by and of objects which are themselves charter members of the public world.

Suppose I hear—as every philosopher must—the siren suggestion that, since my senses do sometimes deceive me, it must be at least conceivable that they are always deceiving; and that the sum of things is perhaps only the private dream— or private nightmare—of one incurably lonely thinking substance. Then I—and we—must give to this seducing siren firm replies: that I—and we—can only know that our senses sometimes deceive us on condition that we also know that this is not always so; that the suggestion of the idealist dream-philosophy could not be understood save on condition that we have sufficient reason to know that it is false; and that, to point out that on any particular occasion I conceivably might have been mistaken, is not even to begin to show that on that particular occasion in fact I am. Much less is it to establish the general and comprehensive conclusion that I never really know. The systematic Cartesian doubter cannot consistently give grounds for, or even express, his wholesale conclusions. In detail his opponent can point to case after case in which people are in a position to know, claim to know, and are in fact correct: they, therefore, actually do know.

(ii) Finally, something direct has to be said about the extraordinarily fascinating model to which Lenin himself remained always in thrall.[34] For it does embrace at least two essential truths about perception. First, if someone is to be said to have (consciously) perceived some object, then they must have had an appropriate experience; and the presence of that object must have been a causally necessary condition for their having that experience. Second, if someone is to be said to have perceived some object, then they must have acquired some information about that object; and its presence must have been a causally necessary condition of that acquisition. To establish that these are indeed both logical truths about perception it is sufficient to consider an imaginary case in which a subject is in the presence of some object effectively blindfolded, and then caused by suitable direct manipulation of the central nervous system to have the experience, and to acquire the information, which he would have had, and acquired, had he been permitted to look at the object without any blindfold. Clearly it would be incorrect, and for the two reasons indicated, to say that our subject had perceived our object.

However, notwithstanding that the representative model does embrace some essential truths about perception, it should not be employed in such a way that its implication is that true perception does not and cannot occur at all. It is in fact so employed whenever those private sensory experiences, which surely are logically necessary conditions of the occurrence of (conscious) perception, are treated as if they were themselves its objects. For it is a third essential truth about perception that its objects are and can only be mind-independent public realities. If I claim to be able to see leprechauns in front of me now, and there are in fact no leprechauns present and visible, then that is by itself sufficient reason for saying that I cannot actually see any. For in this case the most which I can (not truly see, but with a sneer) 'see' are certain mind-dependent expressions of my own delirium, probably tremens. It was, therefore, monstrously misleading: for Berkeley to maintain that the only sensible things are ideas; for Hume to describe his two categories of private experience as perceptions of the mind; and for our own immediate predecessors to label as *sense*-data experience which was in this understanding specifically defined as not necessarily sensory.

So, if we are to continue to employ any of the pictures of The Representative Theory of Perception, we must be quite clear, and make it clear to others, that and why they belong to physiology and not to epistemology. It is all very well, in describing the mechanisms involved in actual seeing, to say that the presence of the visible object causes (not a Cartesian ghost but) the flesh-and-blood subject to have visual experience. But it is the root of all evil in the philosophy of perception, first tacitly to assume that perception does not and cannot in fact occur, and then to proceed to erect or to fail to erect some account of our knowledge of the public world founded not on our perceptions but on my havings of sense-data.

There is, to conclude and to repeat, no substitute for seizing and throughout insisting upon the crucial fundamentals. Although we do in all our (conscious) perceiving have sensory experiences, we do not, because we cannot, perceive private experiences. We are not in fact, nor could we be, confined to the inspection of copies, photographs, reflections, or representations—not even to such as might be certified faithful by either the known goodness of God or our own constant action. We do, and can only, perceive realities which are public, mind-independent, and—in this sense—material. That is, after all, what we ourselves are.

EPILOGUE

I n the Prologue I said that I should in these essays be expounding and defending an Aristotelian as opposed to Platonic-Cartesian view of the nature of man; and that the emphasis throughout would be on the fact that we can, and cannot but, make choices. Having, I think, fulfilled that promise I now conclude with a final illustration to show how relevant such considerations can be to typical contemporary discussions of social policy. This object lesson comes from a work which I happened to receive for review just as I was about to complete the present book. The work is *Equalities and Inequalities in Education*, proceedings of the Eleventh Annual Symposium of the Eugenics Society, held during 1974 in London. The particular contribution which it is here useful to consider is by Jean Floud, who is well regarded both as a social scientist and as a policy adviser.

The title is significant: 'Making Adults more Equal: The Scope and Limitations of Public Educational Policy.' She makes it clear from the beginning that she is one of those—it often seems that they are nowadays a majority among educationalists able to command a hearing[35]—who see educational policy as concerned essentially not with learning and teaching but with (egalitarian) social engineering. Her interest is directed towards equality of outcome rather than equality of opportunity; the latter being an old-fashioned ideal, which must for most of us lose most of its appeal if we are to be assured that whatever opportunities anyone takes or fails to take the outcome is to be made as near as may be the same. Thus, in drawing conclusions from a model provided by J. E. Meade, she says: 'To obtain the maximum equalizing effect from a given amount of public educational resources, the distribution must be not only independent of, but negatively related to, the distribution of inherited inequalities of fortune, *including genetic make-up*' (Floud, p. 50: italics supplied). She is also, though she has a forceful point to make about one methodological limitation, clearly happy with what she sees as an implication of the Jencks work: 'we must see to it . . . that the link between vocational success and living standards is effectively broken' (ibid., p. 38: and compare pp. 40–3).

In pursuit of this surely ruinous ideal she introduces the expression 'life-chances'. It has in fact become a cliché among the new egalitarian 'clerisy of power' (Nisbet, 1976). She defines it in terms of 'people's economic and social opportunities' (Floud, p. 37). But then, like so many others, she proceeds forthwith to identify differences of educational opportunity with differences in achieved education, and life-chances with actual lives. For what she is talking about is correlations reported by Jencks between achieved education and achieved income. Yet she calls differences in the former differences in educational opportunity, while differences in the latter are correspondingly equated with differences in life-chances: '. . . differences of educational opportunity do not explain much of the variation in individual incomes. Measures of the independent influence of educational opportunity on people's life-chance give different results . . .' (ibid., p. 41).

There is no need to add more here to what has already been said about the general temptations which may seduce both professional social scientists and ordinarily self-indulgent lay people to ignore, or even to deny, the realities of choice. But it is worth noticing a special attraction of the particular confusion between life-chances and actual lives. The fact is that, whether for better or for worse, equality of opportunity has a much wider appeal than equality of outcome. So, if you really want to equalize not life-chances but lives, you will find the going easier if, when you should be speaking of actual lives, you choose instead to discuss, with a suggestion of sociological expertise, life-chances.

The Aristotelian thesis that we are essentially corporeal is equally relevant. For who—in Floud's 'distribution of inherited inequalities of fortune, *including genetic make-up*'—is supposed to inherit a total genetic constitution? Certainly my genetic constitution is not something which I have earned. But neither is it an inheritance, nor a windfall which I have been so fortunate or unfortunate as to (have to) pick up. It is, rather, something which is itself essential to what I am.

Of course, I can suppose that my genes had been in some

modest way different; just as I can suppose that I had been born on a slightly different date, or raised in a different way. But any drastic supposition in either direction ceases by that token to be a supposition about me. For I just am the person who was born to such and such parents, with such and such a constitution, and so on. Although I can understand what it is like to be a very different person, very differently circumstanced, I cannot by that token understand a suggestion that I might myself either be or become a person born at a different time, and in another country, and to other parents. It is rather like the case, which I have argued elsewhere, where, although I can imagine what it will be like to witness my own funeral, I cannot imagine what it would be like for me to witness my own funeral (Flew, 1976a, IX).

The relevance of all this to Jean Floud and her craving to equalize can, and must, be put very briefly. Whatever may or may not be true of that new fangled party political shuttlecock social justice, traditional without-prefix-or-suffix justice is a matter of people getting and keeping, and allowing or helping others to get and to keep, their various and often different deserts and entitlements: 'Suum cuique tribuere'; which, being translated, is 'To each their due'. What is thus due is frequently disputatious. But certainly it must always depend at last in part upon the peculiarities of the individual. People are entitled to, though they have not earned and may not even need, parts of their own bodies: where half the people are born with two eyes and half with none it is charity not justice which requires that the two-eyed make one of their eyes available for transplant. They have claims on me because they are my daughters, claims which no one else has. Something is owing to her because she has served well; and something different is due to him, because he has deserved ill. And so on.

The upshot is that justice is essentially concerned with certain human particularities; and that it is, in a way, an essentially backward-looking notion. Equality of outcome, on the other hand, attends to particularities only in order to abolish or to neutralize offensive occasions of social inequality; and it is, in a corresponding way, an essentially forward-looking ideal. It is, therefore, egregiously mistaken, although nowadays almost universal, to identify these two incompatible objectives; and to speak as if 'equality' and 'justice', or at any rate 'social justice', were as near as makes little or no matter synonymous.

We have here the beginnings perhaps of another book. So let this one end with the suggestion that egalitarians of outcome should, albeit at the cost of sacrificing a powerful propaganda advantage, present their profoundly authoritarian, illiberal and bureaucratic ideal as, what it truly is, a rival to what they should see as the reactionary, backward-looking, anomalous, gothic notion of justice. This after all is exactly how, in the special and particular sphere of the criminal, some forward-looking and scientifically oriented reformers do put their proposals. Thus Dr. Karl Menninger, for a long time the chief spokesman of American orthopsychiatry, wrote in a book characteristically entitled *The Crime of Punishment*: 'The very word "justice" irritates scientists. No surgeon expects to be asked whether an operation for cancer is just or not. No doctor will be reproached on the grounds that the dose of penicillin he has prescribed is less or more than justice would stipulate. Behavioural scientists regard it as equally absurd to invoke the question of justice . . . This sort of behaviour has to be controlled; it has to be discouraged; it has to be stopped. This (to the scientist) is a matter of public safety and amicable coexistence, not of justice' (Menninger, p. 17).

NOTES

1 It is curious that in his Plutarchian comparison between Locke and Darwin, Sir Arthur Keith altogether failed to notice this most important continuity (Keith, *passim*). As an example of philosophical work in scientific theorizing Darwin's analysis and reinterpretation of the concepts of species, variety, and genus might be compared with Albert Einstein on motion and simultaneity in relativity theory. In both cases the analysis is required by the theory. In both cases it had been to a greater or lesser extent anticipated by a philosopher before it was reworked and put to use by a scientist. But whereas Darwin seems never to have read Locke, Einstein certainly did read Ernst Mach; and acknowledged indebtedness to him. Notice, by the way, that after Locke chemists did discover natural kinds in their bailiwick.

2 In the Cambridge of my boyhood people used to quote the arrogant, exhilarating, but erroneous words of Lord Rutherford: 'In science there is only physics—and stamp collecting!'

3 In the *Autobiography* we read that at Cambridge in Darwin's day it was 'necessary to get up Paley's *Evidences of Christianity* . . . This was done in a thorough manner . . . The logic of this book and as I may add of his *Natural Theology* gave me as much delight as did Euclid' (Darwin, 1887, p. 59).

4 John Searle does appear to misconstrue Hume to be saying this, thus completely missing the irony of that now so often quoted paragraph (Searle; and compare Hume, 1739-40, III(i) 1, pp. 469-70).

5 Yet John Passmore retells a tale of hair-raising callousness: 'One of the brethren, taken ill, told Francis' disciple Jonathan that he had a longing for pigs' trotters. "In great fervour of spirit", Jonathan cut the trotters off a living pig. Francis . . . urged him, only, to apologize to the owner of the pig for having damaged his property' (Passmore, p. 112).

6 And some baseless gossip also: 'it is intriguing to discover that certain individuals with a demonstrably vast lust for power suffered from physical sexual abnormalities. The autopsy on Hitler, for instance, revealed that he had only one testicle' (Morris, 1970, p. 118). Maybe Adolf Hitler did share this deficiency with the legendary Henry Hall. But, if he did, this fact was not revealed by the autopsy. The bodies of Hitler and Eva Braun were burnt immediately after their suicides (Trevor-Roper, VII).

7 I owe this point to the second of Julian Huxley's *Essays of a Biologist*, a collection which should be read again before anyone thinks of opening *The Naked Ape* or *The Human Zoo*.

8 I well remember how in his regular Oxford lectures on the history of political thought, which I heard in 1946, G. D. H. Cole saw nothing here save an object for mockery. His socialist commitments, commitments which most of his hearers at that time shared, blinded us all. Had Cole continued the quotation with two later sentences we should still not have appreciated then what is now the aptest application of the second. Smith goes on: 'By pursuing

his own interest he frequently promotes that of the society more effectually than when he really intends to promote it. I have never known much good done by those who affected to trade for the public good.'

The not unmixed benefits of the division of labour are, Smith contends, again unintended consequences of intended action: 'This division of labour, from which so many advantages are derived, is not originally the effect of any human wisdom, which foresees and intends that general opulence to which it gives occasion. It is the necessary, though very slow and gradual consequence of a certain propensity in human nature which has in view no such extensive utility; the propensity to truck, barter, and exchange one thing for another' (A. Smith, 1776, I(iii), Vol. I, p. 12).

9 Darwin's reference to what he prefers to call 'prudential restraint', in the passage quoted at the end of Section 1 above, suggests that he read the *Second Essay*. Ruse, 1973b, Note 5 asserts, no doubt truly, that he 'read the 6th edition which appeared in 1826; but Ruse here provides no evidence for this assertion.

10 See his 'Mathematical Dissertation', in Godwin, 1820.

11 For reference to some recent calculations showing the enormous returns in poverty reduction offered by investment in birth control programmes, see Flew, 1970, p. 42. But be warned that to use your brains in this way is to invite the charge of heartlessness: you will surely be denounced as a public enemy by most of the loudest voices in both the Third World First and the domestic poverty lobbies.

12 The points made in the last three paragraphs of Section 1(ii) are more fully developed and defended in Flew, 1961, VI. The inadequacies of Hume's account are related, I think usefully, to the question 'Could an Effect Precede its Cause?' in my fiercely youthful contribution to the symposium under that title in the *Proceedings of the Aristotelian Society* Supp. Vol. XXVIII (1954).

13 Monsignor Ronald Knox in his 'Studies in the Literature of Sherlock Holmes', picked out a special form of epigram, the Sherlockismus. A typical example would be such exchange as: Holmes—'Let me call your attention to the curious incident of the dog in the night-time'; Watson—'The dog did nothing at all in the night-time'; Holmes—'That was the curious incident'. Or again: Holmes—'I was following you, of course'; Watson—'Following me? I saw nobody'; Holmes—'That is what you must expect to see when I am following you' (Knox, pp. 145 and 175).

14 For some development of this constantly confounded distinction between prescriptive and descriptive senses of 'expect', see Flew, 1975, §§5.9 and 6.11.

15 The unfamiliarity of this description of corporations which were set up and are now maintained primarily if not only in order to obtain a monopoly price for (some sort of) labour provides one indication of how far the British climate of opinion is shaped by uncritical and uncriticized Labour reflexes. Compare and contrast the way in which large private firms are as such constantly miscalled monopolies. It seems indeed that no Labour Party conference is complete without much applauded speeches urging this or that industry 'should be taken into public ownership'—made, that is to say (although this is never said), a state monopoly—on the self-contradictory

ground that it is dominated by three, or four, or whatever, big monopolies.

It is sad to find such a doctrinally motivated, strictly mendacious misuse of the word 'monopoly' even in George Orwell, who was usually so sensitive to and scrupulous to avoid all ideological and other corruptions of language. Thus, in 1945 he wrote: 'A few of the big monopolies, such as I.C.I. . . . are Jewish-owned or partly Jewish-owned' (Orwell, Vol. II, p. 378). But though I.C.I. may have had exclusive patent control over some products and processes there were of course then as now other firms in the chemical industry, and there was some competition from imports.

16 The passage just quoted in the text, and others, seem to me to make it quite clear that in this section of the first *Inquiry* Hume did hold such a 'unity of science' thesis. But Donald Livingston has recently drawn our attention to passages in the *Early Memoranda* of 1729–40 and in the essay 'Of Some Remarkable Customs', first published in 1752, four years after the first *Inquiry*, in which Hume at least suggests a different, better and incompatible view (Livingston, especially IV). Perhaps Hume, like Hempel and so many others, came to his official view because he thought that this was how things must be; and then, when he was thinking as a historian, quasi veritate coactus, said different things without noticing the inconsistency.

17 This is the first sense distinguished in Chapter XI of R. G. Collingwood's *An Essay on Metaphysics*. An earlier and in some ways better version is to be found in his paper 'On the So-called Idea of Causation' (Collingwood, 1940, and 1938).

18 It is most unfortunate, and should be remarked, that in *The Poverty of Historicism* Popper's official definition of 'historicism' buries its one glancing reference to what is for him the essential scandal under irrelevant and confusing mentions of other less noxious notions. His real enemy—and the Public Enemy—is unmasked in the Dedication: 'In memory of the countless men and women . . . who fell victim to the fascist and communist belief in Inexorable Laws of Historical Destiny' (Popper, 1957, pp. 3 and v). It will be obvious from the text that I believe that Popper should have attacked not only this notion but the whole idea of any natural laws of human action, as such.

19 No one, and least of all so eminent an authority as E. H. Carr, has any business to speak in this sort of context of the February Revolution and the Bolshevik coup in October as both together 'the Russian revolution of 1917' (Carr, p. 91). There are already too many ignorant and infatuated Radicals speaking of that coup as if it had been what the February Revolution was, without our leading Soviet historian giving them encouragement. It cannot be too often emphasized that the weak and too often ruinously tolerant government which the Bolsheviks overthrew was actively preparing free elections for the long longed-for Constituent Assembly, and was presided over by a man who would in our contemporary understanding of that term rate as a social-democrat. Nothing like this could truly be said of the Chiang Kai-shek régime, driven off the mainland by the Chinese Communists.

20 Not for the first nor the last time it has to be said that no one has any business to plunge into print with a discussion of philosophical questions about freewill unless they have subjected themselves to the propaedeutic of

some catholic course of classical reading. One good but still entirely manageable programme would be to read both Schopenhauer's prize *Essay on the Freedom of the Will* and the relevant portions of all the earlier works mentioned therein.

21 Anyone who infers that I myself want to minimize the importance of this special case, or to deny its possible relevance to the contemporary secular discussion, may be referred to Flew, 1973, Part III and Flew, 1976a, VII.

22 Although everyone has always attributed this conclusion to Descartes, and although it certainly does follow from positions to which he was most clearly and categorically committed, I cannot put my hand on any passage in which he himself actually states, beyond all possibility of alternative interpretation, that the brutes are in fact insensible; that, scandalously, none of them are in any way any more conscious than are sticks or stones.

Thus, and typically, in a letter to Henry More (23 November 1646) Descartes argues against the 'prejudice . . . that dumb animals think'; and, since his official definition of 'thought' apparently includes all and only modes of consciousness, this at first appears decisive. Yet in the penultimate paragraph of that letter he warns: 'Please note that I am speaking of thought, and not of life or sensation. I do not deny life to animals . . . and I do not deny sensation, in so far as it depends on a bodily organ' (Kenny, pp. 243 and 245). It is at least not unequivocally certain that 'sensation' has here to be construed in a metaphysically behaviourist sense. Perhaps Descartes never actually faced and answered the question of whether—say—a throbbing pain in a dog's foot would not be something of which the dog is sensible even though the dog's consciousness might never involve that full-blooded, articulate self-awareness which is for Descartes the preferred paradigm case of cogitatio.

23 I have seen some discussion of this sort of proposition by philosophers, but none of this has been in the mainstream professional journals: I mention for instance, G. E. M. Anscombe's 'A Reply to Mr. C. S. Lewis' Argument that "Naturalism" is Self-Refuting', in *Socratic Digest IV* (Oxford: Blackwell, 1949); Margaret Knight, 'Consciousness and the Brain', in *Science News 25* (Harmondsworth: Penguin, 1952); and Antony Flew, Ernest Gellner, and Antony Flew again, on 'The Third Maxim', 'Determinism and Validity', and 'Determinism and Validity Again' in the *Rationalist Annuals* for 1954, 1957, and 1958, respectively (London: C. A. Watts, 1954, 1957, and 1958, ditto).

My references to the Lewis book mentioned in the text are to the first paperback edition not to the original hardcover (London: Bles, 1948). In the paperback the third chapter, which is devoted to the present argument, has been largely rewritten in an attempt to meet the criticisms which Miss Anscombe deployed in the article mentioned in the previous paragraph. Neither the author nor his publisher provides any indication either that these substantial changes have been made, or why.

The retraction by J. B. S. Haldane is to be found in the *Literary Guide* (predecessor to *New Humanist*) for April 1954.

24 Compare the similar, and similarly unfortunate, concentration on such manipulation cases in his 'Determinism' in *Mind* for 1957: criticized in

Discussion Notes by both Antony Flew and M. C. Bradley in *Mind* for 1960.

25 Compare Bertrand Russell in 1921: 'A desire is "conscious" when we have told ourselves that we have it . . . it only differs from an "unconscious" desire by the presence of appropriate words, which is by no means a fundamental difference' (p. 31).

26 See, for instance, Andrei Vyshinsky's final speech in 'the trial of the bloc of Rights and Trotskyists', a speech delivered on 1 March 1938: 'In our country, rich in resources of all kinds, there should not have been and cannot be a situation in which a shortage of any product should exist . . . It is now clear why there are interruptions of supplies here and there, why, with our riches and abundance of products, there is a shortage first of one thing, then of another. It is these traitors who are responsible for it' (Quoted in Conquest, 1968, p. 418).

27 In the latter case the inclination is further strengthened by the fact that any professional expertise of the analysts derives almost exclusively from study of neurotic patients in a therapeutic situation.

Incidentally: experience teaches that observations of this sort, even with all overtones removed, often give offence both to professional analysts and to lay spokesmen for the enterprise. Yet it must be, to put it no higher, imprudent for friends of the profession to suggest that it is engaged in giving expensive and time-consuming therapy to patients who in fact enjoy rude mental health. Nor will it do, notwithstanding that it is all too often done, to begin to play the popular metaphysician by suggesting that *really* every one of us is a neurotic. For then the substance of the original observation re-emerges as the point that analytic patients are, presumably, egregiously neurotic. As John Wisdom used to say: 'When the metaphysician says that everything is really so-and-so, what he really means is that it is not; not *really.*'

The whole business may be instructively compared with the reluctance of many psychiatrists, and many enthusiastic lay spokesmen for orthopsychiatry, 'to accept the medical model' of mental disease. For if patients diagnosed as mentally diseased are not in fact suffering from conditions in crucial respects analogous to those of physical disease, how can their psychiatrists pretend to be practising as doctors, and upon what bases are they enjoying the high status and emoluments traditionally and quite rightly awarded to genuine healers (Flew, 1973, *passim*)?

28 Tibor Szamuely in 'The Birth of Russian Marxism' (*Survey* for Summer 1972) quotes the response of a Russian Populist to his first reading of *Capital*: 'The knowledge that we feeble individuals were backed by a mighty historical process filled one with ecstasy and established such a firm foundation for the individual's activities that, it seemed, all the hardships of this struggle would be overcome' (p. 69).

29 For a choice collection of such orthopsychiatric statements see, again, Flew, 1973, *passim.*

30 I welcome on these issues the strong and entirely independent support of Winston Nesbitt and Stewart Cavendish. When they completed their 'On not being able to do otherwise' for publication in *Mind* for 1973 they had certainly not seen any of my papers in this area: the materials recycled in Chapter Nine were not collected from any of the regular philosophers' trade journals.

31 Recently some of today's philosophical Radicals—persons of a Leninist rather than a Benthamite allegiance—seem to have been exploiting the same confusion in the reverse direction: arguments, and often mere abuse, calculated to dispose of empiricism in the private interpretation have been mis-taken to disembarrass these ideologues of the new absolutism of the uncomfortable requirement to expose their own cherished theories to the harsh test of brute and public fact. See, for instance, Flew, 1976d, and 1976e.

32 Lenin's too short way with idealist dissent is reminiscent of an oft-told tale of the incomparable doctor. Boswell writes: 'After we came out of the church, we stood talking for some time together of Bishop Berkeley's ingenious sophistry to prove the non-existence of matter, and that everything in the universe is merely ideal. I observed, that though we are satisfied his doctrine is not true, it is impossible to refute it. I shall never forget the alacrity with which Johnson answered, striking his foot with mighty force against a large stone, till he rebounded from it, "I refute it *thus*"' (Boswell for 6/VIII/1763: italics original).

33 Those concerned to develop a neo-Wittgensteinian account of the fundamentally and essentially social character of all knowledge must, however, be careful—much more careful than they usually are—to provide for the possibility that someone in a minority of one may be in fact, and can surely also know that he is, right. When G. E. M. Anscombe first published her account of time I faulted it for giving unwitting aid and comfort to Ingsoc's Ministry of Truth (Anscombe, and compare my review in the *Philosophical Quarterly* for 1953). Similar comment needs to be made on such works as David Bloor's *Knowledge and Social Imagery*. In a word: remember Winston Smith and *1984*!

It is one of the shining merits of *The Theory of Moral Sentiments* that Adam Smith confronts head on a parallel problem of deriving the possibility and possible legitimacy of individual dissent from social attitudes. Of conscience he writes: '. . . if we inquire into the origin of its institution, its jurisdiction, we shall find, is in a great measure derived from the authority of that very tribunal, whose decisions it so often and so justly reverses.' (Quoted in Raphael, p. 91: I give the reference thus deviously as my thanks to Raphael for there directing me to Smith's other masterpiece.)

34 The leading 'Old Left' (i.e. frankly Muscovite) Marxist philosopher wrote: 'The ghost of the "sense-datum" has been haunting philosophy for a long time. Of course it never troubled Marxists. But the others are to be congratulated that, after the linguistic criticism, this ghost has been laid' (Cornforth, 1965, p. 150). Since, as we have seen, and as was further shown by Paul, Lenin in fact never succeeded in extricating himself from such Cartesian toils, this Marxist freedom from care appears to be purchased at the discreditable price of either incomprehension or frivolity. Were Cornforth not so committed to the totalitarian Stalinist principle that philosophical innovations are acceptable only when made by the approved political leaders, he could more generously have hailed such 'linguistic criticism' as what it is—a major contribution to solving problems of materialist philosophy.

35 Compare for instance Tyrrell Burgess, who writes in his Preface to the

British edition of *Inequality*: 'To almost any proposal for education we can now ask "did it survive the Jencks test?" And, if not, we can further ask: "What explicit steps are proposed to fend off failure this time?" . . . A clue to the way we ought to do this can be found in the experience of the schools. Their failure as engines of social change . . .' (Jencks, pp. 1 and 2).

BIBLIOGRAPHY

This is intended to cover all, but only, the works to which reference is
made in the text, the over-all aim being to produce an adequately full
and precise but economical and unobtrusive system of reference.

ANSCOMBE, G. E. M. 'The Reality of the Past', in M. Black (ed.),
  Philosophical Analysis (Ithaca, N.Y.: Cornell University Press,
  1950), pp. 38–59.
AQUINAS, ST. T. *Summa Theologica*, translated by the Fathers of the
  English Dominican Province (London: Burns Oates and Wash-
  bourne, 1920).
AUSTIN, J. L. *Philosophical Papers* (Oxford: Clarendon Press, 1961).
AYER, A. J. *The Foundations of Empirical Knowledge* (London:
  Macmillan, 1940).
BAIER, K. 'Action and Agent', in *The Monist* for 1965, pp. 183–95.
BELOFF, N. *Freedom under Foot: The Closed Shop in British Journalism*
  (London: Temple Smith, 1976).
BERG, C. (1944) *War in the Mind* (London: Macaulay, 2nd edition
  1944).
—— (1946) *Deep Analysis* (London: Allen and Unwin, 1946).
BERKELEY, G. *A Treatise concerning the Principles of Human Knowledge*,
  in *The Works of George Berkeley Bishop of Cloyne*, Vol. II, edited by
  T. E. Jessop (Edinburgh: Nelson, 1949).
BLACK, M. 'Making Something Happen', in S. Hook (ed.), *Deter-
  minism and Freedom* (New York: New York U.P., 1958), pp. 15–30.
BLOOR, D. *Knowledge and Social Imagery* (London: Routledge and
  Kegan Paul, 1976).
BOHR, N. 'On the Notions of Causality and Complementarity', in
  Dialectica for 1948.
BORGES, J. L. *Antologia Personal* (Buenos Aires: Sur, 2nd edition
  1966).
BORST, C. V. *The Mind/Brain Identity Theory*, edited by C. V. Borst
  (London and New York: Macmillan, and St. Martin's Press,
  1970).
BOSWELL, J. *Boswell's Life of Johnson*, edited by G. B. Hall and
  further edited by L. F. Powell (Oxford: Clarendon Press, 1934).
BRILL, A. A. *Psychoanalytic Psychiatry* (New York: Lehmann, 1948).
BROMBERG, W. *Crime and the Mind* (London and New York:
  Macmillan, and Collier-Macmillan, 1965).

BUCKLE, H. T. *History of Civilization in England* (London and New York: Longmans, Green, 1903).

CARMICHAEL, J. 'German Money and Bolshevik Honour', in *Encounter* for March 1974, pp. 81–90.

CARR, E. H. *What is History?* (London: Macmillan, 1961).

CARROLL, Lewis *Through the Looking Glass*; illustrated by John Tenniel (Harmondsworth: Penguin, 1948).

CHAMBERS, R. *Vestiges of the Natural History of Creation* (London and Edinburgh: W. and R. Chambers, 12th edition 1884).

CHANDLER, R. *Trouble is my Business* (Harmondsworth: Penguin, no date given).

CIOFFI, F. (1970) 'Freud and the Idea of a Pseudo-science', in R. Broger and F. Cioffi (eds.), *Explanation and the Behavioural Sciences* (Cambridge: Cambridge U.P., 1970).

—— (1972) 'Wollheim on Freud', in *Inquiry* for 1972 (Vol. XV), pp. 171–86.

—— (ed.) (1973) *Freud* (London: Macmillan, 1973).

COLLINGWOOD, R. G. (1938) 'On the So-called Idea of Causation', in the *Proceedings of the Aristotelian Society* for 1937–8, pp. 85–112.

—— (1940) *An Essay on Metaphysics* (Oxford: Clarendon Press, 1940).

CONQUEST, R. (1968) *The Great Terror* (London: Macmillan, 1968).

—— (1972) *Lenin* (London: Collins Fontana, 1972).

CORNFORTH, M. (1946) *Science versus Idealism* (London: Lawrence and Wishart, 1946).

—— (1965) *Marxism and the Linguistic Philosophy* (London: Lawrence and Wishart, 1965).

COTTINGHAM, J. 'A Brute to Brutes? Descartes' Treatment of Animals', in *Philosophy*, forthcoming.

DARWIN, C. (1859) *The Origin of Species*, edited by J. W. Burrow (Harmondsworth and Baltimore: Penguin, 1968). Page references are to this, as perhaps the most widely available version. It reprints the text of the first edition of 1858.

—— (1871) *The Descent of Man* (London: Murray, 1871).

—— (1887) *The Autobiography of Charles Darwin*, edited by Nora Barlow (London: Collins, 1950). It is important to employ this first complete edition, since both the original printing of 1887 and later reprints from this omit material which Darwin's widow and others close to him thought it better to suppress.

DARWIN, F. and SEWARD, A. C. *More Letters of Charles Darwin* (London: Murray, 1903).

DESCARTES, R. (1637) *A Discourse on the Method*, in *The Philosophical Works of Descartes*, translated by E. S. Haldane and G. R. T. Ross (Cambridge: Cambridge U.P., 1931).

—— (1644) *Principles of Philosophy*, in *The Philosophical Works of*

Descartes, translated by E. S. Haldane and G. R. T. Ross (Cambridge: Cambridge U.P., 1931).

DEUTSCHER, I. *Stalin: A Political Biography* (London: Oxford U.P., paperback edition, 1961).

DENZINGER, H. (ed.) *Enchiridion Symbolorum* (Freiburg-im-Breisgau: Herder, 29th revised edition, 1953).

DODDS, E. R. 'Why I do not believe in Survival', in *Proceedings of the Society for Psychical Research* (London), Vol. XLII (1934), pp. 147–72.

DODWELL, P. C. 'Causes of Behaviour and Explanation in Psychology', in *Mind* for 1960, pp. 1–13.

DONAGAN, A. (1964) 'Historical Explanation: The Popper Hempel Theory Reconsidered', in *History and Theory*, for 1964, pp. 3–26.

ECCLES, J. C. 'Hypotheses Relating to the Brain-Mind Problem', in *Nature* for 1951, pp. 53–6.

EDWARDS, P. and PAP, A. (ed.) *A Modern Introduction to Philosophy* (New York: Collier-Macmillan, Second Edition, 1965).

EYSENCK, H. J. *Uses and Abuses of Psychology* (Harmondsworth and Baltimore: Penguin, 1953).

FLEW, A. G. N. (1953a) (ed.) *Logic and Language* (Oxford: Blackwell, second series, 1953).

—— (1953b) 'The Question of Survival', in *A New Approach to Psychical Research* (London: C. A. Watts, 1953), and (revised) in T. Penelhum (ed.), *Immortality* (Belmont, Calif.: Wadsworth, 1973).

—— (1954) 'Can an Effect Precede its Cause?', in *Proceedings of the Aristotelian Society* Supp. Vol. XXVIII (1954), pp. 45–62.

—— (1961) *Hume's Philosophy of Belief* (London, and New York: Routledge and Kegan Paul, and Humanities Press, 1961).

—— (1964) *Body, Mind and Death*, edited by Antony Flew (New York and London: Collier-Macmillan, 1964).

—— (1966a) *God and Philosophy* (London and New York: Hutchinson, and Harcourt, Brace, and World, 1966).

—— (1966b) 'Again the Paradigm', in P. Feyerabend and G. Maxwell (eds.), *Mind, Matter and Method* (Minneapolis: Minnesota U.P., 1966), pp. 261–72.

—— (1967) *Evolutionary Ethics* (London, and New York: Macmillan, and St. Martin's Press, 1967). This monograph has since been republished, along with others in the same series, as Volume Two of W. D. Hudson (ed.), *New Studies in Ethics* (London: Macmillan, 1974).

—— (1970) Introduction and Notes to Antony Flew (ed.), *Malthus: An Essay on the Principle of Population* (Harmondsworth and Baltimore: Penguin, 1970)

—— (1971) *An Introduction to Western Philosophy* (London and Indianapolis: Thames and Hudson, and Bobbs-Merrill, 1971).

—— (1973) *Crime or Disease?* (London and New York: Macmillan, and Barnes and Noble, 1973).

—— (1975) *Thinking about Thinking* (London: Collins Fontana, 1975).

—— (1976a) *The Presumption of Atheism* (London and New York: Pemberton/Elek, and Barnes and Noble, 1976).

—— (1976b) *Sociology, Equality and Education* (London and New York: Macmillan, and Barnes and Noble, 1976).

—— (1976c) 'Three Questions about Justice in Hume's *Treatise*', in the *Philosophical Quarterly* for 1976, pp. 1–13.

—— (1976d) 'Ideology and "a New Machine of War"', in *Philosophy* for 1976, pp. 447–53.

—— (1976e) Review of M. Hollis and E. Nell, *Rational Economic Man*, in *Philosophical Books* for 1976.

FLOUD, J. 'Making Adults More Equal: The Scope and Limitations of Public Educational Policy', in P. R. Cox, H. B. Miles, and J. Peel (eds.), *Equalities and Inequalities in Education* (London: Academic Press, 1975), pp. 37–51.

FREUD, S. (1901) *The Psychopathology of Everyday Life*, translated by A. Tyson (London: Hogarth, 1960).

—— (1910) *Leonardo*, translated by Alan Tyson (Harmondsworth: Penguin, 1963).

—— (1919) *Totem and Taboo*, translated by A. A. Brill (Harmondsworth: Penguin, 1938).

—— (1921) 'Psycho-analysis and Telepathy', in *The Complete Psychological Works of Sigmund Freud*, under the general editorship of James Strachey, Vol. XVIII, pp. 177–93 (London: Hogarth, 1955).

—— (1928) *The Future of an Illusion*, translated by W. D. Robson-Scott (London: Hogarth, 1928).

—— (1933a) *Introductory Lectures on Psycho-analysis*, translated by Joan Rivière (London: Allen and Unwin, 2nd edition 1933).

—— (1933b) *New Introductory Lectures on Psycho-analysis* (London: Hogarth, 1933).

—— (1939) *Moses and Monotheism*, translated by Katherine Jones (London: Hogarth, 1939).

—— (1948–50) *Collected Papers*, translated by Joan Rivière and others (London: Hogarth and the Institute for Psycho-Analysis, 1948–50).

GILLISPIE, C. C. *Genesis and Geology* (Cambridge, Mass.: Harvard U.P., 1951).

GODWIN, W. *Of Population* (London: 1820).

HALDANE, J. B. S. *Possible Worlds* (London: Chatto and Windus, 1927).

HAMLYN, D. W. 'Behaviour', in V. C. Chappell (ed.), *The Philosophy of Mind* (Englewood Cliffs, N.J.: Prentice-Hall, 1962).

HANNAFORD, R. V. 'Who's in Control Here?', in *Philosophy* for 1976, pp. 421–30.

HAYEK, F. A. (1944) *The Road to Serfdom* (London: Routledge and Kegan Paul, 1944).

—— (1967) 'The Results of Human Action but not of Human Design', in his *Studies in Philosophy, Politics and Economics* (London: Routledge and Kegan Paul, 1967).

HEMPEL, C. G. (1947) 'The Function of General Laws in History', in P. Gardiner (ed.), *Theories of History* (Glencoe, Ill., and London: Free Press, and Allen and Unwin, 1959).

HIMMELFARB, G. *Darwin and the Darwinian Revolution* (London: Chatto and Windus, 1959).

HOBBES, T. (1642) *De Cive, or The Citizen*, edited by S. P. Lamprecht (New York: Appleton-Century-Crofts, 1949).

—— (1651) *Leviathan*, edited by C. B. MacPherson (Harmondsworth and Baltimore: Penguin, 1968).

HOOK, S. *The Hero in History* (New York: John Day, 1963).

HOSPERS, J. and SELLARS, W. (eds.) *Readings in Ethical Theory* (New York: Appleton-Century-Crofts, 2nd edition, 1970).

HUME, D. (1739–40) *A Treatise of Human Nature*, edited by L. A. Selby-Bigge (Oxford: Clarendon Press, 1896).

—— (1748) *An Inquiry concerning Human Understanding*, edited by C. W. Hendel (New York: Liberal Arts, 1955).

—— (1779) *Dialogues concerning Natural Religion*, edited by N. K. Smith (Edinburgh: Nelson, 1947).

HUXLEY, A. *Brave New World* (London: Chatto and Windus, 1931).

HUXLEY, J. (1923) *Essays of a Biologist* (Harmondsworth: Penguin, 1939).

—— (1953) *The Process of Evolution* (London: Chatto and Windus, 1953).

JEANS, J. *Science and Music* (Cambridge: Cambridge U.P., 1937).

JENCKS, C. and others *Inequality* (London: Allen Lane, 1973).

JONES, E. (1920) *Papers on Psychoanalysis* (London: Baillière, Tindall and Cox, 1920).

—— (1924) 'Free Will and Determinism', in his *Essays in Applied Psychoanalysis* (New York: International Universities Press, 1924).

—— (1953–7) *The Life and Work of Sigmund Freud* (New York: Basic, 1953–7).

—— (1956) 'The Achievement of Sigmund Freud', in *The Listener* for 1956 (Vol. LV, No. 1415).

—— (1959) *Free Associations* (London: Hogarth, 1959).

KANT, I. *Prolegomena to any Future Metaphysics*, translated and edited by P. G. Lucas (Manchester: Manchester U.P., 1953).

KEITH, A. 'Darwin's Place among Philosophers', in *The Rationalist Animal 1955* (London: C. A. Watts, 1955).

KENNY, A. *Descartes' Philosophical Letters* (Oxford: Clarendon Press, 1970).

KIRK, G. S. and RAVEN, J. E. *The Pre-Socratic Philosophers* (Cambridge: Cambridge U.P., 1957).

KNOX, R. A. *Essays in Satire* (London: Sheed and Ward, 1928).

KOESTLER, A. *Arrival and Departure* (London: Cape, 1943).

KUHN, T. *The Structure of Scientific Revolutions* (Chicago: Chicago U.P., 1962).

LENIN, V. I. (1908) *Materialism and Empirio-Criticism*, no editor or translator named (Moscow: Foreign Languages Publishing House, 1952). This is Vol. XIV of the *Collected Works*.

—— (1914–15) *Philosophical Notebooks*, translated by Clemens Dutt and edited by Stewart Smith (Moscow: Foreign Languages Publishing House, 1961). This is Vol. XXXVIII of the *Collected Works*.

LEWIS, C. S. *Miracles* (London: Collins Fontana, 1960).

LIVINGSTON, D. 'Hume and the Problem of Historical and Scientific Explanation', in *The New Scholasticism* for 1973, pp. 38–67.

LOCKE, John (1690) *An Essay concerning Human Understanding* edited by P. H. Nidditch (Oxford: Clarendon Press, 1975).

LOVEJOY, A. O. (1904) 'Some Eighteenth Century Evolutionists', in *Popular Science Monthly* (New York) for 1904 (Vol. LXV), pp. 238–51 and 323–40.

—— (1936) *The Great Chain of Being* (New York: Harper, 1960).

LUCAS, J. (1970) *The Freedom of the Will* (Oxford: Clarendon Press, 1970).

LUCRETIUS, T. *de Rerum Natura*, translated by W. H. D. Rouse (Loeb Classical Library: London and Cambridge, Mass.: Heinemann, and Harvard U.P., 1947).

LYELL, C. *Principles of Geology* (London: John Murray, 1830–3).

MACCORQUODALE, K. and MEEHL, P. 'On a Distinction between Hypothetical Constructs and Intervening Variables', in the *Psychological Review* for 1948, pp. 95–107.

MACINTYRE, A. C. (1960) 'Commitment and Objectivity', in *The Sociological Review Monograph No. 3: Moral Issues in the Training of Teachers and Social Workers* (Keele, Staffordshire, 1960).

McKELLAR, T. P. *A Textbook of Human Psychology* (London: Cohen and West, 1952).

MALTHUS, T. R. (1798) *An Essay on the Principle of Population*,

edited by J. Bonar (London: Macmillan, 1926). This is a facsimile
edition. I cannot pretend that the editorial material in Flew 1970
is not fuller and better.
—— (1803) *An Essay on the Principle of Population* (London: 6th
edition, 1826). This *Second Essay* is today most widely available in
the Everyman Library edition by M. P. Fogarty.
—— (1830) *A Summary View of the Principle of Population*, reprinted
in D. V. Glass, *An Introduction to Malthus* (London: C. A. Watts,
1953).
MANSER, A. R. 'The Concept of Evolution', in *Philosophy* for 1965,
pp. 18–34.
MARCHANT, J. *Alfred Russel Wallace: Letters and Reminiscences* (New
York and London: Harper and Bros., 1916).
MELDEN, A. I. *Free Action* (London: Routledge and Kegan Paul,
1961).
MENNINGER, K. *The Crime of Punishment* (New York: Viking, 1968).
MILES, T. R. *Eliminating the Unconscious* (Oxford: Pergamon, 1966).
MINK, L. 'The Autonomy of Historical Understanding', in W. Dray
(ed.) *Philosophical Analysis and History* (New York: Harper and
Row, 1966).
MOORE, G. E. 'Proof of an External World', in *Proceedings of the
British Academy* for 1939, pp. 273–300.
MORRIS, Desmond (1967) *The Naked Ape* (London: Corgi, 1968).
—— (1970) *The Human Zoo* (London: Cape, 1970).
NEWTON, I. *Principia Mathematica*, edited by F. Cajori (Berkeley:
California U.P., 1946).
NISBET, R. (1974) 'Rousseau and Equality', in *Encounter* for Sept-
ember 1974, pp. 40–51.
—— (1976) 'The Fatal Ambivalence of an Idea', in *Encounter* for
December 1976, pp. 10–21.
O'CONNOR, D. J. *Free Will* (New York: Doubleday Anchor, 1971).
ORWELL. G. *1984* (London: Secker and Warburg, 1949).
—— (1970) *Collected Essays*, edited by Sonia Orwell and I. Angus
(Harmondsworth: Penguin, 1970).
PALEY, William (1801) *Natural Theology: or Evidences of the Existence
and Attributes of the Deity collected from the Appearances of Nature*, in his
Works (London, 1830).
PANTIN, C. F. A. *A History of Science* (London: Cohen and West,
1953).
PARKINSON, C. N. *Parkinson's Law* (London: Murray, 1958).
PASSMORE, J. A. *Man's Responsibility for Nature* (London: Duckworth,
1974).
PAUL, G. A. 'Lenin's Theory of Perception', in Margaret Mac-
Donald (ed.), *Philosophy and Analysis* (Oxford: Blackwell, 1954).

PEARS, D. F. *Freedom and the Will*, edited by D. F. Pears (London: Macmillan, 1963).

PETERS, R. S. *The Concept of Motivation* (London: Routledge and Kegan Paul, 1958).

PLATO, *The Dialogues*, translated by B. Jowett (Oxford: Clarendon Press, 1953).

PLEKHANOV, G. V. *The Role of the Individual in History*. No translator mentioned (London: Lawrence and Wishart, 1940).

POE, E. A. *Tales of Mystery and Imagination*, edited by P. Colum (London and New York: Dent, and Dutton, 1921).

POPKIN, R. H. *The History of Scepticism from Erasmus to Descartes* (Assen: Van Gorcum, 1960).

POPPER, K. R. (1953) 'Science: Conjectures and Refutations', in his *Conjectures and Refutations* (London: Routledge and Kegan Paul, 1963).

—— (1937) *The Poverty of Historicism* (London: Routledge and Kegan Paul, 1957).

PUTNAM, H. 'Minds and Machines', in S. Hook (ed.), *Dimensions of Mind* (New York: Collier, 1961).

RAPHAEL, D. D. 'The Impartial Spectator', in A. S. Skinner and T. Wilson *Essays on Adam Smith* (Oxford: Clarendon Press, 1975), pp. 83–99.

RUSE, M. (1973a) *The Philosophy of Biology* (London: Hutchinson, 1973).

—— (1973b) 'The Nature of Scientific Models: Formal v. Material Analogy', in the *Journal of the Philosophy of Social Science*' for 1973, pp. 63–80.

RUSSELL, B. A. W. (1920) *The Practice and Theory of Bolshevism* (London: Allen and Unwin, 2nd edition 1949).

—— (1921) *The Analysis of Mind* (London: Allen and Unwin, 1921).

RYLE, G. *The Concept of Mind* (London: Hutchinson, 1949).

SARGANT, W. *Battle for the Mind* (London: Pan, revised edition 1959).

SARTRE, J.-P. (1943) *Being and Nothingness*, translated by Hazel Barnes (New York and London: Philosophical Library, and Methuen, 1956 and 1957, respectively). The second page reference is in every case to the French original *L'être et le néant* (Paris: NRF-Gallimard, first published in 1943 under the German occupation).

—— (1960) *Critique de la Raison Dialectique* (Paris: NRF-Gallimard, 1960).

SCHOPENHAUER, A. (1819 and 1844) *The World as Will and Idea*, translated by R. B. Haldane and John Kemp (London: Trench, Trubner and Kegan Paul, 3rd Ed. 1896).

—— (1841) *Essay on the Freedom of the Will*, translated and edited by K. Kolenda (Indianapolis: Bobbs-Merrill, 1960).

SEARLE, J. R. 'How to derive *ought* from *is*', in W. D. Hudson (ed.), *The Is/Ought Question* (London: Macmillan, 1969).

SEARS, R. R. *Survey of Objective Studies of Psychoanalytic Concepts* (Social Science Research Council Bulletin No. 51: Washington, D.C., 1943).

SENIOR, W. N. *Two Lectures on Population* (London: 1829).

SKINNER, B. F. (1938) *The Behavior of Organisms* (New York: Appleton-Century-Crofts, 1938).

—— (1948) *Walden Two* (New York: Macmillan, 1948).

—— (1971) *Beyond Freedom and Dignity* (New York and London: Knopf, and Cape, 1971 and 1972, respectively).

SMART, J. J. C. (1963) *Philosophy and Scientific Realism* (London and New York: Routledge and Kegan Paul, and Humanities Press, 1963).

—— (1968) *Between Science and Philosophy* (New York: Random House, 1968).

SMITH, A. *An Inquiry into the Nature and Causes of the Wealth of Nations* edited by E. R. A. Seligman (New York and London: Dutton, and Dent, undated).

SMITH, K. *The Malthusian Controversy* (London: Routledge and Kegan Paul, 1951).

SMYTHIES, J. R. *Brain and Mind*, edited by J. R. Smythies (London: Routledge and Kegan Paul, 1965).

SOLZHENITSYN, A. *The Gulag Archipelago* (London: Collins/Fontana, 1974–).

STEBBING, L. S. *Philosophy and the Physicists* (Harmondsworth: Penguin, 1944).

STRAWSON, P. F. (1950). 'Persons', in H. Feigl, M. Scriven, and G. Maxwell (eds.) *Minnesota Studies in the Philosophy of Science*, Vol. II (Minneapolis: Minnesota U.P., 1958).

—— (1959) *Individuals* (London: Methuen, 1959).

SZAMUELY, T. *The Russian Tradition* (London: Secker and Warburg, 1974).

SZASZ, T. *The Myth of Mental Illness* (New York: Dell Delta, 1961).

TORR, D. *The Correspondence of Marx and Engels*, selected, edited, and translated by Dona Torr (London: Martin Lawrence, 1934).

TOULMIN, S. E. (1953) *The Philosophy of Science* (London: Hutchinson, 1953).

—— (1954) 'The Logical Status of Psycho-Analysis', in M. MacDonald (ed.), *Philosophy and Analysis* (Oxford: Blackwell, 1954).

TREVOR-ROPER, H. R. *The Last Days of Hitler* (London: Macmillan, 1947).

URBAN, W. M. *Beyond Realism and Idealism* (London: Allen and Unwin, 1949).

VALLA, L. 'On Freewill', translated by C. E. Trinkaus, in E. Cassirer, P. O. Kristeller, and J. H. Randall (eds.), *The Renaissance Philosophy of Man* (Chicago: Chicago U.P., 1956).

VENDLER, Z. 'Word and Concept' in G. Vesey (ed.) *The Proper Study* (London, and New York: Macmillan, and St. Martin's Press, 1971).

WARNOCK, M. *The Philosophy of Sartre* (London: Hutchinson, 1965).

WETTER, G. A. *Dialectical Materialism*, translated by Peter Heath (New York: Praeger, 1958).

WHATELY, R. *Lectures on Political Economy* (London: 1832).

WILLIAMS, M. *Brain Damage and the Mind* (Harmondsworth: Penguin, 1970).

WINCH, P. (1958) *The Idea of a Social Science* (London: Routledge and Kegan Paul, 1958).

WITTGENSTEIN, L. (1953) *Philosophical Investigations*, translated by G. E. M. Anscombe (Oxford: Blackwell, 1953).

WOOZLEY, A. D. Introduction to an abridgement of Locke's *An Essay concerning Human Understanding* (London: Collins Fontana, 1964).

YOUNG, P. T. *The Motivation of Behaviour* (New York: Wiley, 1936).

INDEX OF NAMES

This index of personal names does not attempt to cover the Bibliography. It also excludes deliberately the names of legendary or fictitious persons, publishers, and—for reasons suggested in the text—putative incorporeal persons, whether or not divine.